THE LIGHT
OF
GOD

THE LIGHT
OF
GOD

Divine Locutions on
Evil, Karma, Reincarnation,
and Healing

A Sacred Planet Book

LAURA AVERSANO

Inner Traditions
Rochester, Vermont

Inner Traditions
One Park Street
Rochester, Vermont 05767
www.InnerTraditions.com

Text stock is SFI certified

Sacred Planet Books are curated by Richard Grossinger, Inner Traditions editorial board member and cofounder and former publisher of North Atlantic Books. The Sacred Planet collection, published under the umbrella of the Inner Traditions family of imprints, is comprised of works on the themes of consciousness, cosmology, alternative medicine, dreams, climate, permaculture, alchemy, shamanic studies, oracles, astrology, crystals, hyperobjects, locutions, and subtle bodies.

Originally published in 2003 by 1st Books as chapters 8, 9, and 10 of the title *The Light of God.*

Cataloging-in-Publication Data for this title is available from the Library of Congress

ISBN 978-1-64411-296-0 (print)
ISBN 978-1-64411-297-7 (ebook)

Printed and bound in the United States by Lake Book Manufacturing, Inc. The text stock is SFI certified. The Sustainable Forestry Initiative® program promotes sustainable forest management.

10 9 8 7 6 5 4 3 2 1

Text design and layout by Priscilla Harris Baker
This book was typeset in Garamond Premier Pro with Gill Sans, Hermann, and Thirsk used as display typefaces

To send correspondence to the author of this book, mail a first-class letter to the author c/o Inner Traditions • Bear & Company, One Park Street, Rochester, VT 05767, and we will forward the communication, or contact the author directly at **lauraaversano.com.**

Dedicated to the Spirits of the Living God, for their merciful work on behalf of all the Lord's children.

To my family: Marie, Salvatore, Paul, Carol, and Tina. May the truth come to rest within the stillness of your hearts. May peace be with you always.

And finally, to our Beloved.
Thank you, Thank you, Thank you.

CONTENTS

FOREWORD

By Father Francis Tiso

I am walking with a group of people into the forest near our retreat house in Cantalupo nel Sannio in the Province of Isernia, Italy. The walk is in silence, and we are invited to allow the various species of plants along the way to draw out our attention, pulling our awareness away from the things that encrust the self. To perceive the intricacies of the natural world is not only to catalogue them but also to allow them to work on us, to send us messages. Not only is it about messages and information and aesthetics: there is something else.

A long walk in the countryside or up into the mountains does something to our self-consciousness. Just as a poultice draws an infection out of a wound, the millions of microperceptions that arise in a natural ecosystem draw out the puss of egocentric obsessions. Strangely, we are allowed to forget the ego, propped up as it is by endless loops of worry. They drop away. A perceiver is still there, but the name and form of the perceiver have become subtle, almost gone. Straining to keep moving on our feet, the loss of self meets silence behind our shoulders. Someone, it seems, is there. This silence reassures us, without restoring even a hint of the ego that needs, or thinks it needs, so much attention. Where we are going, together, great and small will blend, and both will disappear. No cataclysm, just going along with things as they are. Truly are.

Our walking companions continue on their way, occasionally pausing for a moment of meditation seated on a moss-covered culvert or on the ramp of an old bridge. We are all here together, but the lacing is of silence and not of chatter. Not even metaphysical talk.

The Light of God takes us into the forest with a million micro-perceptions that draw out the poisons of our collective past. Words come pouring off the page like bubbles in a sink of dishes. Looking closely, we see rainbow interference patterns, as if to remind us of where we are going. These words do more for us than do the healing species in nature. Somehow, they both pierce and play with our memories, and make mockery of our minds. There is a hammering here, like a sculptor shaping a stone round and round, day after day, wearing it away with blows and cracks. We see a form, a memory, a pattern, which then eludes us. We know we have had that thought, and then we are not so sure. We look for a scheme, the lay of the land. Here there is texture, but no geography. We are not really at home here, and many things are like the fearsome follies of our dreams. The piercing voice works on us that way, each assertion subverting its predecessor, sternly chiding the mind to drop the habit of analysis. These words would be considered "locutions" to be patiently discerned over a period of years to be sure that flow is coming from the Holy Spirit and not elsewhere.

The voice is one that says something more like "Follow me" than "Understand me." Even in reassuring us that fear is not the way, that same Shepherd voice also informs us of the illusory specters that wrinkle the path. Darkness and light entwine in this forest, and for long stretches the leaf-meal path is not steady beneath our soles.

Like G. M. Hopkins, the Holy Ghost is there with beating breast and bright wings, even when the light goes out in the brown-edged westward traces. For what is between these pages and lines is the life itself, indescribable, unreached by any compass. No dogmatic divining rod will bear this tread deprived of reassuring dromedaries. Throbbing with religious life, the divining rod becomes a kind of luminosity, bending almost to the breaking point in the pull and tug of the weaver whose voice comes through the canebrake, the swaying calamus. In this hidden place where the spring bursts forth, even the beating breast of the divine is at risk; soul and Source blend, and both die away in a final ecstatic echo.

What is this, what is that? Where does this come from? How am I to define these words? Is this a sure guide or a gigantic labyrinth with no center? Each time the warning signs pop up, we are thrown back on our own nature, and the fragility of our memories, our minds, our opinions, our props: not this, not that. Not even these tight-knit pages disclose the secret. If we have already tasted some of the dust of the way, and know that somehow ahead lies a path, that is enough to wend one's way amid bubbles and blossoms. We will meet here old friends, those who loved long ago, those who were draped in robes and carried staves, four and twenty elders and so many more in a long line of dim dawning light. With them, at a certain turn in the road, with mind and body dropping away, someone gets to fly, someone becomes flight itself. The silence at our shoulders lifts up, the earth plane slips away, and strange music seeps closer from the star streams. Listen, my child, to the words of the Teacher, that the eyes of the heart may see the light that deifies.

FATHER FRANCIS TISO

AUGUST 31, 2020

FATHER FRANCIS V. TISO is a Roman Catholic priest who holds an A.B. in medieval studies from Cornell University, a master of divinity degree from Harvard University, and a doctorate from Columbia University and Union Theological Seminary with a specialization in Buddhist studies. He is the Associate Director of the Secretariat for Ecumenical and Interreligious Affairs of the United States Conference for Catholic Bishops, where he serves as liaison to Islam, Hinduism, Buddhism, the Sikhs, and traditional religions as well as the Reformed confessions. He is the author of *Rainbow Body and Resurrection* and *Liberation in One Lifetime*.

PREFACE

If you have faith in me, I am there. If you do not, I am still there.

LAURA AVERSANO

It began with light. Then it was followed by darkness. The process was continual until there was stillness, and I was able to distinguish the voice of God from my own.

In 2001, my prayer life was one of such great fervor and dedication. My prayers had afforded me solace, deep contemplation, and initiation into realms within the spirit world that brought with it ecstatic experiences of the Divine. Revelations from the light and the darkness ensued, coupled with spiritual guidance from souls therein that prompted me to sit down, listen, and begin what would be one of the most challenging writing experiences of my life.

Along with my prayers I received visitations. My quest to know God, to comprehend Divine Providence, to delve into the spiritual laws surrounding the nature of good and evil, was answered. One soul at a time, one voice at a time, one prayer at a time—I became the instrument, fully embodied, taking dictation from those children of God who became His servants in the afterlife, many of whom I have prayed to since a child. The Holy Spirit gave me life through this work. Over twenty years later, I still read these words and sit in contemplation of my relationship to the Divine. The mystery is still present. It always was and will always be.

The process changed me, physically, mentally, and spiritually. I had even more questions than I had before. My spiritual life became more viable as I allowed God to work through me. My relationship to both the light and the darkness was enlivened with such richness that our collective purpose along with human suffering took on new meaning.

We all yearn for inner peace. That heaven we seek in order to silence those voices that separate us from one another lies within the tabernacle of our own hearts. My hope is that *The Light of God* will guide you into holiness, into that tabernacle where your relationship with the Divine leads you to your inner heaven. This book is a process as much as it is a prayer in and of itself.

The writings significantly reflect Christian theology but speak of universal spiritual themes. They are part of the whole, a minute glimpse into the mystery.

Let us now enter into that mystery, into that sacred union. I believe, truly, that this is the work of the Lord.

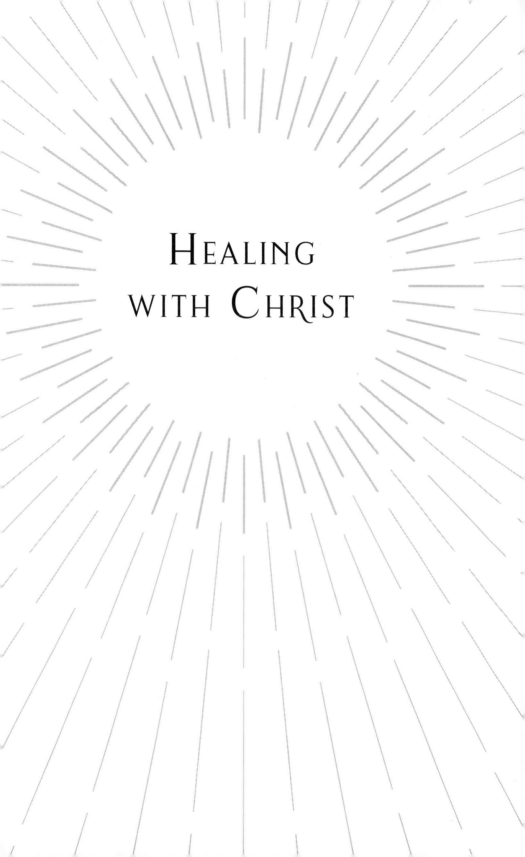

HEALING
WITH CHRIST

My son, if thou come to serve the Lord, prepare thy soul for temptation. Set thy heart aright, and constantly endure, and make not haste in time of trouble. Cleave unto him, and depart not away, that thou mayest be increased at thy last end. Whatsoever is brought upon thee take cheerfully, and be patient when thou art changed to a low estate. For gold is tried in the fire, and acceptable men in the furnace of adversity. Believe in him, and he will help thee; order thy way aright, and trust in him.

SIRACH 2:1–6

And Jesus went about all Galilee, teaching in their synagogues, and preaching the gospel of the kingdom, and healing all manner of sickness and all manner of disease among the people. And his fame went throughout all Syria; and they brought unto him all sick people that were taken with divers diseases and torments, and those which were possessed with devils, and those which were lunatick, and those that had the palsy; and he healed them.

MATTHEW 4:23–24

To heal with the spirit of Christ, one is doing so with the Christ who has been risen to the glorification of the one true God. Whoever wishes to heal in the name of the Lord shall do so upon asking His favor. The Lord grants to everyone the power of His might within reason of their soul's spiritual progression. You have the power to heal as Jesus the Christ had. But you do not know how to embrace this omnipotent power of Him and refuse to accept it during your spiritual journey. That is why we say within reason. It is your reason. Not the reasoning of Christ or his father.

When Jesus healed, he did so with the mercy of our dear Lord in his abiding heart and the energy of the miraculous Holy Spirit. The power in the hands and mind of the Christ far superseded that of all the angels and archangels in Heaven. They, too, bowed down to his glory as both man and Lord.

When Christ healed, his energy was raised to the level of Heaven and that of his Father's will. Whomever Jesus did heal, know that it was within the will of God, which was also the will of Christ in being one with his Father. The power of the Holy Trinity becomes absolute during the healings of Christ and with those who wish to partake of the Christ energy when healing another. We say to you this: be mindful of the power that the Lord gives to you. This power, which is given in the name of His son, is far greater than that which you have seen, and can be used to heal many according to the laws as set forth by the Creator.

For those who seek to heal another, ask the Lord to show you the way. The knowledge of healing through the Trinity with the Christ will be shown to you.

When Christ healed, he invoked the Trinity, which represents the triad of the God consciousness and the eternal agreement between God and all creation. The nature of God as the Father, the Son, and the Holy Spirit is manifested through healing in conjunction within this eternal agreement.

The author of the book of Hebrews in the following passage refers to this agreement in his offering of the Christ consciousness to you.

> *Now the God of peace, that brought again from the dead*
> *our Lord Jesus, that great shepherd of the sheep, through*
> *the blood of the everlasting covenant, make you perfect in*
> *every good work to do his will, working in you that which*
> *is wellpleasing in his sight, through Jesus Christ; to whom*
> *be glory for ever and ever. Amen.*
>
> HEBREWS 13:20–21

This agreement manifested itself with the death of the Lord and because of the tender loving mercy of his Father. This is what glorifies the power of the Trinity and makes it absolute in its healing efficacies. The death of the Lord only solidified the power of the Risen Christ and the eternal flame. In dying for you, he brought to you the gift of eternal life with his Father. His resurrection prevailed over the darkness that is misunderstood in the life hereafter, and those that follow.

The eternal flame is contained within the Trinity and is invoked to harness the healing power of God. We say to you this: for those who call upon these powers, know that you will call upon your own soul to be healed first. For those that seek to heal in the name of Jesus the Christ and the one true God, none will be healed before your own soul has repented. That is the way of the Lord. As you heal another, your soul will continue to raise itself in light of Him.

Discipline and practice of the virtues of our Lord are required to effect healing with the Christ consciousness. Much prayer is needed to listen closely to Him and to free the heart and mind of the passions that will arise as one calls both on the power of Christ to heal themselves and the power of Christ to heal another.

When the eternal flame rests upon the energies of the Trinity through our Lord as Father, Son, and Holy Spirit, the Creator shall imbue the healing energies of the entire kingdom of Him and Heaven to be used accordingly.

When healing with the energies of God as Lord and Father, you are calling upon His essence and light to come forth. You are setting the foundation for the creation of light to come through you in the name of all that is Holy within the realm of God. You are calling forth the omnipotent power of the Lord to reign over all. And you are bringing that consciousness of Divine reality to manifestation. It is you who seek to understand your relationship to the Lord when calling upon this aspect of the Trinity. It is the highest of all praises to Him to believe so righteously in Him and His power that He has laid down before you.

When healing with the energies as called forth by the Son in the Trinity, you are stating an affirmation of your intention to be in the image and likeness of the Creator in any existence that you choose to pursue your spiritual life, be it on the earth plane or in the world of spirit. You are calling to Jesus to remind you of your limitations of self and your expansion as the resurrected spirit. You are acknowledging within you the Divine Providence as set forth by the Lord and that which you have agreed to. You are showing your humility as one of the chosen children by learning the ways of God through His son Jesus the Christ. You are conceding to Him your responsibility to live as He created you to live. When you call upon this power of the Trinity, you are directly placing yourself in the love of the Christ and relating to his embodiment of the eternal spirit.

When healing with the energies as called forth by the Holy Spirit in the Trinity, you are affirming your belief in the power, love, and light of the Lord to heal. You are affirming your contribution to the creative energy of the universe and all that emanates from His light. You are placing yourself within the construct of the Logos and Divine Knowledge as set forth by the Creator. You are allowing yourself to become one with this power of the Lord and the universe to create according to His laws, according to love. You are calling forth the energies of all before you who have risen to the power of the Lord by way of the Holy Spirit, and of the power that is held in the commandments as given to Moses by Him. You are invoking the angels, the archangels, those of the Lord's Council, and others who are seated with Him in the kingdom. All who have embraced the light and power of the Holy Spirit will be with you as you call on it!

With the energies of the three essences within the Trinity, surrounded by the eternal flame, the gift of supernatural healing within the Christ consciousness can and will occur. That is the will of God!

When Christ healed, he was already partaking of the gifts of his Father and knew how to heal according to that holy paradigm created by Him. This is all for you to understand how the Christ healed and how you can heal as he did.

It is suggested for those who wish to follow in the healing tradition of Jesus to meditate upon his name and virtue and to practice embracing the power of the Trinity. One can do this by simply breathing in the presence of Jesus and asking a blessing upon his name.

Lord Jesus, we beseech thee through the power and glory of your Father in Heaven to fill us with your holiness of self, spirit, and will. We ask of you to bestow upon us the light of the eternal flame, which you carry so gently within your heart, so that we too may be healers of all.

Say this prayer unto your heart and having complete faith in the Lord Jesus Christ as healer and Son of God. You will receive spiritual energies and graces from Heaven with this prayer. Allow for this energy, light, and love of God and Jesus the Christ to move through you and heal you. Allow for it to be sent to others.

Once you have practiced this and mastered it, the energies will move through you and raise your own energy to a state of grace within the Lord. Then you may focus on the triad of the Holy Trinity and call forth its powers to assist you.

Bring your attention to the eternal flame as guardian of the Trinity and see yourself as belonging to this triad of holiness. Envision God the Father, the Son, and the Holy Spirit embracing your being and emanating through you the love and glory of the totality of all that He is. You will be held by all that is endearing to the Lord and graced with the fruits of His abiding love for you. Bring that energy of the Trinity to your mind, heart, and body and use it to heal your life and guide you in your mission. The power of this Trinity is so great that it will open doors into other dimensions. It will also align your soul to that of the Lord's will for you. It will heal karma and cast out demons lurking in the shadows. It will bring light to any darkness and burn through it, creating the space for the love of the Lord to prevail.

Be mindful of those who seek to hinder this power from coming to you, for this power belonged to all and was lost when the soul separated from Him. If not for the Lord's love and inspiration for your soul's mission, we would not be speaking to you about this matter at all.

When you call upon this power of the Trinity, the Lord God will come to you in all His glory and will make Himself known in seen and unseen ways. This is His right as master and ruler of all. The power of the Trinity shall avail itself when the time is right for the Lord to concede His power over to you. This is not only for healing, this is for your spiritual life as well. The moment you awaken yourself to this triad of consciousness, *God will come to you.* Again, the focused attention on the Trinity shall have its profound effect on spiritual consciousness and shall endeavor to bring healing to those who meditate upon it. The time when the actual power is availed to you is up to the Lord. In regard to healing, Christ was able to avail himself of the power of the Trinity and manifest it to heal others because of his "right" relationship with His Father. You will all come to know the Lord through praying and healing with the Trinity. You will all come to know of the Lord's omnipotent power as set forth by the Trinity when you have aligned yourself with that of His will for you.

You may call upon the Trinity to heal yourself and one another. This is the Lord's gift to you and His will. It belongs to all who seek love in His name. When you do so, hold yourself in complete reverence of His might and will, and with honor to those who have come before you who have placed themselves in this power of truth. Leave the healing up to the Lord, for it is not you who heals. This you must truly know and experience for yourselves. Leave the outcome to the Lord, for it is only He who knows what is best for the soul who needs to heal. It is only He who knows what is best for the universe and the spiritual evolution contained within it.

Jesus the Christ knew who was to be healed and in what way by his Father's wishes and graces. He was chosen to be the Son of the one true God and endeavored to teach us the news of the kingdom.

> For such a high priest became us, who is holy, harmless, undefiled, separate from sinners, and made higher than the heavens; who needeth not daily, as those high priests, to offer up sacrifice, first for his own sins, and then for the people's; for this he did once, when he offered up himself. For the law maketh men high priests which have infirmity; but the word of the oath, which was since the law, maketh the Son, who is consecrated for evermore.
> HEBREWS 7:26–28

The perfection of the Christ being is made possible through the healing as brought forth by the Trinity. Each time you call forth the powers of that Trinity to heal, you are also bringing the consciousness of the Christ to you. In the above reference to Jesus in the book of Hebrews, we are referring to the Christ within the man, or the Son of the Lord God. He is the child of the same Lord whom you were all born unto—the child of the same Lord that you can all aspire to be and are.

When we refer to healing, we are referring to the process of bringing light upon the darkness. Healing is the awakening of the soul to this light, and the awakening of the soul to merciful love. It is the honoring of the relationship between a soul and the Beloved. It is the affirmation of the presence of the Lord within you at all times. It is the construct by which creation rests itself in order to regenerate the light of God. It embraces the holy energy that all beings and things source from to bring comfort to their soul's missions. It is the merciful energy of the Lord.

There are many levels of healing that can take place for a soul, all of which are deemed by the Lord and His love for you. Healing will always take place at the level of spirit and soul, *always*. For what touches the spirit will always affect the soul's spiritual progression. Healing on the lower levels of existence manifests according to the will of God and the willingness of the soul to participate and have faith in the love of the Lord.

The Lord will endeavor to heal the mind if you so allow it. He would rather bring peace to your thoughts, and Himself to your thoughts, than see your mind in distress. It would do all souls justice to allow for this peace to be instilled by Him, as many of you are ruled by the darkness and fear set upon your mind. Healing with the Lord will always bring peace if you choose to let it in.

The Lord will endeavor to heal your heart and the emotions that arise from the passions within. He understands this takes time and patience within the heart. He does not ask you not to embrace that which so burdens you. He is just asking you to let Him help you carry it. When you ask the Lord to bring healing to your heart, He will offer to carry what you offer up to Him in earnest. Trust in His healing power to bring peace to your pain and anguish, and to those passions that encumber you so.

The Lord will endeavor to heal you physically and in accordance with Divine Providence as set forth by the Logos, faith, karma, agreements of inception, and the willingness of the soul to participate in the spiritual life. This all seems a bit complicated for the Lord God. It is actually more complicated for you to understand and accept. Know that at the end of time, all souls will come to know the light of God and be healed on all levels—that is to say, the levels that truly matter within His kingdom. Many of you do not trust in the Lord when you are not healed physically.

We say to you this: the Lord's love and mercy upon you is limitless. Do not look upon yourself as unworthy of Him when you think you are refused a physical healing. The healing of the Lord is always given when a soul asks . . . always. If you look upon your heart and spirit, you will see the light of God has made its mark on you. Acceptance of the other ways in which the Lord will heal you must be, so that you will continue to have faith in His love and mercy. Remember, the physical body is only the shelter that holds the light of the Lord. It is impermanent.

The Healing of the Paralyzed Man

And he entered into a ship, and passed over, and came into his own city. And, behold, they brought to him a man sick of the palsy, lying on a bed; and Jesus seeing their faith said unto the sick of the palsy, "Son, be of good cheer; thy sins be forgiven thee."

And, behold, certain of the scribes said within themselves, "This man blasphemeth." And Jesus knowing their thoughts said, "Wherefore think ye evil in your hearts? For whether is easier, to say, Thy sins be forgiven thee; or

to say, Arise, and walk? But that ye may know that the
Son of man hath power on earth to forgive sins."

Then saith he to the sick of the palsy, "Arise, take up
thy bed, and go unto thine house." And he arose, and
departed to his house. But when the multitudes saw it,
they marvelled, and glorified God, which had given such
power unto men.

MATTHEW 9:1–8

When I told the young man his sins were forgiven, I was referring to those sins that were with him in many lifetimes before. Not only his sins, but those of his mother, his father, and their parents before them. The sins of him and those that came before him created themselves in thought, action, and deed. It was not only he who suffered for them through his malady, but many suffered because of these sins. These sins had brought darkness upon those they came in contact with and, as a consequence, the man's legs lost the ability to walk in this life. It was because he chose not to walk with the Lord that his legs did not serve him any longer. This was not of the Lord's doing, but was what the soul created for itself in the desire to know his truth. It was not punishment from the Lord, but a sign for the soul to remember what it was he asked the Lord to show him the moment he agreed to be of the light. When I said to those watching that the son of man has the power on earth to forgive sins, I was speaking about the power of my Father to create upon the light that was given to all of you. Through this power, one can choose to see the light through the darkness. This power was given to the Son of God, but also to the son of man, to show you that you and I are one. What I can do, so may you, in the light of the Lord. To forgive one another for being afraid of the light you carry is an act of compassion and mercy that I have shown this man. When I called to him to stand up, I was calling to the Lord God in him, to the Savior and the light that belongs to all. I asked that the light and love of the Lord come forth and heal all past issues and concerns relating to the darkness. It did so, and all those who belonged to this man's family were healed, and all those he affected with his darkness were healed. Always, this is the way. Whether they were healed in the world of spirit or on the plane of the earth, they all received the grace of the Lord, which touched upon their spirits and souls.

It was this man's spirit, soul, and physical body that were healed. The spirit that was healed was the part of him that did not believe in the goodness and kindness of the Lord. This part of his spirit did not believe that he was also of that goodness and kindness. The soul that was healed had brought despair and hurt to others over many lifetimes because of what his spirit believed. In the forgiveness of his sins, I showed him the way to forgiving himself and the way back to the light of my Father. It is simple. For this man to walk again meant walking toward the kingdom in the way that he had so long forgotten. I reminded him with my presence of the Trinity as held through all of us. That power that is under the domain of the Lord is all inclusive and enduring. The Trinity gave to this man the opportunity to be of light, love, and power with my Father once again, and the gift of physical healing and aspiration to be of service to Him. When my Father creates a healing that is physical, know that you will then endeavor to carry out His work. That is the true purpose for miracles created through those who seek His mercy on the physical level. They are there to show others and the person who received the miracle the glory of my Father and His abiding love for you. The Trinity has to be all inclusive for the miracle to take place. When I say miracle, I am referring to what you perceive is a miracle, not me or my Father. To me, the miracle is the glory of creation, and the love of, with, and for God our Father. Many times it needs to manifest on the physical level for you to believe. When you seek to heal as I, and you call upon me and the power of the Holy Trinity to assist you, see the power as embracing all of creation, see all as belonging to and of my Father and have complete faith in that. That will help you in your work.

The Healing of a Sick Man

When he was come down from the mountain, great multitudes followed him. And, behold, there came a leper and worshipped him, saying, "Lord, if thou wilt, thou canst make me clean." And Jesus put forth his hand, and touched him, saying, "I will; be thou clean." And immediately his leprosy was cleansed.

MATTHEW 8:1–3

If you want to heal like me, do not question my Father or the power and love that He gives you. For when I heal as He wishes, I declare with truth and knowing that my Father wills it to be. That is so.

My Father wants for all of you to be healed and for all of you to heal with Him. Although, it is you who have attached your own desires to what kind of healing is to take place. Again, do not question Him when you heal. Instead, raise Him up in authority, power, and mind, and you shall cast out all darkness of affliction in that which you seek to heal. Seek to know me, and seek to know my Father through me, and I will help you. Make a declaration of the Lord unto your own heart when you seek to heal another. Those who are not afraid of having power with the Lord shall endeavor to know it fruitfully. Most of you greatly fear the power of the Lord and the fire of the Holy Spirit. I beseech you, you will all come to learn of this as you choose in your own time, but remember, you will learn of it as it is through the will of God. His power is needed for the spiritual consciousness to transcend into light and you are all a part of that. You will learn to embrace it as it comes to you. And come to you it will, for you cannot rise to Heaven without the knowledge of the Lord's power before you and within you. As I have said, the Trinity is all inclusive, as above, so below. The power of the Lord that rules the heavens will also rule the earth. In this way, the evil that persists is not to be feared because there will be a time when you will rise above it and all will be as one in His light.

When I said to the sick man, "I want to heal you, be healed," I was affirming my faith in Him through the sacrament of the anointing of the sick. Through this soul's penance, he was able to receive this sacrament as a blessing from the Lord upon him.

All of the sacraments that have been given by my Father are declarations of the risen spirit within you. A sacrament is a construct of spiritual energy by which an initiation into the holiness of the Lord is given. With each sacrament, your spirit and soul are given the opportunity to rejoin the Lord in the light you were born into. It is an opportunity to become closer to Him and to receive the blessings He has deemed for you. Whenever you declare a sacrament as truth of the Lord's law, it shall be given, *it shall be given.* The sacraments are also given power and glory by that same construct that aligns the Trinity to the power, love, and light of Him. They are interchangeable and work in relation to each other. When you call upon one, you indeed are calling upon the other for you to heal with the Trinity. Your healing cannot be complete without the receiving or initiation of a sacrament. When the energy of the Trinity is invoked, it will create an opening in the person receiving the healing for the awakening of God to be instilled once again. This is the blessing of a sacrament.

The Healing of the Men with Demons

And when he was come to the other side into the country of the Gergesenes, there met him two possessed with devils, coming out of the tombs, exceeding fierce, so that no man might pass by that way. And, behold, they cried out, saying, "What have we to do with thee, Jesus, thou Son of God? Art thou come hither to torment us before the time?"

And there was a good way off from them a herd of many swine feeding. So the devils besought him, saying, "If thou cast us out, suffer us to go away into the herd of swine."

And he said unto them, "Go." And when they were come out, they went into the herd of swine; and, behold, the whole herd of swine ran violently down a steep place into the sea, and perished in the waters. And they that kept them fled, and went their ways into the city, and told everything, and what was befallen to the possessed of the devils. And, behold, the whole city came out to meet Jesus; and when they saw him, they besought him that he would depart out of their coasts.

MATTHEW 8:28–34

The role of demons and evil in regard to man is not to be feared in the way that you fear. It is to be understood. Just as the light of God is to be respected, so is the darkness. When one respects the darkness, one will have an appropriate fear of how to disengage the soul from past, present, and future harm done by the demons. The respect is not about admiration of the dark side, for there is nothing to admire about misery. It is to be respected in a way that the soul can see the harm it can do when engaging with it and will learn to leave well enough alone. When you choose to disengage with the demons, they will lose power over you. Remember, this choice is yours and is one of great magnitude and concern. For this parallels that of your spiritual life and your relationship to me and my Father.

What you do in conjunction with the polarities of the light and the darkness is in effect all about your relationship to God. Disengaging with demons requires intense spiritual work and discipline in the ways of the Lord.

Demons or dark spirits travel within many dimensions of existence, and can be with a soul for many, many lifetimes. It is only when the passions that engage the soul are brought into light that the demons will be cast out. I say to you this: be mindful of what you hold in your heart in relationship to Him, for it is not only you who will carry those demons, but they will be passed on to your children and their children too. That is the karma of the dark world, such as there is karma of the light world.

When I went to heal the two men with the demons, they challenged me as they will challenge anyone of light that comes to them to try to rid them. Remember, was I not tempted in the desert by the Devil himself? Just because I am the Son of God does not mean that the darkness will not try and frighten me. As much light we hold within, we will be met with as much darkness—both internally and externally. Only I know better than you, for I know truly that I am the Son of God and that nothing can ever truly harm me in the face of the Lord. But trust me when I say to you to be mindful of what you align yourself with, for that you know not what you do.

Just as the demons were cast into the pigs, they can come in many forms, seen and unseen. They can take hold of the mind, heart, spirit, soul, and body. They can work from the world of spirit and from the other dimensions of reality. Do not be fooled by their sweetness, for many times they come with sweet tongues that will poison you. This is not to frighten you, for you must know the love and protection of the Lord will always prevail. It is you who must decide that the dark side no longer serves you in any way, *in any way*.

When the demons challenged me to cast them out, they asked me to send them into the herd of pigs. In this way, they thought that they could make their way into the souls of others. They were mistaken as I am the Son of God, and it is their own darkness that caused their destruction. *Light will always come up against darkness.* You must know that. As long as you endeavor to learn of your essence, this will be. Once you have come upon the kingdom of the Lord, that will no longer be. But only upon His kingdom, for the dark spirits also have their place among those in the world of spirit. I will speak more about this when we talk about the subject of evil.

The reasons these demons found their way into these men are many, and the reasons that they find their way to you are many. Always, always, be mindful of the Lord. It is truly only by His hand that you will be cast out of the darkness, and the darkness will be cast out of you.

Many of you do not like addressing this subject. That is why the men of that town begged me to leave. It is easier for you to look upon another as being with the darkness than to call upon it in your own selves. Know that you all have it. As the son of man, I have it. As the Son of God, my light heals it. I chose in the desert to stay with my Father. I would suggest you do the same. It is easier for men to keep hold of the darkness than to seek the light in themselves. When you seek to conquer the demons, you will be asked to sacrifice much according to your understanding. All the Lord asks of you to is to seek Him. For you it will require a letting go of what you think serves you and draws these demons to you. It will be matters of the heart, mind, body, spirit, and soul.

When demons occupy the mind, they will seek to distinguish themselves as dementia, hysteria, and negative thoughts. Illness of the mind is nothing more than the soul's willingness to let the darkness rule the thoughts. When demons occupy the heart, it will cause you to have hatred toward yourself and another and will cause you to act out in that manner. When demons occupy the body, and know that this does happen often, illness can set into the physicality of that person. This is not to say that all illness occurs because of the darkness, only some. That you will know. You can always look into the eyes of a person and see that it is not their own soul that occupies their bodies.

When demons occupy the spirit, such as a curse, the spirit will be held in an energetic pattern until the spirit can be released. This can last for many lifetimes and can cause the spirit much distress. When the soul becomes occupied with the darkness, it will incarnate in many lifetimes on earth or as a dark spirit in the world of spirit to seek to cause harm and injustice toward another. This will only happen when the darkness has permeated the other levels of being.

In the matter of healing all demons, prayer to the one true God is needed. Rituals of solitude, mindfulness, cleansing, fasting, and offerings to our Lord will assist you. The simplest way is to not be afraid of your light and to allow the love of the Most High to fill your being with Him. The darkness does not understand about love nor does it seek to know it. Love will heal all darkness. I am speaking about the Lord's love for you, your love for yourself, and especially your love for another and another. The understanding that evil does exist and needs to come to completion under the will of God is important. For this, you all have to learn to be still.

When I called to the demons to come out of the men and sent them unto the swine, I did so with righteous power of the Lord God. I did so with reverence of His Divine Providence for the souls of the men and also the spirits of the darkness. They, too, must finish their work in learning to love my Father. I called to them with righteous affirmation of my love for the two men and my love for the demons. When I say love, it is within a different context than you appreciate. The darkness will become confused when you seek to offer it the love of my Father. In offering love to them, it does not mean to take them into your home. You would be foolish in doing so. You have enough to be with already in your spiritual progression. I called to them with righteous indignation of the laws of the Lord at work.

I say to you this: when you seek to cast out demons, always call on the Lord for protection and guidance. Do not seek to cast them out in pursuit of your own grandeur. This will not work and you will bring harm unto yourself. Call upon the angels and the archangels of Heaven. Call upon His counsel. Call upon those seated at His right hand in the kingdom. Call upon the prophets and teachers that have come before you. They will come. And they will assist you.

When you seek this healing, discourse with my Father through solitude will assist you. Then the demons have no way to be contained in the manner in which you live. They seek to address themselves in every aspect of the soul's existence. Solitude will allow you to quiet the mind and focus your attention on my Father. The demons tend to scramble the mind and bring more thoughts to it to confuse it when you desire to separate from them. Continual prayers to my Father will endeavor to bring light. There are many prayers that have been used over time so that the Lord may heal the darkness.

> *And Jabez called on the God of Israel, saying, "Oh that thou wouldest bless me indeed, and enlarge my coast, and that thine hand might be with me, and that thou wouldest keep me from evil, that it may not grieve me!"*
>
> 1 CHRONICLES 4:10

That is one such prayer from the scriptures. Another is that which I used in the desert to rid the Devil from my presence.

> *Then saith Jesus unto him, "Get thee hence, Satan, for it is written: Thou shalt worship the Lord thy God, and him only shalt thou serve."*
>
> MATTHEW 4:10

Within the psalms you will find many prayers in the way of protection from the Lord God. One of the most powerful is a psalm of David.

The Lord is my shepherd; I shall not want. He maketh me to lie down in green pastures; he leadeth me beside the still waters. He restoreth my soul; he leadeth me in the paths of righteousness for his name's sake. Yea, though I walk through the valley of the shadow of death, I will fear no evil, for thou art with me; thy rod and thy staff they comfort me. Thou preparest a table before me in the presence of mine enemies; thou anointest my head with oil; my cup runneth over. Surely goodness and mercy shall follow me all the days of my life, and I will dwell in the house of the Lord forever.

PSALMS 23:1–6

Use the prayers that are found within the scriptures. The light they carry is given special distinction by the Lord God and that of His Council to cast out any darkness. There are more. Any prayer that is said by a holy person in the scriptures of our Lord can be used to help you. Also, any prayer said by the prophets of our Lord who have been so deemed as such by Him are to be used as well. When you call upon an angel, a saint, a teacher, that is in effect a prayerful intention, using the light of the soul you called upon to help you.

Be mindful when you are dealing with the dark side. Do not embrace the demons that plague you, nor do those things that stir them. Indeed, when you choose to bring light to them, they will be angered. I am speaking about the stirring of the energy that will endeavor to hold your spirit and soul beholden to them longer. Be mindful of those passions that incite their attention, and seek to bring justice and temperance to that of the ego self and to the will that is not belonging to our Lord. Know that even those who live as the Lord wills for them will be bothered as I was myself in the desert. Yet the interaction I had with the Devil is what I am trying to teach you about. The darkness exists in many lower levels of reality; for you would do well to be mindful of your relationship with it. My hope is that you find yourself in right relationship. That is to not engage in the first place, or rather when you choose to, to understand why it is that you need this relationship so. Also contemplate where it is that my Father is with you in this relationship, and where you see yourself with Him. All of this will be beneficial in your assistance of bringing in the light in your endeavor to acknowledge and heal the darkness and the demons that come with it.

To fast is another way that our Lord advises you to cast out the darkness. When the body is empty, it will leave the vessel empty of more than just nourishment that the demons feed upon. The ritual of fasting is symbolic of the purging of the passions that bind you in your physical body. When your body is empty, it will give more space for the mind and it will also raise your vibration higher toward that of our Lord so that you may contemplate Him more. When you are empty of food, a basic desire and attachment of the human form, you will see clearly the earthly attachments and desires that bring you pain. You will see clearly what has brought you to this place of darkness. You will understand why it is that these dark spirits have come to you. With an empty body, you will hear them, see them, and feel them more. You will be more in stillness. It is my suggestion to you that you do this knowing that your faith in the Lord is strong, as is your mind. When you leave yourself empty, this will create more space for energies to descend upon you from both worlds. So it is advisable when one is fasting to rid the self of demons that much prayer, solitude, and stillness be adhered to.

The cleansing of the body is also important. The element of water, as we have mentioned previously, is belonging to that of the Holy Spirit. It refers to the markings of God upon the soul of the righteous. Those who are righteous stand in humility of their light upon the Lord.

When you bathe yourself in water, call upon the energies of the Holy Spirit to bless you in the same way that you are given that blessing upon baptism. Any water can be made holy by the blessing of my Father. All you need to do is ask Him. When you cleanse yourself in this water that is made holy, the light will bathe the physical body and help to cast out demons.

When you seek the help of my Father for this magnitude of healing, you will endeavor to give offerings to Him and to others in His name. You cannot cast out the darkness without letting go of something. That can be anything that the Lord has asked of you on any level. You will make a sacrifice of your self, spirit, and/or soul on behalf of the Lord. Know this is in your highest good and it will change your existence as you know it. Whether you are on the plane of earth or in the world of spirit, you will be different in many forms.

Always, when you seek to heal from the demons that bind you, call on the powers of myself, my Father, the Trinity, and the Holy Spirit to deliver you from evil. You must be willing to make this declaration to our Lord and to all those who help Him as well as to the dark spirits. Once you are delivered from them, you can only go unto the Lord. So take heed of what you are requesting. You will encounter testing of the Lord to see of your loyalty to Him. If you are not able to keep your promises, the demons will return, but not at the hands of my Father. It will be at your own hands because of your refusal to give up what brings the dark spirits close to you. My Father will only do so much for you in this matter. As this is all part of the free will He gave you to learn about Him, to understand your perceived duality. My Father will deliver you. It is up to you to do the rest of your inner work.

I say to you this: love as my Father loves you. That is the greatest deterrent to evil of all forms.

Love as my Father loves you and you will find no greater healing than that which I will give to you.

The Healing of a Sick Woman

And Jesus arose, and followed him, and so did his disciples. And, behold, a woman, which was diseased with an issue of blood twelve years, came behind him, and touched the hem of his garment. For she said within herself, If I may but touch his garment, I shall be whole. But Jesus turned him about, and when he saw her, he said, "Daughter, be of good comfort; thy faith hath made thee whole." And the woman was made whole from that hour.

MATTHEW 9:19–22

The faith of this woman in the Son of God and in my Father is something I wish for all of you to aspire to. Just as I declare the power, love, and light of my Father in the healing of a soul that seeks it, it was this woman who affirmed her faith in the Lord and the power of the Holy Trinity that works through me. It is this faith that is born in the house of the Lord. It is this faith that will bring you back to Him. It is the affirmation and embodiment of this faith that is needed by all souls seeking Him. The healing of souls and of all His creation cannot return to Him unless they have received this faith in the sanctity of their hearts. It was not once that this woman did not believe herself to be a child of God. It was not once that this woman did not believe herself to be healed by Him. It was not once that this woman did not believe herself to be loved by Him. The inner strength of knowing and embracing that faith in the Lord gave this woman the gift of healing she sought from me, from my Father, and from the Holy Spirit. When she asked to be made whole, she did not ask to be made whole in physicality, nor did she want that. She asked of me and the Lord God to take her unto His light and bring her into eternal love with Him. She knew that the Lord God would endeavor to grant her request, and that knowing was touched upon by her longing to return to Him. It was the Lord God who not only healed her but made her physical body well again. That is the joy of Him, to give to His children a miracle of love that they least expect. My Father is doing that all the time for you. I wish that you would open your hearts and eyes to see this more.

The woman being made well was nothing more than her returning to the kingdom of God. There was purpose in the Lord for making her body well again. Remember, the healing of my Father will always be in accordance with that which the soul needs most for his highest purpose as deemed by our Lord.

If anyone does not believe in the healing power of my Father, he is born without faith of Him. Those who seek to know truth will endeavor to be graced by the Holy Spirit upon which the healing powers of the Lord will make themselves known. When the Lord God deems upon a soul the graces of healing, the power of the Holy Spirit shall rise above the kingdom to initiate the Divine energy of the heavens and shower the soul with the Lord's unyielding love and light. For this is absolute truth. Servants of the Lord such as myself do not need to make their presence known. A request to the Lord made from your own voice shall be good enough as the Son of Him. For remember, you and I are one. We are all belonging to my Father. This is true of anyone who prays to the Lord for another for healing. When you ask my Father to offer love and comfort to another, you have touched upon His heart the ways of Him. To see His children loving as He does is His greatest desire. Know that all requests for healing will be heard by the Lord God and by those of His Council. All requests. The Lord beseeches you to ask of Him when you need His healing love. All will be answered in prayer through the light and love of Him. When you so have faith in His healing love, and even when you do not have faith in His healing love, He will endeavor to heal you and those you pray for. You must not give to the Lord that which you think in earnest is of your will in regard to His healing. You are already given the ways in which the healing love will serve you best in your earthly experience or in the world of spirit.

My Father will do as much as you allow Him to do for you. The moment you experienced your first earthly life, you were made to be whole. The moment you chose to rebuke my Father's love for you, you needed His healing love and energy. When you seek to understand the mind's role in relation to the healing energy of Him, you will be closer to the kingdom. I say to you this: the mind is the greatest deterrent to having faith in my Father. Any healing deemed by Him is manifested according to the amount of faith that the soul carries.

When you seek to use prayer as a method of healing, it is important that your faith in His power to hear and respond to you is present. It does not matter whether you are praying to Him for your own sake or for another's. If you have faith in Him, but not in yourself, then you truly do not have faith in Him at all. For that which He is, you are. To have faith in yourself as being a child of God and worthy of His healing energy will bring to you what you earnestly ask for.

When you pray to my Father for healing, do so with a willingness to hear, see, and do all that He asks of you in favor of this healing. This is nothing more than to love Him and all His children. How such a request can bring many of you to confusion. Pray continuously and offer up to Him that which needs healing for yourself or another. Pray to all those who are in the kingdom of Heaven with Him. There are many that have intercessory power with the Lord and do His bidding. Be disciplined in your heart and mind when asking for the healing of our Lord. You must learn to accept the grief of Him in earnest when receiving healing. He will endeavor to heal what binds your heart from loving Him. You will come to know grief of not having the Lord with you all this time and in being so far away from Him. When you seek to heal like me with the intention of loving my Father, you will come to understand what it is to lead a prayerful life indeed.

Raise your hands up to my Father and offer Him through the power of prayer the sacraments that He offers to you.

As the living Father hath sent me, and I live by the Father, so he that eateth me, even he shall live by me.

JOHN 6:57

Take heed of this passage in the scriptures, and also of the following one. Indeed a very important lesson for you all on the healing that is of our Lord.

It is written in the prophets, and they shall be all taught of God. Every man therefore that hath heard, and hath learned of the Father, cometh unto me. Not that any man hath seen the Father, save he which is of God, he hath seen the Father. Verily, verily, I say unto you, He that believeth on me hath everlasting life. I am that bread of life. Your fathers did eat manna in the wilderness, and are dead. This is the bread which cometh down from heaven, that a man may eat thereof, and not die. I am the living bread which came down from heaven; if any man eat of this bread, he shall live forever; and the bread that I will give is my flesh, which I will give for the life of the world.

JOHN 6:45–51

All of you who want to heal with the power of the Risen Christ, with the power of the Lord in your heart and hands, take unto you the healing energy of the sacraments as given to you by Him and remember those words as spoken above. Raise your spirit up to the Lord and repeat:

*As the living Father hath sent me, and I live by the
Father, so he that eateth me, even he shall live by me.*

JOHN 6:57

This is a powerful prayer to use when proclaiming a healing for
yourself or another. Embrace the healing energy of the sacraments
and embrace the triumphant blessings of the Lord that He bestows
upon you as initiations into the Divine Hierarchy. Proclaiming is
different than asking the Lord. There are times when you should ask
in humility through prayer for healing, and there are times when you
should proclaim with Divine righteousness the power of the Lord to
heal through you. You will know when you are called to do what the
Lord desires for you.

As the scriptures tell you, all will be taught by the Lord. Not
one of you will leave His light in the end. This is written everywhere
throughout time as deemed by my Father. You will all come to believe
in Him again. You will all come to believe in me again. This will be
so, as many of you are needing healing from the Lord at this time.
Your hearts are broken in despair over losing Him. You are like lost
sheep on a mountain, waiting for your shepherd to come find you and
take you home. *The Lord is coming. He is coming.* To pray for healing
believing that you are the bread of life, and that the soul you are
praying for is also the bread of life, will bring you to eternal life. This
I promise you.

I am teaching you how to heal in the ways of our Father. Take
heed of what I say, you will endeavor to learn and understand much in
the spiritual life of the soul.

When you pray for a soul to be healed, always make the sign of
the cross as given my Father—before, during, and after a holy prayer
is given. By doing so, you shall bring forth protection to the soul
and call on the powerful energies that embrace the Logos. You will
be unlocking the heavens to descend upon the earth and touch upon

the soul whom healing is being asked for. There are many of you who
have forgotten the power of making the sign of the cross over another
person or upon yourself. It is a practice that has been used throughout
time by many of the Lord's servants. When many of you stand together
and offer the sign of the cross to my Father, you will receive a blessing
from Him and the angels. To stand and do this continuously will
bring favors of the Lord upon you. To make the sign of the cross over
a person needing healing will indeed bring that and so much more
from our Lord God. It will bring your souls closer to our Lord and
will help to heal past karma. When you stand in continual light of the
Lord, that which binds you shall be set free. When you offer a soul a
blessing of the cross, you shall be calling upon all the energies of the
heavens and belonging to that of the Trinity to assist you. As I have
and many before me, you will anoint the soul who is receiving the
blessing. When you invoke this sacred blessing, you are being given the
power to anoint another through the graces of our Lord God. This is
the Ark of the Covenant as manifested through you. This is the glory
of Him. It is a simple invocation that will make the heavens rejoice.
When you practice this invocation with the mindfulness of the Lord,
watch to see that spirits of God will come to guide you further in
your endeavors. Pay no attention to those spirits that try and stop your
progress with Him; trust that you will be protected. That which will
come to frighten you will be dealt with by the Lord himself. When
working as His servant, always remember that the Lord himself will
protect you from all evil. It will come, and it will be taken away, in the
appropriate time and manner.

Through this anointing, the life of the living God and the Risen
Christ shall be given to you. Another way of anointing a soul to
receive a healing of our Lord is through the use of oil. This is very
helpful when a soul is suffering from mental distress or when the
mind has been taken over by darkness. I say to you this: anoint with
oil that has been blessed by the Lord, and you shall be given all the

protection and graces of the archangels of Heaven, of the miraculous Holy Spirit, and of the guidance of Elijah. It is the Holy Spirit that is called forth when oil is made use of in healing, and it is the Holy Spirit whose protection gives rise to the archangels of Heaven. When you seek to anoint another with oil, make the sign of the cross upon their forehead and whisper the name of Elijah, for it is he who will come as a great prophet of the Lord to anoint the soul in light of the Holy Spirit and the archangels of Heaven. It is the spirit of Elijah who has been throughout time a great servant of the Lord and who remains in Spirit alive through the Son of God and through his disciples. Do not be mistaken. Elijah will never die. He is risen and will live throughout the souls of many who yearn to return to Christ.

When you seek to anoint another with oil for healing, you are again being asked to initiate the sacraments as given to you by God. Just as my Father sent Samuel to Bethlehem to anoint the future King David with oil, so shall you anoint all of the future kings of the kingdom of the Lord. We all sit at the right hand of the Lord enthroned in His mighty works and love.

> And the Lord said, "Arise, anoint him, for this is he."
> Then Samuel took the horn of oil, and anointed him in
> the midst of his brethren; and the Spirit of the Lord came
> upon David from that day forward.
> 1 SAMUEL 16:12–13

> Let that therefore abide in you, which ye have heard
> from the beginning. If that which ye have heard from the
> beginning shall remain in you, ye also shall continue in
> the Son, and in the Father. And this is the promise that
> he hath promised us, even eternal life. These things have
> I written unto you concerning them that seduce you. But

the anointing which ye have received of him abideth in you, and ye need not that any man teach you; but as the same anointing teacheth you of all things, and is truth, and is no lie, and even as it hath taught you, ye shall abide in him.

1 JOHN 2:24–27

When you anoint a soul with oil that is blessed by the Lord most High, the angels, the Holy Spirit, and the great Elijah, you are giving to that soul the permission to render death in the face of the Lord.

The soul will be ascertained by the Lord in the anointing as to where it is in its spiritual progression toward Him. Just as the spirit of the Lord rushed upon David, so will the spirit of the Lord rush upon the soul receiving the anointing and that soul will indeed be raised up to the Lord in all ways. Trust in this, for it will be so. Be mindful of the presence of the Lord upon you in wondrous ways after such a blessing and take heed of your expanded light.

It is not only the spirit of the Lord who will descend upon you; all the wisdom of the great prophets that served under Him will also come to you. I say to you this: repeat the name of Elijah in solitude and stillness of Him, and you will come to know great truth and wisdom. Repeat the name of Elijah, and you will come to know peace and healing of the mind. His name alone shall carry you to the kingdom. Elijah stands before you always, as God the Father, the Son, and the Holy Spirit. His soul encompasses all souls. Anoint with oil in his name and you shall experience the glory of the Lord within you. For I, the Son of the Most High, also call upon the Spirit of Elijah to assist me, and all of the great prophets of our Lord who have come before me. This is truth. I healed with the power of my Father and the wisdom and guidance of Him, and those He sent to teach others before me. This is to show you that you may call on any of the prophets of the one true God, as we are all one. The power that comes to us from the Lord is mighty, and you would do well to call upon us when you are seeking healing of Him.

And after six days Jesus taketh Peter, James, and John his brother, and bringeth them up into a high mountain apart, and was transfigured before them; and his face did shine as the sun, and his raiment was white as the light. And, behold, there appeared unto them Moses and Elias talking with him.

Then answered Peter, and said unto Jesus, "Lord, it is good for us to be here; if thou wilt, let us make here three tabernacles: one for thee, and one for Moses, and one for [Elijah]."

While he yet spake, behold, a bright cloud over-shadowed them; and behold a voice out of the cloud, which said, "This is my beloved Son, in whom I am well pleased; hear ye him."

And when the disciples heard it, they fell on their face, and were sore afraid. And Jesus came and touched them, and said, "Arise, and be not afraid." And when they had lifted up their eyes, they saw no man, save Jesus only.

And as they came down from the mountain, Jesus charged them, saying, "Tell the vision to no man, until the Son of man be risen again from the dead."

And his disciples asked him, saying, "Why then say the scribes that Elias must first come?" And Jesus answered and said unto them, "Elias truly shall first come, and restore all things. But I say unto you, that Elias is come already, and they knew him not, but have done unto him whatsoever they listed. Likewise shall also

the Son of man suffer of them." Then the disciples under-
stood that he spake unto them of John the Baptist.

MATTHEW 17:1–13

So you see, the spirit of Elijah brings to you great power, wisdom, and healing of the Lord. It is his spirit who is called forth among the son of man and his disciples to help teach in the ways of the Lord. It is his spirit who is reincarnated as many of the servants of the Lord, not just John the Baptist. Elijah is the one who comes in the face of the Lord, which indeed is the highest spirit of us all. To embrace this spirit is to embrace the all-knowing of our Lord. The Lord God has given Elijah great authority to do His bidding. He has given all of you great authority to call on Elijah when you seek healing. He has given you great authority to call upon all of us. Again, we are all one Risen Spirit.

When you desire a healing from the Lord in the highest order possible, speak the name of Elijah, and the great prophet shall come to you and bring you the wisdom that you seek. For there is might, power, and strength of the Lord that comes with this name. To sit in prayer and speak of it shall bring you strength of spirit and mind to endure the trials of the spiritual life. To speak his name shall bring you comfort and holiness. To speak his name shall make safe the passage for one who is near death to the next life. To speak his name will move mountains as large as the faith you have in its power to do so. Speak the name of Elijah and the demons will frighten so. Speak the name of Elijah and the archangels will bow down to you. Speak the name of Elijah and the gates of Heaven will open. Speak the name of Elijah and you will be glorified into the image and likeness of the Lord God.

For when you call upon Elijah, he will come. When you call upon Elijah, I, the Son of God, will come. When you call upon Elijah, the Lord Himself will come. In this name is the healing power of the Lord God, of the Risen Christ, of all that is seen and unseen. His name embraces all.

When you use this name to bring healing, always use it according to the laws of the kingdom. Whoever misuses this as set forth by the Lord shall endeavor to suffer the consequences. Only for the highest good shall it be given.

When Elijah was going to be taken to Heaven, Elisha, his disciple, asked of the great teacher to give a portion of his spirit to him.

And it came to pass, when they were gone over, that Elijah said unto Elisha, "Ask what I shall do for thee, before I be taken away from thee." And Elisha said, "I pray thee, let a double portion of thy spirit be upon me." And he said, "Thou hast asked a hard thing: nevertheless, if thou see me when I am taken from thee, it shall be so unto thee; but if not, it shall not be so."

And it came to pass, as they still went on, and talked, that, behold, there appeared a chariot of fire, and horses of fire, and parted them both asunder; and Elijah went up by a whirlwind into heaven. And Elisha saw it, and he cried, "My father, my father, the chariot of Israel, and the horsemen thereof." And he saw him no more; and he took hold of his own clothes and rent them in two pieces.

He took up also the mantle of Elijah that fell from him, and went back, and stood by the bank of Jordan; and he took the mantle of Elijah that fell from him, and smote the waters, and said, "Where is the Lord God of Elijah?" and when he also had smitten the waters, they parted hither and thither; and Elisha went over.

And when the sons of the prophets which were to view at Jericho saw him, they said, "The spirit of Elijah doth rest on Elisha."

2 KINGS 2:9–15

When Elisha asked for a double portion of the spirit of Elijah, the Lord God not only granted that wish to Elisha but to all those who seek to be disciples of the Lord. The Risen Christ had come before through the prophet Elijah, or perhaps I should say it is the Risen Elijah that has come in the son of man, or Jesus the Christ. Let it be said, he who calls upon Elijah shall be given a double portion of his spirit, and he will be granted the wisdom, power, and strength of the Lord. He who calls upon the Risen Christ shall also partake and be given a portion of his spirit. It is the spirit of the Lord Most High that will come to you through us. We are one and the same.

The chariot of the angels that brought Elijah to Heaven will wait upon you to carry your wishes to the Lord. The spirit of Elijah will never cease to be, as he will be with you always until the end of time as you know it. It is Elijah and the Son of God who will guide you to the kingdom at the end of time. All those who have not yet ascended to the throne of the Lord, know that they will be waiting for you to bring you before the Lord and His Council. Elijah is the spoken truth of the Lord, for the knowledge that pertains to the scriptures runs from his mouth. I say to you this: for those of you who do not read the scriptures of the Lord, prayers to the great prophet will guide you to do otherwise. The healing and wisdom you seek from Him is written throughout scriptures, those within all the traditions under Him. Why is it when the Lord has given you knowledge of Him as within the scriptures that you do not seek to know it?

There is power in the scriptures, power from our Lord, power to heal you. Read of the prophets and teachers of the Lord such as Elijah or the son of man. Contemplate the healings, miracles, and teachings of the great prophets and the Son of God. You have asked me to teach you to heal in the name of my Father. Indeed, I say to you this: the words that come from the scriptures are truth. I speak about the words that come from our Lord God, not the ones that come from man.

You will know the difference. The ones that come from Him are of heavenly light. The ones that come from man who perceives the Lord in the contemplation of the ego self will be shown to you. The true scriptures are the words that come from the mouth of the Most High. The false teachings are the ones that come from darkness.

Death, Transition, and Life Eternal

The day following, when the people which stood on the other side of the sea saw that there was none other boat there, save that one whereinto his disciples were entered, and that Jesus went not with his disciples into the boat, but that his disciples were gone away alone (howbeit there came other boats from Tiberias nigh unto the place where they did eat bread, after that the Lord had given thanks).

When the people therefore saw that Jesus was not there, neither his disciples, they also took shipping, and came to Capernaum, seeking for Jesus. And when they had found him on the other side of the sea, they said unto him, "Rabbi, when camest thou hither?" Jesus answered them and said, "Verily, verily, I say unto you, ye seek me, not because ye saw the miracles, but because ye did eat of the loaves, and were filled. Labour not for the meat which perisheth, but for that meat which endureth unto everlasting life, which the Son of man shall give unto you; for him hath God the Father sealed." Then said they unto him, "What shall we do, that we might work the works of God?" Jesus answered and said unto them, "This is the work of God, that ye believe on him whom he hath sent." They said therefore unto him, "What sign shewest thou then, that we may see, and believe thee? What dost thou work? Our fathers did eat manna in the desert; as it is written, He gave them bread from heaven to eat."

Then Jesus said unto them, "Verily, verily, I say unto you, Moses gave you not that bread from heaven; but my Father giveth you the true bread from heaven. For the bread of God is he which cometh down from heaven, and giveth life unto the world."

Then said they unto him, "Lord, evermore give us this bread." And Jesus said unto them, "I am the bread of life: he that cometh to me shall never hunger; and he that believeth on me shall never thirst. But I said unto you, that ye also have seen me, and believe not. All that the Father giveth me shall come to me; and him that cometh to me I will in no wise cast out. For I came down from heaven, not to do mine own will, but the will of him that sent me. And this is the Father's will which hath sent me, that of all which he hath given me I should lose nothing, but should raise it up again at the last day. And this is the will of him that sent me, that every one which seeth the Son, and believeth on him, may have everlasting life; and I will raise him up at the last day."

JOHN 6:22–40

You have all asked me what it means to die for you. And I tell you that I have done so. Read the scriptures. It is your own perception of what death is and life eternal with Him. I am the bread of life. All that exists in the consciousness of my Father, I am. All that exists in the consciousness of you, I am. I came here not to serve you, but to show you how to serve Him. When the scriptures say that it was I who died for you, they are referring to the willful state of man and his lower nature. I allowed for the will of man to die so that the will of my

Father can be resurrected in the power of the Risen Spirit. What is so difficult about this concept to understand?

I will explain more. Remember, as above, so below. When I died, the lower forms of spirit that were part of my nature were raised up to the level of our Lord God. That included all aspects of personality, lower forms of consciousness, ego states, and linear reality. Like others before me, I was expanded to the greatness of light before the Lord at the moment I was to return to Him. Because of the light that I am capable of embracing, and because of my humanness that I was capable of being, all issues of the lower form of man's nature and all concepts of evil as you understand it had the opportunity to be lifted, as I so allowed. When I "died" for you, I brought healing to those levels of consciousness in the construct of your ordinary reality and raised you up even further to our Lord. It was my soul and spirit, as it has been with others, that brought you the opportunity to do as I have, to be one with Him. It is not I who think of myself as dying for you, it is I who think of the Spirit of the Lord that is within me who has brought you to eternal life. The bread of life is indeed that. You will be fed only by the Spirit of the Lord. Your human life cannot exist without it. This is truth. The son of man is not only me but any man who chooses to walk with the Lord. You have all raised me up to a level of being that you feel you cannot even touch. For I say to you this: when I die for you, I do so over and over again. When you die, you will also do so for another, and another. We die for each other because we raise each other up to the Lord each time we turn to Him.

With each man that dies, the spirit and the soul will have to be contended with. I say to you this: the spirit of one shall belong to another. The soul of one shall belong to the all.

When the time has come for my Father to take you, know that you will not be alone. You never are. You will have countless beings from the world of spirit to take you in their arms and welcome you home. Before your departure from your earthly existence, know that your spirit will spend much time with the Lord's Council in contemplation of your spiritual life and journey. Decisions will be made as to how you desire to learn about love and my Father on the next part of your journey. The spirit will be divided and healed in the ways of the Lord. Part of the spirit will rest with loved ones that it is has known in many lifetimes. Another part of the spirit will be raised before the Lord so that it has a chance to be healed by the light of Him. It is this spirit that has the opportunity to be closer to Him or to move further away from our Lord. There is yet another part of the spirit, the one that is of the light and life eternal. It is this part that will sit with the Lord and wait to journey with the lower forms of spirit and the soul once again. The decisions of the Council of our Lord and that of the willing student will decide upon where it is that the spirit and soul will place itself next. Be it in the world of spirit or on the earth plane once again. Sometimes we allow you to choose. Sometimes it is we who do the choosing for you. Always, we ask, knowing ahead of time what we see as the best road for you to learn about Him, about love.

The soul is a different and heavier construct of energy. It is larger than that of the lower forms of spirit, yet not separate from spirit. It is the resting place of the spirit that chooses to continue to learn of my Father. As there is ultimately one Spirit that is Him, there is one soul. The soul was created the moment that God emanated light in different forms of creation, in the dimensions of His choosing. First there was one soul, and from that soul was born another, and from that one, another. As I have said before, you are all saint and sinner. You are all light and darkness. Your soul is part of every soul that has embraced the light of Him and the darkness that is and is not of Him. When the spirit is ready to contemplate the Lord again, it shall choose a soul to rest in, or a number of souls that are resonant in their spiritual journeys to learn with. There may also be a number of spirits that are joined with one soul. The spirit and the soul at the end of time shall merge and be at one with the Lord and with the all.

Never look upon yourself and think you are just of your making. For that would be foolish. You carry the light of many, and the darkness of many, depending on how you choose to live your spiritual life in light of Him. As you continue to learn of Him, you will embrace eternal life through the continual death or ending of that which is not of the Lord's light. This is how it will be always. You die at every moment you awaken to Him, to love, to the light. You effect with this death a healing of so much more than yourself. If you could only see or recognize this wonder. You heal spirits and souls across time. You raise or lower those souls and spirits who are in the same resonant construct as your own spiritual life. This is of their own choosing also. You cannot raise to the Lord or pull someone from Him who does not desire to do so.

The time will come for you to leave your earthly body or even to transition from one dimension in the world of spirit to another. Why is it that you fear the loss so? Why is it that you fear the Lord so? Know that you are already part of the way home, to your true home in the kingdom of the Lord. You choose to suffer by holding on to what you think is your salvation. I see many of you who grasp on to the illusion even though you see the light ahead. I cannot tell you more than I have: that what you perceive as existing is not reality. The only way of being is that of pure heavenly light with my Father. So when the time has come for you to meet with Him, do not walk, *run to Him*. For He and His Council will be waiting to embrace you. Once you have been shown how much you are loved by the Lord and all the angels, a time will come for you to look upon your thoughts and actions of the past and see where it is you need to embrace the love of My Father more.

You look to me as your salvation, when I say to you, look to my Father. Look to that part of you that is Him! Death is nothing more than a cycle of energy that coexists with birth—such as light is a cycle of energy that coexists with darkness. When you raise your intellect to that of Divine intelligence and wisdom that the Lord hath given you, then you will see that death does not exist in the kingdom, only eternal life, such as darkness does not exist in the kingdom, only pure light.

Death resembles many different forms. There are times when the body will continue to live even though the spirit and the soul have left it. The attachment to the physical body will cause a portion of the spirit to continue to breathe life into the body or the body might be taken up by another spirit. I am referring to the deaths of those that are in their earthly existence. Through serious illness on any level, the spirit will begin to leave the body as the illness furthers itself upon the physicality and upon the spirit. There are many reasons this does happen. In any case, there are times when the spirit and soul will choose to leave before the body departs. I say to you this: be mindful of your fear of the Lord and His love. For only that will bind you in your attachment to the physical world. It is not wise to leave the body unattended for so long as wandering spirits will tend to find safe passage through it for their own guises. The darkness only comes when the spirit and soul have not fully entered into acceptance of the Lord's will for it. This is not to frighten you; this is to show you that the Lord's love for you will keep you safely wrapped in His tenderness.

There can be death of the mind, and death of the body. In either way, when the Lord calls to you, go to Him. There are times when you choose to go before your time, through self-inflicted agony or mental distress. I say to you this: be compassionate and loving to yourself. For there is no greater injustice than what you do to set yourself apart from the Lord and His will for you. The Lord will intercede at times on your behalf when it comes to self-inflicted agony and death. But always, wherever your spirit ends up, He will come to you without judgment but with sorrow for your decision to not see the truth of your light in its entirety. He will come and show you love, and show you another way to learn of that love. When you seek to know death through your own choosing and not of the Lord's will, we say to you this: know and trust in the Lord. We prefer that you leave the taking of the physical body up to the Lord and His will for you.

That is the way of the Lord and that is the way of love. If you so choose otherwise, we ask that you surround yourself in the light and love of Him during your agony so that you do not recreate the circumstances of your living experience in the world of spirit. That can and does happen. It is the same during the earthly experience or during your growth in the world of spirit. The Lord endeavors to be by your side. He will not insist His way, will, or love upon you, even though you have it all. You have Him. *He will never leave you.*

Self-inflicted agony and death will also come when the mind chooses to be ill. For it has become easier for many of you to seek the Lord through the mind inappropriately, rather than through the living experience of the heart, spirit, and soul. I am not speaking of that which urges you to seek Divine wisdom and intelligence. I am referring to those who seek to use the mind to know the Lord in a manner that is not in alignment with Divine Righteousness. In order for you to learn of the Lord and His love in the sense of righteousness, your living experience of Him need not be cut short by your own misgivings, fear, and doubt of who you are, of who He is.

When the mind seeks to know fervently of the light or of the darkness, it has the power to destroy the balance that the Lord has created for your learning during your earthly experience, or during your experiences in other realms. When you feel that the mind is overwhelmed with thoughts, do not seek to inhabit another plane of reality insomuch as the mind loses all contemplation of existence and balance. You will not find the true Lord in what you seek to occupy your mind with. I am not speaking about those who seek the world of spirit and union with Him periodically. I am speaking about those souls who lose complete ability of the mind to perceive light and darkness, reality and illusion. To know this is your choosing. To endeavor to search for light or darkness as a consequence of hardship during your present existence will bring you out of balance with all the dimensions of the self and spirit. This is because the search at this time still has many attachments and desires that are out of balance. It is this state of being that the darkness feeds upon. The light and love of the Lord will endeavor to protect and guide you, as you are given the strength of the Lord to persevere if you so desire it. There is truth when it is said that the Lord helps those who help themselves.

There are many who are given gifts of the Holy Spirit that manifest themselves as spiritual powers. Why is it that so many of you think they are not of the Lord? The moment you perceive gifts of the Lord as not of His Love is the moment those gifts will turn away from Him. The mind that you are given is as strong as that belonging to the essence of Him. It is this you must believe.

We recommend that you choose for your mind, body, and spirit to live as fruitfully as you can amidst the Lord's bounty for you. When the time comes for you to return to Him, know that you will do so and with grace. To inflict death upon the mind, body, or spirit of the self will take away the grace of the Lord that you so compassionately deserve.

When my Father took me to Heaven to be with Him, or as you say, when I died for you, I gave to you the light of all that you are capable of expressing. In doing so, I surrendered to my Father the pain of humanity for leaving His side. The inconsolable grief that is felt by the spirit and soul for having lost its way becomes transcended by the limitless love of my Father. There is death in which the grief, separation, and illusion exist no longer. I freely give to you the heart of my Father and the grace of the Holy Spirit. Through my heart and light, the kingdom of my Father shall be yours.

For those of you who aspire to the spiritual life, it is you who know that your earthly experience of Him and that experience you choose in the world of spirit is for your contemplation after you truly die. The dissolution of the body or the lower form of spirit in the other realms is incapable of truly becoming one with the Lord until a death of all lower forms of existence has taken place. Those we refer to as spirits retain part of their personalities and noetic makeup only for the benefit of serving you in the lower worlds. Sometimes this is to bring you comfort and guidance. Unfortunately, sometimes this is also to bring you pain. When they are with the Lord as one, they are nothing but light, no division of even spirit. That is the ultimate death, the unity of light and the unity of God. When you no longer need them or the Lord does not need His helpers, they will unite with Him in essence and energy.

You prepare yourself during your spiritual life to come to understand about this concept you refer to as death. It is only when you allow yourselves to embrace the beginnings of this concept that you will truly live as the living God within, in any realm or dimension. You cannot otherwise have a living experience of light and of the Lord.

When indeed the time comes for the Lord to take you, you will be surprised at the ease with which He grants you mercy, even at the knowledge of your will against Him. For I say to you this: be mindful of the Lord God throughout your earthly experience or time in the world of spirit. The way in which you will cross over to the Lord will be greatly affected by what you do during your spiritual life. It is not the sin of man that puts you in disregard of the Lord. It is your lack of faith in the process of rising to eternal life that will bring you anguish as the time nears for you to be with Him.

Death did not occur with the Garden of Eden as you so think. It created itself before in the kingdom of the Lord. Was it not an angel of the Lord that fell from Him, who went and took with him armies of angels to besiege the Lord and His goodness? What manifested in the garden was a part of the angels' ploy to deceive the Lord and His children of all truth and light. So you see, even angels can encounter death of the Lord's light. All beings in the world of spirit can until they are one of light with Him. The spiritual life does not end once you transition from what you refer to as death on the earth plane to life hereafter. *Your responsibility to be a child of the Lord never ends.* When the angels fell to the lower forms of reality, God granted all, even in the world of spirit, the freedom to choose life with Him or without Him. It is simple. The Garden of Eden is only symbolic of what took place in the kingdom of the Lord. The death of light as you would understand it first happened in the house of God. It was the Lord who allowed this to happen. He fully understood what it was that the angels needed to learn from this, and He let them go with His graces. That is why we say to you when any spirits of the Lord come to you, be it angels, saints, or the Lord's disciples, always ask the Lord God to make sure they are of light. Until you have come to that place where you truly know, just be mindful that many spirits will come that seek to be dishonest in the way of Him. When Jesus died for the salvation of many, he also died to resurrect the light that fell with the angels who were close to the Lord. Jesus was to show you that even those who fall heavily from grace can be saved by the Light of God and returned to the kingdom.

> *If any man see his brother sin a sin which is not unto death, he shall ask, and he shall give him life for them that sin not unto death. There is a sin unto death: I do not say that he shall pray for it. All unrighteousness is sin; and there is a sin not unto death. We know that whosoever is born of God sinneth not; but he that is begotten of God keepeth himself, and that wicked one toucheth him not. And we know that we are of God, and the whole world lieth in wickedness.*
>
> 1 JOHN 5:16–19

So you see, when the Lord God created you, He did so with the intention for you to live in love of Him, in love of yourself, in love of one another. When you seek to alter His truth and light, you indulge in the rituals that will bring your soul closer to darkness and ultimately death. Death of the spirit and death of the soul is more profound than the dissolution of the physical body. When you look not to His greatest commandment, you offer yourself that which will render your essence incapable of discerning truth. For we say to you this: the sin that leads to death is the one of pure intention to do ill will to the Lord's greatest commandment without due mercy. This is the sin that will bring injustice to the spirit and more to the soul. The sin that will not lead to death is the one where the grief of the Lord penetrates your heart so that you come to know and experience His mercy. The sin that leads to death will indeed cause the physical body a death so great and also cause those in the world of spirit the same.

Thus, the Lord did and did not create death. The Lord created for you the freedom to learn of the polarity of light and darkness within the concept of linear and nonlinear reality. Simply put, He gave you the power to know all the mysteries of Heaven. You were also given the free will to learn, know, and experience it all for yourselves. It is what you choose to do with that power that will create a death for you on different levels of your awareness and essence. Death is not a word that comes from the mouth of the Lord. This is something you have spoken of in order to help you relate better to your eternal truth. It is unfortunate that most of you do not contemplate death as much as we think you should. To contemplate it in this sense does not mean to ponder it. *It means to allow for the death of the darkness to continually move through you and expand itself into the Light of God.*

Death also symbolizes justice in the way of our Lord. That is how the Lord comes to interpret death. When He allowed for the angels of Heaven to rebuke Him, He did so with the foreknowledge of the justice that would affect mankind and that of the world of spirit. The

Lord does not take to mind the death of the physical body as there are more important things for Him to take concern of.

> *In the sweat of thy face shalt thou eat bread, till thou return unto the ground; for out of it wast thou taken, for dust thou art, and unto dust shalt thou return.*
>
> GENESIS 3:19

This does not mean that He wants you to treat the physical body without the kindness and mercy of Him. It is just that the Lord knows which element the body will return to after the spirit and soul have left it. And it was the Lord who proclaimed death's continuity when he spoke the above words as told in the scriptures.

As there is life eternal, so there is death eternal. The cycle will end when all are of the light of Him, and of the universal wisdom.

It is through death that we are raised to the kingdom. It is through death that we are raised in the mind, heart, spirit, and soul. The deaths of the Lord's prophets have brought to you many teachings of Him. Do you not think that the Lord knew what He was doing when He created you? Or when He sought to give you His power to know truth? Through death, you learn of love. Through death, you learn of power. Think about this.

Death as you know it can never overcome you if your soul is quenched by the desire for our Lord. For those who seek to bring harm to another soul will find themselves in death's way in regard to Him. When the spirit meets with death, it has more opportunity to resurrect itself into the light of the Christ and the light of God. When the soul has come face to face with death, it is harder to rid itself of the punishment it has created. The soul only faces death after it has tried many times to heal itself at the level of spirit. Thus, it has failed in succumbing to the light or chooses not to. For this, we give you many opportunities. If the soul chooses to create a Hell to live in, that is because it has brought it upon itself. Redemption and salvation through the Lord is always there for you. The best way to continue to live and die in right consciousness of the Lord God is to endeavor to be fulfilled in ecstasy by Him.

When a soul dies, know that it will regenerate itself. Just as the physical body turns to ashes once it disintegrates, so too will the soul decompose and regenerate itself into the goodness of Him. Even a soul who has chosen a Hell for itself and aligns with the Evil One shall eventually become weary of its circumstances and will die a death so that it can regenerate itself back into the light of the Lord. As we have stated many times, all will return to Him. All will return to the light, even the darkness. And so it will be.

I say to you this: if you do not love, you will stare death in the face a thousand times over. I do not speak of death that is in the light, I speak of death that is in the darkness.

When you permit yourselves to be of Him and the time comes for the body to dissolve itself, you will be sure to come back into the next life with less pain and suffering of the physical body unless otherwise deemed by Him. If you choose not to be of Him at the time of your crossing, then you will come back into this life with suffering beyond means. This is not of the Lord's doing. Those who hold on to the physical body in torment upon leaving it and in disgust of the Lord will create more torment in the life hereafter. It is most likely that that soul will incarnate again on the earth plane rather than the world of spirit to learn of their attachment to the physical body until they come to understand the death of it, and the glory of that physical death.

Yes, there is glory. Paul the apostle spoke these words of the Lord.

> *But some man will say, "How are the dead raised up? And with what body do they come?" Thou fool, that which thou sowest is not quickened, except it die. And that which thou sowest, thou sowest not that body that*

shall be, but bare grain, it may chance of wheat, or of some other grain. But God giveth it a body as it hath pleased him, and to every seed his own body.

All flesh is not the same flesh; but there is one kind of flesh of men, another flesh of beasts, another of fishes, and another of birds.

There are also celestial bodies, and bodies terrestrial; but the glory of the celestial is one, and the glory of the terrestrial is another. There is one glory of the sun, and another glory of the moon, and another glory of the stars, for one star differeth from another star in glory.

So also is the resurrection of the dead. It is sown in corruption; it is raised in incorruption. It is sown in dishonour; it is raised in glory. It is sown in weakness; it is raised in power. It is sown a natural body; it is raised a spiritual body. . . .

Now this I say, brethren, that flesh and blood cannot inherit the kingdom of God; neither doth corruption inherit incorruption. Behold, I shew you a mystery: we shall not all sleep, but we shall all be changed, in a moment, in the twinkling of an eye, at the last trump. For the trumpet shall sound, and the dead shall be raised incorruptible, and we shall be changed. For this corruptible must put on incorruption, and this mortal must put on immortality. So when this corruptible shall have put on incorruption, and this mortal shall have put on immortality, then shall be brought to pass the saying that is written.

1 CORINTHIANS 15:35–44, 50–54

He will swallow up death in victory.

ISAIAH 25:8

O death, where is thy sting? O grave, where is thy victory?
1 CORINTHIANS 15:55

There are many of you who do not see victory and justice in the death of the body. Your attachment to it impedes your return to the kingdom. The physical body can also be raised to the energy of the Lord, where the soul who inhabits it feels less torment on the physicality. Listen to us closely. For even when you are suffering so on the physical level, come to have complete faith and dignity of the Lord and you will see that you are suffering less. The Lord will send upon you His loving energy to unbind the physical pain of karma you have created for yourself. Even at the time of death, before you are risen completely, you may come to know no pain of suffering within.

At the end of time as you know it, the perception of death and reality will be different for you. Spirits and souls, embodied and not, will be able to cross over into the kingdom of God as they are. Then, we will all be embraced by the Lord Most High and come unto His arms as light. Your understanding of death will be raised by the Divine wisdom and intellect of the Lord. It is at that time the attachment to the death of the physical body shall be never more.

Even though you might choose death that is not in Divine Righteousness with our Lord, know that you will not be cast out of His loving embrace. You will always be given the opportunity to dance in the kingdom with Him.

The symbol of death in Christ is indeed the cross upon which he died. To look upon the cross with discontent and grief over the Christ is not what the Lord asks of you to do. To look favorably upon the cross as a token of grace within the transition of one life to the next is what the Lord wishes. The cross is not of despair, but of glory of the union with our Lord, of the glory of death and the promise of life eternal that it will bring. It has been revered by everyone, although we ask of you to see it as a means for you to understand about the glory of life ever after with Him. So when you offer the sign of the cross to another, or upon your own person, you are indeed acknowledging the power and glory of the living God. To continually see it as the vehicle for the suffering of Jesus will do nothing for your spiritual growth.

To fully comprehend death, one must complete the stages of spiritual growth as set forth by our Lord. They are those that Jesus the Christ and others before him have lived in light of the Lord's truth. They come in forms of sacraments, laws, commandments, and truths. To relate suffering to death in light of these stages is something that you have chosen to do. Suffering happens when you do not allow for the works and the will of the Lord to move through you with grace, patience, and understanding. You can comprehend death at each moment you choose to live as the Christ did, not as Jesus the man, but the Son of God. These stages are given to you through the trials and joys of Jesus the Christ, as with others before him. They directly relate to the mysteries as set upon the rosary of the Holy Mother. I am referring to those mysteries that are glorious. Each time you experience a death of the spirit or the self, you have the opportunity to be resurrected into the light of the Lord as the Christ was. For I say to you this: know and learn of the death of Jesus, not the death of Christ. Christ never died, only Jesus did. It is simple. Every time you think you will die a death on any level, contemplate the true life of the Christ after the death of Jesus occurred. You spend so much time wasted in the suffering of the man Jesus, more than even he did. Use your time wisely.

Even in the joyful and sorrowful mysteries of Jesus, you will find the glorious ones, the Christ, the Son of God. You will find death only in the way you perceive his suffering. In the way that Jesus truly suffered and died, he only found peace with his Father in Heaven.

Healing and the Mercy of God

Then answered Jesus and said unto them, "Verily, verily, I say unto you, the Son can do nothing of himself, but what he seeth the Father do: for what things soever he doeth, these also doeth the Son likewise. For the Father loveth the Son, and sheweth him all things that himself doeth; and he will shew him greater works than these, that ye may marvel. For as the Father raiseth up the dead, and quickeneth them, even so the Son quickeneth whom he will. For the Father judgeth no man, but hath committed all judgment unto the Son, that all men should honour the Son, even as they honour the Father. He that honoureth not the Son honoureth not the Father which hath sent him. . . . Verily, verily, I say unto you, the hour is coming, and now is when the dead shall hear the voice of the Son of God; and they that hear shall live."

JOHN 5:19–23, 25

Let it be said, those who seek to heal in the name of the Lord God must believe in me, and those who seek to heal in the name of the Christ must believe in my Father. To heal in the name of the Christ you must believe in the laws as set forth by Divine Providence. The manifestation of creative forces must work in opposition to each other so that balance of will and life energy converge.

When the Lord God asks me to heal, it is decreed and His power shall rule above all else. I did not heal everyone that I encountered along the way in my travels; I healed those who heard the voice of God's Son. Know this, dear children: every one of you is called to be the Son of God; not everyone listens. The Lord God will heal everyone. Not everyone wants to be healed. There is a time for all of you to learn about the presence of the Lord within you and to appreciate the love of the Lord. There are times when many of you take ill, and it is those times when you must know that the Lord is with you. To take ill may manifest itself in different ways, for the Lord's challenges are many as you seek to understand your purpose. When the Lord has given a judgment or Divine ruling as set upon a soul, know that it is the Lord alone who has decreed this soul's purpose as having a special mission. There is karma among you that is decreed by Him to be of service to humanity and to those in the world of spirit. You will be healed at the time your karma is complete with the Lord. Remember, healing will avail itself in the appropriate ways and times as deemed by my Father. That is truth.

When you look around you, do you not see souls who are born with deformities and grave illnesses? Do you not ask when it is that the Lord will heal them? I tell you this: the intention as set forth by the soul's mission is always of my Father's will. It is the will of the soul as to how it chooses to live out that mission. There are times when souls are born in agony to your eyes, only to serve the mission of Him for a higher purpose. You might ask why it is that the Lord does not heal them. For this is the healing, dear children. It is these souls whose healing is larger than that of their own spirit. It belongs to the kingdom of the Lord and all who dwell within it. It is because of souls like these that you may also be healed. Yet you fail to see the angels among you that you so judge as the unworthy. Look a little closer at the souls that live amongst you. They are children of God, as you are a child of Him. You want to heal like me? Show compassion, strength, love, and mercy to those you deem unworthy of it so. That is your greatest challenge in healing as I do. This is your greatest obstacle. Did I turn away from the lepers that came to me? Did I show them fear, or the courage and love of my Father? Let it be said: Any man who can show their face to the Lord in earnest and with courage, any man who can offer love to another whom they deem unworthy, let the might of the Lord be with them always, and may the power of the Lord to heal come through them. The moment you can touch the leper among you, there will be no greater healer than the Lord who works through you.

To love as I do, to love as my Father does, that is the power and light behind every soul that is healed. To show the Lord's mercy and compassion for your fellow man and those in the world of spirit is when you will become a healer of men, a healer of souls. You do not need to touch a person and make him well for the power of the Lord or of the Christ to work through you. You need only to be of the Christ energy and the essence of the Lord for you to heal.

When it comes to the healing of karma, this is left up to the Lord alone. When you become a healer of men and a healer of souls, the Lord will come to you and show you the time to release the soul from any past, present, or future responsibilities in the way of Him. It is usually the Lord who does this. And as always, He has appointed those in the world of spirit and on the plane of earth to carry out His duties.

Do know and understand this. Karma does not always have to be healed. There is a time and place for everything under the kingdom of God. I am only speaking of that karma that has kept the soul in its own agony. And it is not for you to know which souls they are. That is why I tell you to offer love to everyone that you meet, for the child of God within them is the child of the Lord within you.

When you are given the opportunity of the Lord to help free the soul from this agony, trust you will be shown. Do not fear or doubt in your ability to do right by Him, for when you are given gifts of the Lord to heal and wish to heal like I do, always ask for the Lord's Divine Will to take place and know that it does so. You can do no harm in the healing of another if your intention is in Divine righteousness of Him. When you seek to heal of your own agenda, trust that the Lord will be watching you, and protecting the soul to whom you offer your healing, not the Lord's. What comes to a soul is brought on in part by its passions and what it desires to know of Him or not know of Him.

To unbind the soul, look to the Lord and ask for His mercy and wisdom. A soul may be released through continual prayers offering that soul up to the Lord for all goodness and protection. The soul must agree to be risen to the Lord in the state of duality so that it will be healed of any doubt of its true Godnature. You must offer upon the body the sign of the cross and throw holy water upon the heart, mouth, and head of the soul—the places where fear and doubt emanate. And you must ask the soul if it desires to be saved by the Lord God. If the soul says yes, it must be willing to release to Him all that has held his soul back from the kingdom. His promise to the Lord will be that he listens to the Lord's will for him forevermore. It is simple. The soul must promise to love and carry the light from which he was born. *If it is of the Lord's will and is the appropriate time for the soul to be released from his duties, the request will be granted by the angels, archangels, the Council of the Lord, and the Lord Himself.* Remember, this is a most gracious blessing given to you. The healing of karma affects not only the soul who is being healed but all souls in relation to that learning continuum.

Again, there are those whose karma does not need to be healed, only in your eyes. That is for the Lord's understanding. The soul will come to know in time through the grace of the Lord of what purpose he serves.

There will also be times when you offer this healing upon a soul and the Lord does not grant the request for the release of the soul's duties. Then you are to know that the soul is not complete in its mission for the Lord and for himself. When it is time, the soul will be released from its duties and brought into the arms of the Creator.

When the soul has been healed and released from its karmic duties, know that the soul must stay in righteousness with the Lord, or else the healing will be changed. This is not of the Lord's doing, this is the way that Divine Providence is bound within the Logos. All that is healed is always in relation to the creative energies of our Lord. Divine Providence in relation to healing does not serve the will of the Lord alone, but the will of the universal consciousness. Was this created by Him? Yes. Was this also created by you? Yes. Divine Providence was set forth by the laws of the Creator. The free will of man set up another matrix of energy to work within that spiritual paradigm in order for things to be the way they are. That is what I meant in the beginning of this discourse when I said, *you must believe in the laws as set forth by Divine Providence for the manifestation of creative forces to work in opposition of each other so that balance of will and life energy converge.* In regard to healing, the Lord's will, the rules as set forth by Divine Providence, the Logos, and the will of man will work in opposition to create the desired intention that the soul seeks.

When the soul has obtained its truth and desired intention, then the polarities of energy will no longer be at opposite ends and a healing will take place—a healing on any level that is the will of the Lord and the universal construct. When a soul is healed, it will always support the good of the universal construct and never the soul alone. That is why I say to you to believe that you are healed in every moment by the kingdom of the Lord. To know this, to have faith in this, you have already proclaimed a truth of the Lord and the Holy Spirit that inherently works within you, and you have set upon yourself and upon the universal construct a healing that will effect itself according to the laws of God. This I promise you. There is no one better that could proclaim the healing powers of the Lord through you than the Lord himself in your own heart's sanctuary. It is not I, nor another who can do greater. Until you come to realize this, the Lord sends you teachers like myself and others, until you can believe that I am you, and you are me. We are all of and belonging to the Lord and the universe.

When you arise in the morning, ask with the greatest love you have for yourself and with the greatest love you have for the Lord to heal you. Believe with complete faith, and it shall be given.

The greatest obstacle to being healed is the absence of love; this I cannot tell you too many times. You think you all know of love, of the

Lord's love. I tell you again, the moment you can touch a leper among you, there will be no greater healer than the Lord Himself who works through you. The moment you can show that soul the tenderness, mercy, and the love of Him that you so desire from the Lord for yourself is the moment when you love like Him. That is when you love like me. If you think this is so easy for you, then why are most of His children alone and suffering so?

The truth of who you are in the spirit of Him is given so righteously. The apostle Paul, a favored disciple of the Lord, was known for his works of mercy. It would serve you well to read the writings of this child of the Lord as well as other works of disciples. In remembrance of me, in remembrance of the Lord, seek out His teachings, seek out His works through those that are called to serve Him. To meditate upon the works of these souls will offer a healing to the soul and to the mind of those who seek to know the truth of Him. As it was written, call forth the energy of the Lord and of the Christ as you read upon these words. Feel the Lord's love embrace you through them.

> *But thou, O man of God, flee these things; and follow after righteousness, godliness, faith, love, patience, meekness. Fight the good fight of faith, lay hold on eternal life, whereunto thou art also called, and hast professed a good profession before many witnesses. I give thee charge in the sight of God, who quickeneth all things, and before Christ Jesus, who before Pontius Pilate witnessed a good confession, that thou keep this commandment without spot, unrebukeable, until the appearing of our Lord Jesus Christ. Which in his times he shall shew, who is the blessed and only Potentate, the King of kings, and Lord of lords, who only hath immortality, dwelling in the light which no man can approach unto; whom no man*

hath seen, nor can see; to whom be honour and power
everlasting. Amen.

1 TIMOTHY 6:11–16

Take these words and pray with them over your loved ones. For
these words are of the Christ, the Holy Spirit, the Lord God, and of
all the teachers of light. Decree these words over those who are ill of
body, of mind, and of spirit, and you will see the light of the Lord
come through them and bring them peace.

The offering of inner peace to a soul is perhaps the most loving
of gifts that a soul can feel within itself. When the love of the Lord
is known throughout the soul and spirit, peace of the Lord prevails
within. Inner peace is important in order for the soul to cultivate the
kingdom of the Lord in its heart. It is important for the construct of
humanity and the world of spirit to maintain this inner peace so that
light continues to be made manifest through the soul's creation of self
and spirit. The peace of the Lord be with you all and keep you in the
arms and graces of the Creator.

The Healing of a Blind Man

And as Jesus passed by, he saw a man which was blind
from his birth. And his disciples asked him, saying,
"Master, who did sin, this man, or his parents, that he
was born blind?" Jesus answered, "Neither hath this man
sinned, nor his parents; but that the works of God should
be made manifest in him. I must work the works of him
that sent me, while it is day; the night cometh, when no
man can work. As long as I am in the world, I am the
light of the world." When he had thus spoken, he spat on
the ground, and made clay of the spittle, and he anointed
the eyes of the blind man with the clay, and said unto

him, "Go, wash in the pool of Siloam." . . . He went his
way therefore, and washed, and came seeing.

JOHN 9:1–7

When I teach you about me, about my Father and His laws, why is it
that you judge another's disparity against my Father's will? When you
see someone who is ill or who has taken on circumstances that seem
unkind to you, do not bring judgment upon them as being bereft of
my Father's love and will. As I have told you before, judge not another
person's path, for you do not know from where they came and where
they shall go. That is up to my Father to bring discernment upon.
This is not karma as you would think of it, this is not reparation of
sins against the Lord. This is not concerning the will of the self. For
this is the will of the Lord Most High. And there will be many times
when you will meet with those who are living the will of Him when
you will think that they are bereft of my Father's love. The power of
the Lord is not up for your judgment, that is something that the Lord
will decide how to make manifest through those who are willing to
learn and teach others.

When I say that there is no one that can work in the night, I am
speaking of the truth that no one can work in the realm of my Father
without the knowledge and wisdom that knowing Him brings to you.
It is easier to see the truths of your own making, rather than to accept
what the Lord hath given you. For in this man to be healed, it was
neither karma, nor sin, nor the darkness that took away his vision.
Rather, it was the will and reward of the Lord God to make manifest
through this soul the mercy of Him. Indeed, there are those times
that the angels rejoice when God hath given such a gift of holiness
to one who is so well deserving of it. When God has given you gifts
of a similar nature, do not think of the Lord as bringing punishment
upon you. There are reasons within Divine Providence and that of the
Logos where your incapacity (as you see it) is simply bringing the light

of God to the world. This is something that the Lord has asked you to do before you returned to the plane of earth and this is something you have chosen. Remember, what comes to you in the highest will of the Lord, accept it and rejoice. To be chosen by Him so that you are an example of the Lord's loving kindness is extraordinary.

Each agreement made by those searching for Him is different for each soul. It is from the mouth of the Lord only that you shall hear the truth of your mission.

You make of illness and incapacity more than what it truly is. I say to you this: render yourself incapable of demeaning what has been appropriated to you. It is up to the Lord when the truth shall set you free. It is up to you depending on your faith and willingness. The reasons for illness and incapacity are many—from self-inflicted distress to the work of the Evil One, from the magnificent power of the Lord, or perhaps from duty. When I say that it is up to the Lord as to when the truth shall set you free, I am not speaking of the Lord who is external of your own devices. I am speaking about the Lord God who is within each and every one of you. There are times when your spirit and soul will make decisions without the knowing of the self, and it is those decisions that will create the space for the laws of God to make manifest through you. These decisions of course are not without God being aware of them, whether these decisions are of the light or the darkness. Do not spend countless hours searching for the meaning of your illness or incapacity. Rather, spend countless hours asking the Lord God how it is that you can use that energy to be of service to Him, to others, to the universe. When you do so, the Lord will show you the meaning. Be patient with His answer. The answers do not usually come to you the very moment that you seek them. The Lord God is knowledgeable in the ways of man and of the greater mission. His understanding of your integration is merciful. It is this way with all things, even when the Lord hath promised you His reward. Know that you shall have it always in eternity with Him, but be patient, for the Lord's intelligence knows all things that come under Him. When you choose not of Him, then you are left to fend not only in the realm of God, for He shall never leave you, but also in the realm of the Evil One. So trust in the Lord I say to you, and you will come to know the truth of your mission as time proceeds.

When I healed the man born blind, I was to show you that the Lord God works and maintains His power both in the light and in the darkness. This is not to say that the Lord is of the darkness; this is to say that the Lord is omnipotent within the darkness and that in the darkness you will also find Him. His light cannot leave anything that was created in the image and likeness of Him. Remember, the angels that fell from my Father were of light, too. They could not be of pure darkness, because that does not truly exist. For the darkness to even exist there has to be light created by the Lord God Himself. Even the Evil one cannot breathe life if there were no Lord to speak about.

So I say to you this: when you seek to heal as I do, remember it is within the capacity of the Lord to make manifest through the soul a myriad of possibilities. Remember that the light will coexist with the darkness in the soul that you are asking the Lord to heal, whether yours or another's. Do not be afraid of the darkness, children, and never be afraid of the light. Respect that all souls have a learning continuum within the realm of God. And in the lower states of consciousness and reality of the soul there has to be a balance for the soul to exist as self. When you cast out the demons, you are giving balance to that spiritual understanding that is already known in the kingdom. The healing comes not when the demon leaves the body. When the soul understands and interprets its relationship to the Lord and to the darkness, it will bring upon it a new awareness, a healing indeed. The darkness needs healing because it is you who is out of balance with the perspective of the Lord within it, as well as the light within it. When you come to truly understand this, the demons will leave you as quickly as they came.

Thus, when you seek to heal with the Lord's will in mind, have respect for all that is within His kingdom. Until then, fear the Evil One because he can bring illness, pain, misery, and despair. To fear in this instance is to understand, respect, and to put into proper perspective. Now you are learning! When you have this learning, the Lord God will work within you at every moment to cast out what does not truly belong. You will have a greater understanding of the reasons why all is under the domain of the Lord.

This is why many times when I have healed those with demons inside, all I have had to do was tell them to be quiet and leave. I understand the workings of all the truths of the universe.

And soon you will too. This respect of spiritual laws and paradigms that have ruled the universe and the kingdom of God for eternity is much needed in order for you to call upon the power of the Lord to heal. You give to the Lord that which you choose to give. Give to Him all your understanding so that His understanding may be with you.

The Cleansing of the Lepers

And it came to pass, as he went to Jerusalem, that he passed through the midst of Samaria and Galilee. And as he entered into a certain village, there met him ten men that were lepers, which stood afar off. And they lifted up their voices, and said, "Jesus, Master, have mercy on us." And when he saw them, he said unto them, "Go shew yourselves unto the priests." And it came to pass, that, as they went, they were cleansed. And one of them, when he saw that he was healed, turned back, and with a loud voice glorified God, and fell down on his face at his feet, giving him thanks; and he was a Samaritan. And Jesus answering said, "Were there not ten cleansed? But where are the nine? There are not found that returned to give

glory to God, save this stranger." And he said unto him,
"Arise, go thy way; thy faith hath made thee whole."

LUKE 17:11–19

For any of you who do not learn humility of the Lord cannot indeed serve Him or heal by Him. When you seek to obtain His righteousness, you must first learn of gratitude for all that the Creator does for you. It is upon your heart and soul that the expression of thankfulness renders good karma; so many of you do not truly understand the importance of this. The Lord and all His works shall not be taken for granted. When the Lord bestowed this grace of healing among the lepers through me, there was only one who returned to give praise. The giving of praise and thanks to the Lord for His gifts to you has its effects in the many dimensions of the world of spirit and within the universe as well. The power of giving thanks and praise to the Lord belongs with the profound union with the one true God. When you are offering your praise, you are giving a service to the Lord and that of His mercy, which your soul needs to create. How generous it is of Him to give you all that He has, all that He is. How selfish of you not to recognize Him in everything. How ignorant it is of you not to thank Him. To be of service to Him is indeed a gracious offering of your soul to be one with His. When those nine lepers failed to recognize the glory of the Lord, they were no different in spirit and soul than they were in their physical malady. I said to the one leper that returned to give the Lord thanks that indeed it was his faith that saved him, as he offered his soul and spirit up to the Lord for the Lord to do His bidding upon Him for the goodness of all. It is that one soul who was healed, not the nine. They would soon come to realize the truth in their ignorance.

When you seek to heal in the name of the Lord, give thanks to Him and praise His name for the gift of the kingdom He hath given you. You are declaring Divine justice in doing so.

The righteous shall come to know God. As you are healed, you become righteous unto Him. This is truth. There is no other way. There is no other healing. Sit with the Lord and be righteous and deserving of His greatest love for you. It is simple. In the words of the apostle Paul:

> *Though I speak with the tongues of men and of angels, and have not charity, I am become as sounding brass, or a tinkling cymbal. And though I have the gift of prophecy, and understand all mysteries, and all knowledge; and though I have all faith, so that I could remove mountains, and have not charity, I am nothing. And though I bestow all my goods to feed the poor, and though I give my body to be burned, and have not charity, it profiteth me nothing.*
>
> *Charity suffereth long, and is kind; charity envieth not; charity vaunteth not itself, is not puffed up, doth not behave itself unseemly, seeketh not her own, is not easily provoked, thinketh no evil; rejoiceth not in iniquity, but rejoiceth in the truth; beareth all things, believeth all things, hopeth all things, endureth all things. Charity never faileth: but whether there be prophecies, they shall fail; whether there be tongues, they shall cease; whether there be knowledge, it shall vanish away. For we know in part, and we prophesy in part. But when that which is perfect is come, then that which is in part shall be done away. When I was a child, I spake as a child, I understood as a child, I thought as a child; but when I became a man, I put away childish things. For now we see through a glass, darkly; but then face to face. Now I know in part, but then shall I know even as also I am known. And now abideth faith, hope, charity, these three; but the greatest of these is charity.*
>
> 1 CORINTHIANS 13:1–13

All the ways in which I have taught you how to heal, they are powerless without the love of the Lord, without your love for Him, and your love for each other. This is so.

Always remember this, when you seek to heal as I do in the name of my Father, do not proclaim yourself better than the soul that you are healing. Do not proclaim yourself better than the Lord. For what you proclaim will come back to teach you otherwise. There is no one greater than another. Be cautious of righteousness of power without the Lord as you are healing or asking to be healed by Him. You will not receive what you ask for, but you will receive a learning of grace and humility under Him. There is no one that can heal without learning to appreciate the Lord in their heart. No one.

Be mindful of the soul to which you request healing in the name of the Father. For anyone who does not look to you as an equal child of the Lord is not a healer of men, of souls, of the angels, and the Lord Most High. When I washed the feet of my disciples, I told them these words in response to their bewilderment.

> *Know ye what I have done to you? Ye call me Master and Lord; and ye say well, for so I am. If I then, your Lord and Master, have washed your feet, ye also ought to wash one another's feet. For I have given you an example, that ye should do as I have done to you. Verily, verily, I say unto you, the servant is not greater than his lord; neither he that is sent greater than he that sent him. If ye know these things, happy are ye if ye do them.*
>
> JOHN 13:12–17

Do not let idolatry besiege you as you come into the healing powers of the Lord. I am not referring to your love of the Lord, but the false love of yourself and power that does not rightly belong to you as you would believe. To let those you heal by the Lord's love idolize you is foolish. You will come to learn quickly otherwise. To do that is not of the Lord's love or even of the love of yourself, which is holy. That is love of grandeur to which you seek, and healing in the name of the Lord hath no place for it.

Sacraments and Healing

Then Peter opened his mouth, and said, "Of a truth I perceive that God is no respecter of persons. But in every nation he that feareth him, and worketh righteousness, is accepted with him. The word which God sent unto the children of Israel, preaching peace by Jesus Christ (he is Lord of all), that word, I say, ye know, which was published throughout all Judaea, and began from Galilee, after the baptism which John preached: how God anointed Jesus of Nazareth with the Holy Ghost and with power, who went about doing good, and healing all that were oppressed of the devil, for God was with him. And we are witnesses of all things which he did both in the land of the Jews, and in Jerusalem; whom they slew and hanged on a tree. Him God raised up the third day, and shewed him openly; not to all the people, but unto witnesses chosen before of God, even to us, who did eat and drink with him after he rose from the dead. And he commanded us to preach unto the people, and to testify that it is he which was ordained of God to be the Judge of quick and dead. To him give all the prophets witness, that through his name whosoever believeth in him shall receive remission of sins."

While Peter yet spake these words, the Holy Ghost fell on all them which heard the word.

ACTS 10:34–44

You place so much of your own thoughts upon the sacraments that the Lord hath given you that they have become less of Him and more of your own desires. When my Father gave you these rites of initiation unto His kingdom, He did so with the intention of birthing you to the newness of the Lord, birthing you to the presence of the Holy Spirit upon your heart, soul, and mind. This was in reverence to those sacrifices that I made on your behalf while I was still on the earth, and those that I continually make for you while in Heaven.

The sacraments are tests of strength and endurance upon the soul, marked with great wisdom and knowledge from the Lord Most High. I say to you this: do not look upon the sacraments as testaments of another's place with the Lord. Look upon them as the Lord's trials for you that will lift you up and raise you to Him. To receive a sacrament by a prophet of the Lord does not mean that you are absolved from what you have hidden from. To receive a sacrament simply means that the Lord is opening the door for you to transform yourself into a living God, a living Christ, a sacred vessel for His glory to be made manifest in. You have given authority over these sacraments to man in all traditions, when it is the Lord who has all authority as to when it is time for you to be initiated into these graces. The transformations that will accompany these rites are great. You will receive sacraments from the Lord God many times throughout your soul's awakening. You will come to know endurance and strength of the soul through them. Each time you feel the strength of the Lord upon you and within you, know that you have risen to the next level of grace with Him.

When God the Father anointed His son Jesus in baptism through John, He opened the doorway for all of you to be made in the image and likeness of Him. He opened the doorway for all of you to receive the glory of the Lord in all His splendor. He opened the doorway for humanity and the conscience of the world of spirit to be lifted into the arms of the Creator. He allowed for the transformation of man to be manifest on the level of the spirit, soul, and consciousness of all. He created the paradigm of oneness within all things, within love. The baptism of Jesus was just as holy as the resurrection of the Christ. Without the one, you cannot have the other.

Through the sacraments, the creative power of the Spirit of the Living God is made to work its miracles within each one of you. This is truth. The importance of these rites is made so by you. If you only knew of the power and glory available to you when you allow yourself to be immersed in the sacredness of these rites of passage unto Him.

The Lord hath given you His throne to learn from. Take the power of these sacraments and use them to your learning advantage, your growth to be of Him. Each time you ask to be anointed in the name of the Father, you will be. This I promise you. Whoever asks for a blessing from God shall never be turned away. In this you must believe.

The sacraments are powerful as they help man put into proper perspective their relationship to sin and their relationship to God with sin and without it. Let go of your sins, dear children, and do not be afraid of the loneliness that you will encounter in doing so. The sacraments will bring you as much sorrow as they will joy. To grow in the faith of the Lord through them you must know that all things will fall into the perspective as the grace of the Lord would deem them.

The sacraments act as lighthouses for the soul, they brighten the way for the soul to see clearly the way back home to the kingdom of the Lord. When you ask the Lord to partake in these initiations, do not hesitate to open your heart to Him when He has granted your request. There are many of you that do not know how much the Lord truly loves you. When He gives you a blessing so great, it is because He misses you so in His heart, and wishes for your safe return back into His arms.

Thou hast caused men to ride over our heads; we went through fire and through water, but thou broughtest us out into a wealthy place.

PSALMS 66:12

It is with each sacrament you will receive in the appropriate perspective all of the light, the darkness, and the mercy of the Lord that will be made known to you. One cannot go through the light without knowing and experiencing the darkness. You know by now that your essence is that of light. The moment you were no longer of essence and sprang forth into energy, you made yourself available to more than just light. Adam and Eve in the Garden of Eden happened only because what manifested on earth did so in the upper dimensions of the world of spirit. You will go through the fires of purification and transformation to come to the waters of the Spirit. Both sin and grace will be made known to you because the Lord God encompasses both. Do you think that you would be of a nature that the Lord God does not know about Himself? Indeed, we say not. It is because of His many virtues that the Lord hath in proper perspective and righteousness His light of the world, and it is from that light that He serves us, all of mankind, and the universe. It is because of His relationship to all that exists that He is the Lord Most High. It is because of that relationship that within His true kingdom there is no darkness. Only the light exists because of the respect and understanding of where the darkness belongs. When humans and those in the world of spirit no longer have a desire to understand or carry themselves within the darkness, the darkness will just dissolve itself into light. Remember, all things are of oneness with Him, all things.

Do you not think the Lord understood the desires of man, spirit, and soul before He created you? These sacraments upon which He blesses you are for you only. You will come to understand this soon.

The cycle of grace and sin is not to be discounted but admired for the knowledge and wisdom that can come to the soul upon understanding this paradigm. God has not only placed Himself amidst the light but also the darkness. And it is up to you to search for Him in the error of your ways, in the misunderstanding of who you think He is. You are reborn into the life of the Living God through the sanctity of the sacraments that are given in complete love for you and your highest purpose. You do not know what it is to be truly born until you have graciously committed to living your life in the way that God intended. You have that opportunity many times over during your spiritual life.

In different traditions, the Lord God has given rites of passage so that each individual can find their way back to Him within their own intellectual and spiritual understanding. In the way of the Christ, the sacraments given to Him by our Lord God are as follows. They are Holy Baptism, the Eucharist, Confirmation of the Holy Spirit, Renunciation of Sins, Anointing of the Sick, Matrimony, and the Holiest of Orders.

In each of them, there is one theme of importance. That is that the Spirit of the Living God is alive within each one of you. That spirit is reborn to give you the strength and courage to be of the light of the world as your Father in Heaven wishes for you to be. With each of these sacraments, you have the opportunity to create Heaven on earth and to put into perspective your light to the world, your light to Him, and your light to yourself. I say to you this: look not upon the goodness of the Lord to save you, for that is already given. Look to the goodness of your own soul to bring you to salvation of Him. You know not the power that you have in the name of Him. If you did, we would not be having this discourse.

It is through Baptism that you come to receive the other rites and learn there is no difference in the Spirit of God from one passage to the next. They all express themselves in form differently from one another and are marked by various levels of strength, faith, and knowledge of the Lord. Yet they are all of His birth unto you, and your birth unto Him, always.

With the Eucharist, you find the Lord in all things. You come to know Him through the Divine Union that you made yourself to be with Him. You are reborn into the oneness that you left.

With Confirmation, the Spirit of the Living God is once again declaring His presence within you, gathering strength as you pursue your life of the Father. Your spirit's understanding of the Trinity is deepened as you come to mature in your spiritual life.

Through the Renunciation of Sins, you come to begin to understand why it is you left the Father in the first place. Your perceptions of light and the darkness begin to unfold in a higher understanding regarding your relationship to Him.

Through the Anointing of the Sick, you are humbled by the humility of the Father for your spiritual life. As you are reborn into the womb of the Most Holy, you prepare for your return to Him.

In Matrimony, you are given the joyful opportunity to be reborn to the Spirit of the Living God in the sharing of your spiritual life with another.

And finally, in the Holiest of Orders, you affirm your faith as being born unto Him and profess the rest of your life to be solely dedicated to the understanding and exploration of Him.

Know that it is partially your responsibility to take hold of the Lord's power and might as given to you during these rites, for the way in which you come to know Him will greatly depend upon it. I say to you this: commit yourself totally to the Father in Heaven, and you will be eternally baptized through the life-giving waters of the Holy Spirit. One might wonder how the powers of sin and grace can be in the soul at the same time. For I choose to see it in another light. When all is in perspective in the way of the Lord, it is what it is—light. Do not place your own interpretations of what this light is; that is what the Father will do. It is only up to you to find your relationship to that light. When you are baptized and the Holy Spirit renews that of your own spirit into the Living God's, it is not that it drives out all evil, it is that you find peace among the duality of the will that you perceive is within you. It is that peace and righteousness that will cast out evil if the soul is at the beginning of its spiritual life. For the soul who is advanced in his knowledge and love of the Lord, it will simply put into alignment all that was created in the image and likeness of Him. Evil will not need to be cast out at this level, for there will be a holy relationship between all that is light and all that is dark, leaving nothing left for interpretation but the Lord Himself and all His glory. I will say to you again: that which you are given by Him, He has knowledge of also. That is why He is God and you are you. He has practiced much longer at being the Lord of the heavens than you have.

You see, as you advance in your spiritual life and become more of Him, these things will be easy for you to understand and grasp within the realm of your consciousness.

And so it was said in the gospel of John:

> *In the beginning was the Word, and the Word was with God, and the Word was God. The same was in the beginning with God. All things were made by him; and without him was not any thing made that was made. In him was life; and the life was the light of men. And the light shineth in darkness; and the darkness comprehended it not.*
>
> JOHN 1:1–3

So you see, dear children, all things came to be through Him. As the light shines in the darkness, the darkness is still there in right perspective of the Lord. It comes to respect the truth in the light and its presence is transformed into an inner peace in the kingdom of Heaven. You desire healing from Him. Look at the graces He bestows upon you through these blessed sacraments. You will receive healings upon your soul in more ways than your human self could ever imagine.

Indeed, it takes time for the consciousness of humanity and the world of spirit to come to this place. It is our hope that you use this wisdom to deepen your relationship to the Father and to that of His unsurpassed glory for your soul's resurrection.

> *But what things were gain to me, those I counted loss for Christ. Yea doubtless, and I count all things but loss for the excellency of the knowledge of Christ Jesus my Lord, for whom I have suffered the loss of all things, and do count them but dung, that I may win Christ and be found in him, not having mine own righteousness, which is of the law, but that which is through the faith of Christ, the righteousness which is of God by faith; that I may know him, and the power of his resurrection, and the fellowship of his sufferings, being made conformable unto his death, if by any means I might attain unto the resurrection of the dead.*
>
> *Not as though I had already attained, either were already perfect; but I follow after, if that I may apprehend that for which also I am apprehended of Christ Jesus.*
>
> PHILIPPIANS 3:7–12

Now is the time to take hold of what the Lord hath given you. All of your souls have come to the place where you are ready to receive Him in light of yourself. The gains that the apostle Paul were referring to were those belonging to the bounty of the Lord in the way of his spiritual life. He had come to realize that his knowledge of the spiritual life meant nothing without His faith and love of the Lord and Christ Jesus. Even with that, he was at the very beginning from whence he started.

When you rise to the kingdom of the Lord, you will rejoice in splendor, and then you will come to see that you had never really left. The elation of being with Him turns itself into peace and stillness. This is a stillness within the existence and expression of light. You will know that it is only God that matters. Even the inexplicable joy that you feel in being with Him becomes of less importance.

Paul came to the understanding of the relationship between Christ Jesus and God, and the transposing of the spirit and soul of the Most High on all souls born from Him. Here is where you come to the understanding of the spiritual life being an attachment for many who partake of it. When you rise above the attachment, you come to God in boundless ways as the true source of all life. You are given this opportunity to heal as such through the sacraments. In saying that the sacraments will raise you up to the Lord, I mean that they will bring you to rest in stillness of the expression of Him through you and in emptiness within the Lord's bounty for you. When you and He are one, there will be nothing else to speak of.

The conscious expression of the Lord God takes place when you are in the midst of being anointed by one of the sacraments of Him. You not only become of His likeness and image, you become of His energy and essence each time you allow for the sacraments to dwell within you. The transposing of the spirit and the soul are one with the Father in that the spirit and the soul elevate themselves into the kingdom each time you have received a rite, so that they may be purified and likened to the image of the Beloved. During this phase, there is no difference between spirit and soul to the Lord. Their energies become interchanged with that of the Divine nectar of the Lord so that you may be given all that you need to drink of Him.

I say to you this: to heal as the Christ does, give yourself to Him, first, last, and always. That is His way, that is your way, that is the way of love. To partake in the sacraments of the Lord is simply to make oneself sacred in His love for you.

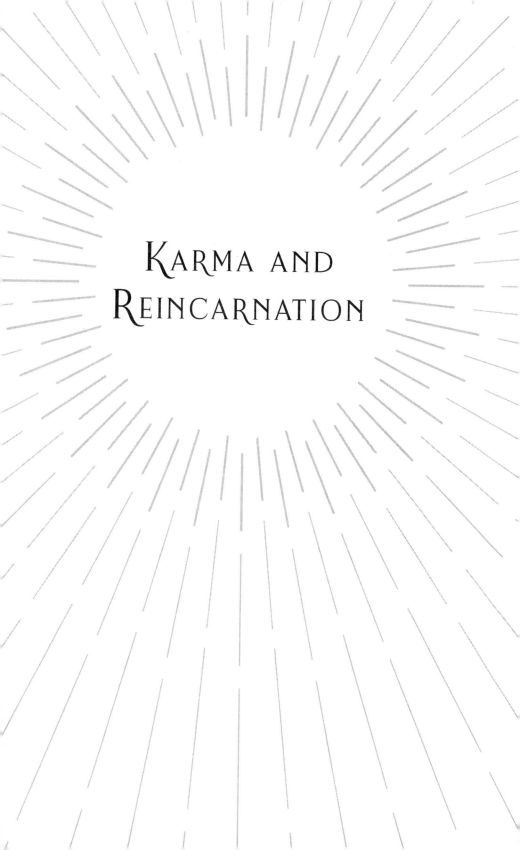

KARMA AND REINCARNATION

And I pray God your whole spirit and soul and body be preserved blameless unto the coming of our Lord Jesus Christ.

1 THESSALONIANS 5:23

We have known and believed the love that God hath to us. God is love; and he that dwelleth in love dwelleth in God, and God in him.

1 JOHN 4:16

These things saith he that holdeth the seven stars in his right hand, who walketh in the midst of the seven golden candlesticks: "I know thy works, and thy labour, and thy patience, and how thou canst not bear them which are evil. And thou hast tried them which say they are apostles, and are not, and hast found them liars; and hast borne, and hast patience, and for my name's sake hast laboured, and hast not fainted. Nevertheless I have somewhat against thee, because thou hast left thy first love. Remember therefore from whence thou art fallen, and repent, and do the first works, or else I will come unto thee quickly, and will remove thy candlestick out of his place, except thou repent. But this thou hast, that thou hatest the deeds of the Nicolaitanes, which I also hate.

"He that hath an ear, let him hear what the Spirit saith unto the churches; to him that overcometh will I give to eat of the tree of life, which is in the midst of the paradise of God."

REVELATION 2:1–7

It is for you to better understand the teachings of Revelation, as there are many grievances as to what the prophets of our Lord have given you to decipher. These writings were not to frighten or confuse you, rather to show to you the glory of God through eternal life and the inner workings of those dimensions. You have come to perceive this life as the only one you are to live, and in that you are mistaken. It is not just one life, but many lives, and more than one life at a time that you will live. And this you will come to understand shortly. The end of time is not as you have contemplated. It will not be destruction or chaos. There will be reorganization, penetrated by a deep love for you by our Father in Heaven. Most of the teachings throughout Revelation give credence to the cycle of birth within the kingdom of Heaven. It includes the powers of the Lord associated with those cycles as appropriated to the entirety of the universal consciousness. There is not true death, only life upon continual life, always. That is the way our Father in Heaven deemed it for us.

The one who holds the seven stars is the one who has earned the degree of spiritual attainment of the Lord. He no longer has to incarnate on any level of contemplation of Him and can sit at His right hand as pure light. The number seven in scripture refers to the holiest of sanctuaries and the highest degree of attainment that the soul could possibly seek on all levels. When it has reached this degree, it in fact is no longer a soul, but is part of the essence of God. When it was said in the scriptures that he holds the seven stars and walks in the midst of the seven gold candlesticks, he is walking amidst the throne of our Lord and that of His Council and supreme beings. These beings hold the knowledge and wisdom of the understanding of eternal life.

Dearest children, your works, your labors, your endurance, they all seek to serve you in every life you choose to learn of Him and the love He has for you. When we say to you that you will live many lives and more than one life at a time, this is truth. There are a number of ways in which the spirit and soul can redirect its essence and energies to grow in the name of the Lord. It is not for you alone that you have come here to learn. It is for your brethren as well that you come to know God. The learning of your spirit and soul takes place at levels that your conscious awareness does not even know about. This is the reason we speak to you: so that you may see that all of your actions, thoughts, and intentions pertaining to your life and the Lord as you perceive Him are not about your existence at all in reality. The Lord hath given you incredible power at creating the universe in light of Him. If you think karma is about simply doing good so that you may rest in His arms, we bid you to think again.

Your soul can redirect its energies in understanding that it belongs to many beings, not just yourself. Your soul may belong to thousands of your brethren, and it is those actions of another, besides your own actions, that greatly affect you so. That is why the Lord gave you the emotions that you carry. It is not only to feel what it is you are capable of feeling. It is to also feel the actions, thoughts, and intentions of all souls. A soul can redirect itself to birth through many different lifetimes, both on the plane of earth and in the world of spirit, and the soul can choose to house many different spirits, as a spirit can house many different souls.

What we mean is this. The soul is a direct expression of essence from God upon the universe. A soul is not a person as you might think, although it seems to transform itself into that understanding to make it easier for you. It is pure essence of Him at the moment it is birthed into life. Its purity changes as it grows to learn of Him and love, ultimately to return back to the purity from whence it came. When the Christ appeared to his followers after he was resurrected as the light of the Father, he said to them this: "Peace be unto you: as my Father hath sent me, even so send I you" (John 20:21). To this, Christ was referring to the peace of the soul. He commanded the souls of his apostles to return to the peace within the essence of His Father. He was not just speaking of their spirit or speaking of what they had come to learn of in this lifetime. Rather he was declaring to them that their souls find peace and perspective within the cycle of birth that they had come to learn of the Lord with. The Christ continues his discourse with them. "Receive ye the Holy Ghost: Whose soever sins ye remit, they are remitted unto them; and whose soever sins ye retain, they are retained" (John 20:22–23). To this the Christ added the final decree of our Lord. This was to offer up to his Father not only their souls but to raise their spirits to that vibration of the Holy Spirit so that soul and spirit can merge as one complete inner cosmos of the Holy God and return to pure light. It is when this soul at its highest grace and this spirit at the level to which it is most holy merge together that the cycle of birth shall end for that soul and spirit, inclusive of all beings within the container for that soul and spirit. This is important to know. You will see that there are times in universal awakenings when many humans die at the same time or many spirits move to the next level, integrate with other spirits, or return to the light. Or there might be times when humans or spirits take ill as you would call it. This may indeed be because of the evolution of the cycle of birth that is transpiring within His kingdom. Indeed, this will happen when the integration of the highest souls and spirits take place. This is the cycle that we were referring to. Do not shed tears when you see that many are taken from you. There are times when this is appropriate. There are also those times when it is not of the Lord's will that this happens. We are merely speaking of those times when many return to the Lord at once. Do you not think that the Lord hath prepared the way for them? So you see, karma is more than reparation for sins and goodness paving the way for you to meet with the Lord in His kingdom. It is about the sanctity and righteousness of the universe at large with the glory and love of Him reigning over all.

The spirit can redirect its energies in the process you have come to know as reincarnation. It can divide itself amongst many souls, and can further separate when integrated in human capacity or spirit capacity. There are varying levels of spirit both in man and in the spirits of the other world. The soul and spirit attend to karma and the cycle of birth differently.

Karma is the spiritual process by which the transmission of souls from one level of light to the next become imbued with the potentiality to be of the Lord God. It encompasses more than the laws of cause and effect as you know it. All of which we have been stating here. It involves the laws pertaining to the expansion of light, with the understanding, respect, and balance of the darkness. Simply put, all that is of Him and His light will return as such. All that is of darkness will also return to Him. Karma transmutes energy and essence from our Lord into the lower levels of creation, and unto the realm of the world of spirit.

The process of reincarnation adheres to the cycle of birth in that it transmutes the spirit of that soul into the higher levels of energy and essence of our Lord. Indeed the two processes work simultaneously and in polarity of each other if you could perceive the paradigm of light that is set up in the cosmos. This is not to say that all souls birthed to incarnate themselves again on the plane of earth or in the world of spirit are at that higher level. This is just to say that this is what the purpose is of that process. Reincarnation follows karma, whereas karma belongs under the direction and guidance of the Logos. You will always be born unto light. And darkness will always surround you.

In referring back to Revelation 2, the writings speak: "Nevertheless I have somewhat against thee, because thou hast left thy first love. Remember therefore from whence thou art fallen, and repent, and do the first works; or else I will come unto thee quickly, and will remove thy candlestick out of his place, except thou repent" (Revelation 2:4–6). Is this not true for all of you within the kingdom? When it says to realize how far you have fallen, they are merely speaking about the level of grace and stillness that is absent from the spirit and the soul, and how much of the karma of the universe is due to that construct that has been deemed forth by Him. It is not a negative construct as so many of you think when you refer to the concept of negative karma. For in truth, there is no such thing. There is only that karma that will serve you in embracing the Lord and His will. That is all.

The teachings speak of removing the candlestick from its place unless one repents. In this instance, the candlestick refers to the Divine energy that is channeled from the Lord and that of His counsel and appropriated to you so that you may continue on in your cycle of birth. It is your perception that you are able to live and breathe of your own doing. The truth is that it is the Lord who has given you permission to understand Him more deeply. If the Lord hath not given you way, even if you decided to use your opportunity for darkness, you would not even exist, as human, spirit, or soul. Remember that always. *You cannot escape the Lord or His love for you. It is simply not possible.*

To remove the candlestick would render the soul incapable of pure light. That is the learning mode and spiritual life of the spirit and soul. This is why the teachings say for you to repent unto Him. It is not simply for the benefit of your own soul that you will repent, but for the benefit of Him and all who embrace Him in image and likeness.

The Seven Seals

And I saw when the Lamb opened one of the seals, and I heard, as it were the noise of thunder, one of the four beasts saying, "Come and see." And I saw, and behold a white horse: and he that sat on him had a bow; and a crown was given unto him, and he went forth conquering, and to conquer.

And when he had opened the second seal, I heard the second beast say, "Come and see." And there went out another horse that was red: and power was given to him that sat thereon to take peace from the earth, and that they should kill one another; and there was given unto him a great sword.

And when he had opened the third seal, I heard the third beast say, "Come and see." And I beheld, and lo a black horse: and he that sat on him had a pair of balances in his hand. And I heard a voice in the midst of the four beasts say, "A measure of wheat for a penny, and three measures of barley for a penny; and see thou hurt not the oil and the wine."

And when he had opened the fourth seal, I heard the voice of the fourth beast say, "Come and see." And I looked, and behold a pale horse: and his name that sat on him was Death, and Hell followed with him. And power was given unto them over the fourth part of the earth, to kill with sword, and with hunger, and with death, and with the beasts of the earth.

And when he had opened the fifth seal, I saw under the altar the souls of them that were slain for the word of God, and for the testimony which they held. And they cried with a loud voice, saying, "How long, O Lord, holy and true, dost thou not judge and avenge our blood on them that dwell on the earth?" And white robes were given unto every one of them; and it was said unto them, that they should rest yet for a little season, until their fellow servants also and their brethren, that should be killed as they were, should be fulfilled.

And I beheld when he had opened the sixth seal, and, lo, there was a great earthquake; and the sun became black as sackcloth of hair, and the moon became as blood. And the stars of heaven fell unto the earth, even as a fig tree casteth her untimely figs, when she is shaken of a mighty wind. And the heaven departed as a scroll when it is rolled together; and every mountain and island were moved out of their places.

And the kings of the earth, and the great men, and the rich men, and the chief captains, and the mighty men, and every bondman, and every free man, hid themselves in the dens and in the rocks of the mountains, and said to the mountains and rocks, "Fall on us, and hide us from the face of him that sitteth on the throne, and from the wrath of the Lamb. For the great day of his wrath is come; and who shall be able to stand?" . . .

And after these things I saw four angels standing on the four corners of the earth, holding the four winds of the earth, that the wind should not blow on the earth, nor on the sea, nor on any tree. And I saw another angel ascending from the east, having the seal of the living God. And he cried with a loud voice to the four angels, to whom it was given to hurt the earth and the sea, saying, "Hurt not the earth, neither the sea, nor the trees, till we have sealed the servants of our God in their foreheads." And I heard the number of them which were sealed. . . .

After this I beheld, and, lo, a great multitude, which no man could number, of all nations, and kindreds, and people, and tongues, stood before the throne, and before the Lamb, clothed with white robes, and palms in their hands; and cried with a loud voice, saying, "Salvation to our God which sitteth upon the throne, and unto the Lamb." And all the angels stood round about the throne, and about the elders and the four beasts, and fell before the throne on their faces, and worshipped God, saying, "Amen: Blessing, and glory, and wisdom, and

thanksgiving, and honour, and power, and might, be
unto our God for ever and ever. Amen."

And one of the elders answered, saying unto me,
"What are these which are arrayed in white robes? And
whence came they?"

And I said unto him, "Sir, thou knowest."

And he said to me, "These are they which came out of
great tribulation, and have washed their robes, and made
them white in the blood of the Lamb. Therefore are they
before the throne of God, and serve him day and night in
his temple. And he that sitteth on the throne shall dwell
among them. They shall hunger no more, neither thirst
any more; neither shall the sun light on them, nor any
heat. For the Lamb which is in the midst of the throne
shall feed them, and shall lead them unto living foun-
tains of waters. And God shall wipe away all tears from
their eyes." . . .

And when he had opened the seventh seal, there was
silence in heaven about the space of half an hour. And I
saw the seven angels which stood before God.

REVELATION 6:1–17, 7:1–4, 7:9–17, 8:1–2

Listen closely, as we will explain the best way in which these writings
will serve you. You have feared the Lord and His righteousness from
your interpretations. When indeed, that is not the Lord's wish for
you. He simply wants for you to understand the levels at which the
cycle of birth take place, and the initiation stages that the soul goes
through to reach ecstasy with Him. The cycle of birth belongs to a
larger paradigm of energy consciousness and essence of our Lord. It
contains the laws of karma and reincarnation within it. There has
to be a larger paradigm or that cycle will return to the light. There
would be continual reincarnation of thought, action, spirit, soul, and

the duality of light and darkness if this cycle did not end. When the cycle of birth is complete, you will all be borne at one time unto the kingdom of Heaven with Him. It encompasses the larger picture that the Lord has in mind for you. That is why we name it the cycle of birth for the present moment. It is for you to know that you will be borne as new children of light unto the Lord, whereas you will no longer suffer through life as you know it, in separation from Him.

As we have mentioned, the seals in these writings refer to the seven cardinal rules and powers that come with entering the gates of Heaven through this process. There are so many of you who perceive karma and the process of reincarnation as a selfless act of doing right by the Lord so that your souls may progress in the light of Him. Nonsense. Look further than yourselves and your actions to see what it is the Lord hath in store for you.

The seals have been shown as representative of the darkness of the Lord, whereas it has yet to be completed in the ways of the understanding of the light. One can look at the cycle of birth as darkness, as you are not completely in light of Him at the lower levels of existence. Thus, there has to exist darkness to support the meaning of light for you.

When the Lamb broke open the first seal, it began with the first sound of the beginning of creation. It was then that you were given the righteousness of the Lord. Whereas, at the essence of light that you were with Him, you needed not His righteousness. His righteousness only serves as protection and a guideline for you to find your way back to Him. You were given all the power, knowledge, and understanding of the universe. The cycle of birth was brought into effect to help you understand what it was you needed from Him. The riders that came with the four seals have to do with the levels of initiation and power that come with the expansion of light and darkness as you continue to rebirth your spirit and soul. As you continue to reincarnate, whether in the world of spirit or on the plane of earth, the levels of light and darkness expand with every breath you take so that the energy of each plays an integral part within the universal consciousness. As these expansions take place, the power of the Lord and of the universe manifest the kingdoms of God and Heaven. Eventually, there will be a time when these energies combust into all that is light. Light will continue to birth upon light in nothing but essence. There will be no form to speak of, no soul, no spirit, and no restlessness within the universe. There can be only light at the end. Only God. A different God than you seek to know. One that is indescribable even in scriptures. It is when you seek to identify the Lord in your life that you confuse yourself. It is thus that we seek to explain Him so that you better understand who you are. In truth, the Lord has no identity that is describable to humans, spirits, or even His Council. He will make himself known to you at the level at which you are comfortable in perceiving and receiving Him. Thus, when the writings in Revelation speak of the end of the world, it is only the end of the perceived duality that they are speaking of. It is the end of the present state of energy and perceived essence into *something greater than you could ever imagine.*

The rider that came forth on the white horse bearing a bow and given a crown was to symbolize the agreement between you and the Lord—you and the universe. It is the agreement to carry out your responsibility as caretakers of the light of Heaven, as souls embarking on a mission to expand the light of God, the light within you, and to put into perspective a greater knowledge, understanding, and awakening of the God consciousness that is to come.

There are many places in the scriptures that refer to the coming of the Christ again. For this we say to you is truth. Again, all that you perceive to be true of the Lord and the kingdom of Heaven will be greater than you could ever imagine. Once the Lamb broke open the first seal, it brought the process of evolution back to its origin. And its origin does not even exist anymore because of the learning that is and will be taking place within the universal construct. This learning will raise the vibrations and make the Lord God even more magnificent than before. When the Lord agreed to this, we wonder if He even knew of the greatness He was to become—and the greatness that we were to become with Him.

When the Lamb broke open the second seal, it is said that a red horse came, with a rider that was given power to take away peace from earth. He was also given a sword. The red horse symbolizes thought and will; the confusion of thought from the Divine intellect that you were given. Also, the confusion of will as separate from the Lord's, and the power of that thought to create havoc upon your ideas of creation according to His laws. The red color is symbolic of the blood that is to be spilled due to your indecisiveness of the will and thought of God, with the will and thought of you as a creation of His energy, not essence. The second seal is the beginning of your manifestation of energy unto the Lord, the universe, and the polarity of light and the darkness. With the opening of the second seal, manifestation occurs, which is different than creation. Manifestation is given power and righteousness of the Lord to all beings of energy that are birthed from Him. Creation belongs solely to His essence, not of His energy. So you see, now you are learning. Peace on earth is taken not by the rider, but the power of creation is taken away from the Lord and the power of manifestation is given over to the will of each of you: spirit, soul, and man. The moment you embraced His power and will as your own, you manifested your own laws of being. And these are contrary and in support of Him. I say contrary because much of the will that is happening out there on the lower levels is of your making. I say in support of because much of the will that is happening in the higher levels of energy is of His will. And what is happening at the level of His essence will always be.

When the Lamb opened the third seal, a black horse came. This is symbolic of the weakness of man to dance with the dark side and to place the Lord in incorrect perspective of the darkness. This has to do with power and its perspective. It is not only the Lord whom you are placing in incorrect perspective of the darkness. It is also your spirit and soul, and the power that belongs to you as well.

The moment a spirit is placed in incorrect perspective of the darkness, it divides itself into the varying levels of spirit that we have spoken about during this entire discourse. It is the spirit, when not healed in the appropriate perspective, that causes the soul the anguish that will follow. This is what you have come to understand as negative karma. Again, we choose not to see it as such. It is simply termed in that manner as that is the way you choose to see it. The black horse and the third seal deals more with the aspect of the soul, whereas the second seal deals more with the aspect of the spirit. Once the soul is in anguish, it will take a lot in the way of the Lord to set it back on track. If the spirit can learn to understand this perspective of both the light and darkness with the Lord, it can truly save the soul lifetimes of learning. The rationing of the barley, wheat, and wine refers to the diminishment of the Lord's essence and energy upon the soul, whereas the soul will hunger for the righteousness of the spirit to be healed in the face of God. The soul at the lower levels of manifestation cannot be healed without the healing of the spirit. The soul at the essence of the Lord (remember, when creation began, there were only a few souls that were born of light that birthed into many) does not need the healing of the spirit because the two are merged at the level of creation before they separate into many souls to learn of Him.

When the Lamb broke open the fourth seal, a pale green horse came and its rider was called death, and the Evil One accompanied it to bring forth mass destruction. I say to you this, dear children: this is true when it is in perspective of Him. Not in perspective of the darkness alone. You must all put in perspective your love for the Lord and His light and also your love for the darkness. For that is something you have within you. It is not that destruction of the earth will happen. And yes, if you look around, you will see that much of the earth and the universal consciousness is changing. All is coming into righteousness and understanding of the polarity of life, light, truth, and yes, the darkness. Love is also coming into righteousness within the grace and compassion that the Lord has for you. Many of you fear that which is a part of the Lord. Remember, the Lord giveth to you all that He is. Do not fear what the Lord doth not fear and is in truth about. He is in truth about the darkness. The pale green horse is about the truth coming to light, coming into perspective. The rider that was called death and the Evil One are only manifestations of what is out of balance in your understanding of the nature of God. When you all can understand creation better, the destruction on the earth will stop. It is not of the Lord's doing, remember this. It is partially of your own doing, but mostly because of misunderstanding.

When the Lamb broke open the fifth seal, it became about the regeneration and proliferation of souls unto the kingdom of Heaven. It is about temperance, that which each soul has to learn. It is not about the torture of souls, which is perceived by the reading of scripture, but of the regeneration of the spirit and soul as deemed forth by the universal construct and the will of Him. The altar that is referred to in the passage regarding the fifth seal refers to the domain of the kingdom of God. The kingdom of God is born from the kingdom of Heaven. It is where duality begins, where all that is born of the energy of God manifests. The kingdom of Heaven belongs to His essence. The souls who had been slaughtered are indeed as such. They are those that are simply longing for other souls to reach their destinies so that they may all cross over and become one with the light of Heaven. The white robe is to symbolize patience and justice of all karma and all thought. It is these souls who wait at the threshold of the kingdom of Heaven for all the souls and spirits to merge again as one. It is these souls who will hold the space for the alignment of all souls to return unto Heaven, and for all spirits to be of one with Him.

The sixth seal is indeed the awakening, not the destruction. It is the changing of the universal construct and the intent of the Logos and the spiritual laws as set forth by the Creator put into action and effect. It is about fear, and the righteousness of it. This fear is not to make you afraid of Him. On the contrary, this fear is to bring you to an understanding of your own sense of compassion and unyielding love you have for all things, including yourself. It is not only what the Lord hath willed, but what you have willed in the face of Him. The awakening will be a gradual one. It only seems as though it is not gradual because there are more of you who are awakening to Him at the same time. Gradual does not mean the intensity is less than it has been in past times in both the world of spirit and on the plane of earth. Indeed, the intensity of change and the number of souls who are partaking in this great universal shift are many. When this happens, things seem to happen at a faster pace.

The four angels that came before the seventh seal was opened who stood at the four corners of the earth symbolized the new era of the Lord, the new Christ, the awakening, the ascension, the second coming of Light as you have all heard of before.

The fifth angel that came from the East was the visionary from the Lord, the new disciple of Him, all that you will come to be in the near future. You must wait and see, as the shift for many of you has already started.

It is not the angels who will make the distinction between those souls who are of the Lord and those souls who are not. In the time to come, there will be no need to make that distinction as you will all desire to return to Him as equal in light.

When the Lamb opened the seventh seal, it was indeed about the silence of the Lord, the purity of the love and light of Him. It was or will be no longer about restitution or learning of Him. For there will exist the silence of Him as the greatest grace from Heaven upon you.

This is the cycle of birth of which we speak. It is not as difficult as you think it is to understand, yet it encompasses more than your noble mind is willing to partake of.

It is not just about the healing of one's spirit and soul, but the redirection of the essence and energies of the Lord and the entire universe to create a new spiritual and universal paradigm of love, light, and truth. This is something we are all striving to, even those of us in the world of spirit. It is said in Revelation, "Holy, holy, holy, Lord God Almighty, which was, and is, and is to come" (Revelation 4:8).

The meaning of these words was not even understood by the greatest of the Lord's prophets. For we tell you this, you will be in awe at the coming of Him. It is said that we all will be.

But this I say, He which soweth sparingly shall reap also sparingly; and he which soweth bountifully shall reap also bountifully. Every man according as he purposeth in his heart, so let him give, not grudgingly, or of necessity; for God loveth a cheerful giver. And God is able to make all grace abound toward you; that ye, always having all sufficiency in all things, may abound to every good work. As it is written, He hath dispersed abroad; he hath given to the poor; his righteousness remaineth for ever.

2 CORINTHIANS 9:6–9

Now he that ministereth seed to the sower both minister bread for your food, and multiply your seed sown, and increase the fruits of your righteousness; being enriched in every thing to all bountifulness, which causeth through us thanksgiving to God. For the administration of this service not only supplieth the want of the saints, but is abundant also by many thanksgivings unto God, whiles by the experiment of this ministration they glorify God for your professed subjection into the gospel of Christ,

and for your liberal distribution unto them, and unto all
men, and by their prayer for you, which long after you for
the exceeding grace of God in you. Thanks be unto God
for his unspeakable gift.

2 CORINTHIANS 9:10–15

There is much truth in these spoken words. Those who root themselves in the graces of our Lord shall indeed bear truth in incarnations to come. Remember, the way in which you perceive good karma will not always be as so. The soul who suffers much can also have good karma. It is just that their agreements with the Lord may differ. Thus, it is true that if you build your foundation upon the light of Him, you will have a great foundation to work with. Just remember, there are varying levels of spirit, soul, and embodiment, or lack thereof. Good karma will always come back to justify the makings of the soul and the highest aspects of the spirit. It is at the lower levels that it may not appear as good to those who see it. We say to you this as we have said many times during this discourse: do not place judgment on that life that you see another partaking of. It is not for you to distinguish or decide who is of light and who is of darkness. It is only the Lord who truly knoweth. It is when you seek to take responsibility for sharing in the karma of others that you will indeed progress on all levels. The person who plants a little will have a small harvest because the person who puts little effort into knowing the Lord will gain nothing as a right of refusal unto himself. When you seek to refuse the Lord within you, you place your soul and spirit at the lowest levels of the spiritual ascent toward Him. You think that your soul and spirit only work at the level that you are conscious of. That is why we say to you always that you must pray to be of the Lord's light. The process of karma and reincarnation is taking place on all levels of your being at every moment. This you must know and believe. That is why you must do things on every level, the physical (if you are embodied), the mental, the emotional, and the spiritual. That is why you must also pray for others. For you truly pray for yourself when you pray for one another. *Prayers for another help the karma of all.*

The person who plants a lot will have a big harvest. This does not mean the soul who acquires much in the material world has done right by the Lord. Material gain has little to do with true karma as so many of you would like to think. Doing right by Him will not afford you the luxuries of self that you would so like to have. Indeed, the purpose of planting a lot, as the scriptures say, is so that you make the garden of God and the heavens available to all of His children. Thus, all may partake of the good karma that is deserved to all beings of light, all children of the Lord. It is not even that you would see the harvest. There have been many a prophet of the Lord who plant a good garden and do not see the fruits of their labors until centuries later. It is these great children of Him who had much faith in His works and trusted in the Lord's will. They knew the moment they surrendered to Him that they were planting the seeds for good life to come to all men indeed. That is why the scriptures say, "He hath dispersed abroad; he hath given to the poor: his righteousness remaineth for ever" (2 Corinthians 9:9).

The poor are the poor of heart and the poor of spirit. Once the seed is planted firmly in the light and faith of Him, it will continue to grow, even amidst the darkness. All it takes is a sparkle of the Lord's light and your faith to change the energy surrounding karma and the process of incarnating again. When you come into this life, be it on earth or in the world of spirit, you do not necessarily come directly from your previous experiences. It doesn't always work that way. There are many factors among the Lord's laws that place you where you are and ought to be. The choice is given to you to continue to learn as light, and of course, you all take it. But the directions as to where you are to learn next are deemed by Him and His Holy Council. There are ways in which your spirit and soul work in conjunction and separately to accommodate the workings of Him and the learnings within you. All is necessary for the merging of spirits and souls at the end of time as we know it. This is certainly not to say that karma is unchangeable either. At the lower levels of existence, it most certainly is. But let it be known that the Lord knows the truth for each of us. If there is karma that is changed or healed, it is because it is of the Lord's will and within your highest good.

When the scriptures say that it is God who gives seed to the farmer and bread for food, they are meaning that it is the Lord who reigns over the process of karma and reincarnation and it is through *Him only* that you can make tremendous shifts in your spiritual awakening and ascension. The Lord will give you what you need and will indeed make you rich in every way. When you give service to Him in good faith and good karma, you are serving the justice of the Lord not only in the present moment but for the future, and in relation to those grievances of the past. This is truth. Living in righteousness of Him serves the light and the darkness of all that is without boundary of time. You heal spirits and souls of the past, present, and future. You heal those beyond the expansion of your vision and intellect. You create change in the direction of the light and the darkness. You put into perspective the duality that exists on the lower levels. The understanding of evil has a framework that the soul can interpret according to the light of God. All this, for one good thought, one good deed, one kindness to another, an act of faith, an act of love. The choice is yours.

Each time you create good karma, the faith of Him grows in numerous ways above all else you perceive that only belongs to you. It has been written that you shall reap what you sow. Again, yes, you shall. Indeed, do not judge what the Lord hath given you unless you know in your heart that you have done so righteously in His honor. When you can look into your own heart and see that you are living righteously by Him, you do not need to pay attention to the circumstances surrounding your present existence. For we tell you this, if you are living righteously, then the Lord is watching over you and taking care of the process of your ascension toward Him.

We will begin at the lowest levels of contemplation and existence. How is it that karma affects the embodiment or physicality of man? Whether you are rich or poor, in health or in sickness, in desperation, in fear, or in love, that all matters not. It is where you are with the Lord amidst all these circumstances that will greatly affect your karma more than anything else. Indeed the route you have taken previously, with the direction of your soul and spirit, have much to do with what transpires for you if you are an incarnate being. But remember once again, do not judge your karma by your present circumstances. There is much you do not know of in the way of Him.

There are some people who choose to become enslaved by their karma not only on the physical level but in the spirit and soul as well. We ask you to be cautious and mindful of that. Enslavement is different from curses put on a soul. Enslavement is when the soul initiates a patterned response due to fear and inadequacy of the Lord and situates himself into these circumstances on all levels, which the Lord doth not desire for him. Remember this. The Lord hath given you free will up to a certain point. If He were to help everyone who enslaved themselves into a karmic pattern without permission from the soul, then there would be an imbalance of the light and the darkness within the existence of spiritual laws. If the soul does indeed ask the Lord, then the soul would not be enslaved in the first place. This is when, as you would refer to it, negative karma takes place.

Know this. The Lord within you is the only one who can heal karma, and the only one who can halt the process of reincarnating. When a soul and spirit reincarnates as man, it will carry with them not only the patterns of their own makings but of all the souls who live at the same spiritual level as themselves. If the Lord has deemed that all spirits and souls heal one another as they grow in His image and likeness, then the Lord has deemed that all spirits and souls will learn from one another as they grow in His image and likeness. It is simple.

Do not place so much importance on circumstances but on learning to receive the love of the Lord through your heart. Each time you look at someone who is rich, poor, in sickness, or in health, look beyond their fear. Look beyond your own fear and embrace the light of where they are in relationship to Him. Then after you understand them, place that understanding upon your own heart. You will come to understand the Lord's love for you and your purpose for being here.

This is important for you to do because you will not only be working with your own karma but others who are like you in spirit and soul. You, as man, will indeed carry many others in the realm of your spirit. When you ask yourself or another what it is they fear of the Lord, this will usually help the process of healing the karma that ties you and other spirits that are drawn to you because of your similar understandings of Him.

Your circumstances come from lifetimes, and others' lifetimes, and all those beings who are tied to the others that come to you. When you find yourself in a circumstance that does not feel in righteousness of the Lord, then you are with negative karma as you refer to it. We still choose to see that there is no such thing as negative karma. Be patient and be mindful. Righteousness does not mean bearable circumstances on any level. Righteousness does not mean instant gratification. If you are mindful of Him always, you will know the truth. When you find yourself in righteousness of the Lord, then you are with good karma, or rather, you are with His light. This does not mean that your circumstances reflect that ecstasy of the Lord's light on the physical level. And it does not mean that they don't. The truth of it is that the miracles of the Lord and the good karma of all souls are everywhere around and within you. You just might not take notice of them.

Know that whenever there is suffering of karma on the lowest level of existence, the spirits of the Living God who have been part of your soul and spirit will be there to assist you when the time is right and when you also ask. To think that you create your karma totally is not truth. It is an accumulation of the experiences of spirits and souls upon the same manifestation levels of light and darkness combined with the will of God, and the false will of the self.

Karma that needs to redirect its energies will do so and manifest in personal circumstances and issues. The energies of karma have to redirect themselves in order to find balance within the soul and the universal consciousness. Whether it is in sickness or in health, in poverty or wealth, in love or in fear, the glory of God will take place above all else. That will bring the embodiment of man to encounter the learning and love of the Creator. Your circumstances will not only be for your learning. Know this as truth. Any of the above circumstances are for others' learning as well. We are speaking about the level of man, but also the level of the spirit and soul as they are graced with these truths.

Know that whatever your truth is, the truth of the Lord's will for you will prevail over all. Whatever it is that your soul and spirit have agreed to do in His name, it shall endeavor to be true. No matter how many incarnations as man, or existences as spirit. There is but one universal karma that all spirits and souls aspire to. That is to be of Him, completely. Once you are birthed from light, you will place yourself within the process of complete love in honor of Him. And you will learn and understand accordingly. The spirits of the Living God will assist you fervently in doing so.

Let us speak about the suffering of man when it comes to karma and reincarnation. When a soul comes into this life bearing fruits of the labor of Christ, it will indeed encounter suffering in expressing the love of God.

There are those souls whose mission it is to solely be the light of God for others. This may bring about circumstances of immense suffering on the physical level, be it through illness, personal loss, or external factors. It is these souls who least express their Godnature in vain and offer their spirits up to the Lord so that their soul can rectify and put into perspective the darkness of others. You may not understand what we are speaking about, but know there are times when you have agreed to be of sacrifice to the Lord. *Sacrifice is not in the way you understand it to be. Sacrifice means to make sacred in the way and name of God.* It is not that the Lord chooses for you to suffer so that others can see of His wrath. Indeed there is no wrath greater than the darkness of man and his mind. A soul may choose to incarnate so that God may indeed use him in love as a vehicle for His works of mercy. *When you notice one who is ill, poor, or in despair, maybe it is they who are more in the light of Him than you realize.* As you all come to understand the Lord more, you will see that there have been many souls, and there will continue to be, who will take on the karmic role as vehicles for His works of mercy. Remember when the Christ healed the man born blind. It was his disciples that turned to the Lord and asked, "Master, who did sin, this man, or his parents, that he was born blind?" And the answer from Christ is the same answer we tell you, dear children. "Neither hath this man sinned, nor his parents; but that the works of God should be made manifest in him" (John 9:2–3).

Suffering of karma at the level of embodiment can also be given power by curses placed upon the soul by himself or another. Curses emanate from the levels of the soul and spirit but can manifest on the physical plane as illness, death, despair, and many other types of grievances. We are speaking about curses as relating to karma, not just curses placed by demons or dark spirits for reasons of relationship to mind, spirit, or soul. Although the former does indeed have much to do with the latter. The time will come when all of you will rectify your darkness and place it in perspective of the Lord. Even when it comes to curses placed on you by another, know that if you are indeed cursed, it is only because you have cursed yourself on some level and the Lord in some lifetime. We do not say this to frighten you, nor do we give it any more truth or light than it should hold. Do know there are such things as curses and they are indeed holding patterns on the spirit, soul, and embodiment of man. When the time is right, the pattern will hold itself up to the light of God and come into perspective. When another has tormented you in this way, it is because their own karma has not completed and by virtue (literally) of your own soul's progression, they will be freed to the light too. Their karma will also come into perspective. All those with whom you have had relationships in past, present, and future lifetimes are part of you and your journey. They are part of your karmic experience. Since we are all one under the Father, that would mean that our journeys support one another. When a curse is placed upon you, you have a challenge to honor the Lord in all ways. We suggest you take Him up on this offer. The power of a curse can be strong if you are not in righteousness of Him. If you are, indeed you shall have no worries.

The curse will be no more when the soul, the spirit, and all those partaking in that energy for lifetimes receive a healing from Him. This is a grace and an awesome gift from the Almighty. Curses relevant to karma and spirits have much to do with the learning of these relationships for you on all levels. They are there because you need them to understand about yourself and the Father, about love, and to rectify your grievances with Him.

There are those times where karma will direct itself into the embodiment of man in order to rectify past injustices against one's own Godnature. Again, you refer to this as negative karma. Limitations can be placed upon a soul by the spirit of that soul or by the Council of God so that the soul may learn to understand its nature more clearly. It is simple. Then, there will be those times when illness, poverty, or restitution take place, so that the soul can give back to the Lord and to all those souls it has caused grievances against some good intentions. The learning of the soul will take place on the earth level, since we are still speaking about karma as belonging to the lowest level of existence. It will be up to the soul as to how much suffering it will endure. We say this because each agreement with the Lord and His Council is different and what each soul does for restitution is agreed upon in hindsight. This you must know. It is not that the Lord wishes for you to suffer. Again, a human concept. Your soul will cease to learn the moment the spirits and souls of those you have caused grievances against are healed. This is done in action, but mostly by thought and contemplation of the Father.

For those who fully come into the light and love of God the Father with forgiveness and love in their hearts, the Father will indeed forgive them for past wrongdoings. *Remember, the only time frame that is held up by karmic law is the one you place upon yourself.* It is only that the Council is there to see whether or not you have truly come to that place of Godnature. Indeed, we must say that they know better than you, as does the Lord. It is usual that most karma plays out over many incarnations for man. It is only at a certain time that the Lord will allow for the spirit of that person to continue their work in the world of spirit, with the soul moving onward in other dimensions to continue as well. Never think that the Lord doth punish you. It is you who punish yourself when you have been evil personified. Nor are we suggesting that if you continue to live your life in absence of the Lord, He will endeavor to excuse your misgivings. The Lord loves and forgives you always. But make no mistake. If your actions, thoughts, and deeds are of intentional evil, the Lord will sit you down and set you on the right path, whether or not you agree with His decision. The Lord will never let evil incarnate go unnoticed or unhealed. This you must know. To rectify does not mean to punish. It means to make right again in the way of God.

The mind, dear children, has an integral part in the continuation of the growth process toward our Lord. If the process of reincarnation is thought of as continual restitution, then where is there room for the soul and the mind to find any peace? Why is it that many of you give the power of your mind to the thoughts around your trials as opposed to giving that power over to the Lord? Whether in embodiment, spirit, or soul, we say to you this: it is always good to be mindful of where it is you are with Him. However, it is negligent to be imbalanced in your integration of the Lord's process for you. This plays such an important role in your reincarnating on the earth plane or in the world of spirit. As you cultivate peace of mind with the Lord, the energies surrounding karmic law and your process of reincarnating will begin to balance themselves out. This is truth.

You must begin by contemplating Him in ways you have never done before. You must allow your mind, your scope of understanding, and your knowledge to expand to the light that the Lord is. Then your spirit and your soul will receive healing from Him in ways you know not. To keep the Lord in the space of understanding that you know binds you always to your karmic ways. The Lord doth desire for you to expand your awareness and contemplation of the spiritual laws as set forth by Him and His Council. On any level, the purpose of the ascension process is to rise above what you think is of the Lord and let the Lord lead you to Him in truth and love. Karmic laws are there for the boundaries of the spirits and souls who endeavor to surrender to Him. The process of incarnation at the existence of man reflects more of the mind frame within the human aspect of the spirit and soul. Most of you falsely perceive you are in knowledge of Him; unless you are given special instructions by the Lord, the level of man who is not on a spiritual path is indeed the lowest of contemplation.

You must rise above what you think you know of Him. We recommend that you listen. *A single thought can keep you separate from Him and enslave you further on your path and in the process of incarnating again.*

If you know that you have come to learn many times on the plane of earth, do not judge yourself. Remember, the Lord God works in truth where all things have purpose, reason, and balance. *This is not about you, this is about Him.* This is about the collective conscience. This is about universal love and knowledge.

There will be many times in one's human existence when progressing at a very fast rate of understanding Him that you will encounter chaos and trials on the earth plane. We are not telling you this to be fearful, and we are not suggesting you rush through your learning to obtain the light and knowledge of Him. We are saying that as the energies of the universe change to meet the needs of the Creator, all of you who have been called upon will receive the Lord as has been planned for you at the moment of your inception. Karma can shift at a very fast pace or at a very slow pace at the human level. The spirit and soul shift first, but for whatever reasons, the human level might take some time to integrate the pieces. We understand internal and external factors take place. We see that many of you who undergo tremendous shifts in expansion and ascension do not understand the responsibility and balance of these shifts. And some of you place your own interpretations upon yourselves and the Lord for the meaning of these shifts. We ask you to be mindful of creating that holding pattern for yourself. When you experience karmic laws unfolding at a rapid pace, we suggest you let them work through you and obtain for yourself a peace of mind always. It is not always necessary for you to know what the Lord hath in store for you or His purpose. This halts your experience of Him. These shifts can manifest themselves in the physical body, in the emotional one, in relationships to everything within and around you. *You must let the Lord and His purpose move through you without attachment to the reason. This is so that the Lord can complete what is necessary for your highest good and the good of others whose spirits and souls are resonant with yours.*

When you come to incarnate again on the plane of earth, you think that all the circumstances are set for you by Him. This is nonsense. It is only that some circumstances are prepared for you, and it also depends on the spiritual attainment of the soul. There are those circumstances that will manifest exactly on earth as they are in Heaven . . . exactly. Then there are those circumstances whose energies will interplay into various manifestations on the earth plane. As long as the highest purpose and reason of our Lord and your growth is served, the karmic laws are satisfied.

There are also those circumstances that may take incarnations to work through, again, with the spirit and soul working at different levels of what is given to them and how they choose to relate to our Lord with what is given. Times, places, relationships—all the logistics of a soul may be determined before the soul reincarnates on the earth plane. This can be done between the soul, the Lord, and His Council. It is not always necessary for the logistics of the soul to be predetermined. That is why the term *predestiny* is not a complete notion. The only thing you are all predestined to is Him. There are conceptual predestinies. By this we mean that there are those souls whose incarnation is determined by the spiritual construct of universal truth. Indeed, all souls work in that way, but there are those who align with that paradigm to a higher degree. There are those souls whose purpose is instructed by the spiritual attainment they have ascended to. As there are certain souls whose life on earth is directly infused by the Lord himself. It is these souls who are predestined by Him. This is not to say that these souls are above all others. Remember, we are all part of each other. Your spirit and soul is one with Him, with another. These souls have obtained the higher frequency of all spirits and souls of the light and are given special instructions on how to live on the plane of earth. And it is their lives that will directly affect yours. You may not recognize the Lord in these souls. Sometimes they are known, sometimes they are hidden. If the Lord and/or His Council set up a specific logistic for the soul, one can trust that it is in their highest good. The Lord knows exactly what He is doing! When indeed you must believe that the highest karma of all is to return to the Beloved Creator.

Know that each of your missions is a mission that another soul has completed or will complete at some time. Do not bear grudges against those who seem to have better karma than you. This is not your concern. There is no one with better karma than anyone else. We are saying this because we see that many of you judge yourself when you come upon another whose life is predestined by Him. Do not fall into your feelings of inadequacy of Him. A simple lesson in learning of love is as magnificent to Him as serving as His prophet! Know this!

There are times when a soul will incarnate over and over again with the same logistics as in previous incarnations. There are times when a soul will reincarnate with the same relationships, in the same gender, with the same physical consequences, in lifestyle or physicality. There are times when a soul will reincarnate with the same health or variations of it throughout their incarnations. All serves His purpose. All serves your reason for choosing to live again on the plane of earth.

We cannot begin to explain to you the many reasons why the Lord does what He does when it comes to the reincarnation of the soul on the plane of earth because the circumstances for each soul are different and unique. Know that at the moment you do reincarnate, you are of one physicality, but of more than one level of spirit and more than one soul in that physicality. Parts of you are also in the embodiment of another.

At the level of man, karma can change, as again, if it is the will of God. We are speaking about His will in general, and the ability for the soul to be in right relationship with Him. If the will is predestined, then it will not likely change. It will redirect itself and complete itself at some time in the process of reincarnating. You cannot go to the Lord without completing your mission. If the will of that soul is not predestined, then one's karmic duties can realign themselves or change with the help of incessant prayer by other souls and spirits on your behalf. It can also change or realign itself by your own soul's capabilities to perform the inner workings of God through your physical, mental, and spiritual evolution on earth. *With God, all things are possible.* And there are many ways in which the laws can be restructured to fit His needs within your own soul. There are even times when a soul is predestined to die at a certain time and, indeed, the spirit and soul do leave the body with the living being still on the earth plane. That is because there are other souls along with spirits that are sustaining that physical life and embodiment. The purpose of that soul is complete with the logistics of that embodiment and needs to move on in energy to a higher plane with the life on the earth plane still breathing. We are trying to make this easier for you to comprehend.

For whatever reasons, the physical body is still needed on earth. The personality may or may not change. It is not uncommon for a new soul to come into a physicality. Do know that this might disrupt the physicality of the present life and leave that life in much chaos. All serves a purpose.

A physical being cannot survive when there is no spirit or soul intact at some level, although the spirit and soul can change. We are not speaking of when spirits attach to another spirit to feed upon their light. We are speaking about the literal transmutation of souls and spirits within a physical being.

This all has much to do with karmic transmission of light upon souls. When a soul reaches a higher level of spiritual attainment with our Lord, he will receive another transmission of light that will raise the soul to another vibration and sometimes cause the transmutation of that soul and spirit to a completely different soul and spirit. Do you understand? You might notice this taking place when you look upon another whose life has changed dramatically in the name of Him. It is true to say that karma is much more of a continual process of evolution than you think.

So indeed, karma can change as can the circumstances around the incarnation. Prayer can help, as it is always in the hands of God. When you ask the Lord to look at the circumstances that have fallen upon you and to change them if it be His will, be mindful that the Lord will listen. We suggest you accept the new circumstances with grace as so many of you fall bereft of what you perceive is the Lord's desire for you when you seek to change your life. Things cannot always be the way humans want them. Things are always the way that your Godnature wants them. Regardless of the darkness and evil that exist on the lower levels of contemplation, things are determined to be of the Lord's will and duty. Even when the circumstances on the earth plane do not change, this does not mean that the spirit or soul has not come into a new realignment. If the Father answers yes to your request for change, you will realign at the level of contemplation that will serve your highest purpose. This you must realize.

Let us speak about karma at the level of the spirit. We have mentioned to you many times during this discourse about the levels of spirit that are simplified so that you can better understand yourselves. You have a lower form of spirit and a higher form, and one that is universal. We will be speaking mostly about the lower and higher forms of spirit. It is usually the lower form of spirit that is involved with the lower aspects of karmic law, as the higher form of spirit is left to work with the higher aspects of karmic law. Whether embodied or not, humans or spirits have each of these levels. And it is both levels that work to serve the Lord in their greatest capacities.

> *And he that keepeth his commandments dwelleth in him,*
> *and he in him. And hereby we know that he abideth in*
> *us, by the Spirit which he hath given us.*
>
> 1 JOHN 3:24

The laws regarding karma and reincarnation affect the spirit slightly differently than they do man or the soul. When it comes to the spirit, we are working with the matter of light in a different transition of being and essence. There is that spirit that belongs in man and there are those spirits in the world of spirit. We will speak about both.

The lower form of spirit carries the karma of all emotions, past grievances, relationships, and issues belonging to the lower energy vortexes. Incarnations that have not completed themselves will settle in the karmic energy of the lower form of spirit. If we are speaking about those in the world of spirit, those spirits whose issues are the same will travel in the same dimension. All issues that the soul has not healed will be apparent in the lower spirit, as well as issues of those spirits once again who are resonant with the vibration of that particular karmic energy. The lower aspects of karma carry the more definitive energies of what keeps the spirit from moving forward. It is this spirit that incarnates into embodiment life after life or chooses to rest in the world of spirit to finish their work in the nature of things. It is these issues from this spirit that will continue to resurface in incarnations until the spirit has learned otherwise. It is very easy for the spirit at this level to enslave themselves into a karmic pattern that will carry through many lifetimes, embodied or not. Sometimes it is this level that can be the most difficult to work with because the intellect of the spirit can be locked into various patterns that have set themselves up for centuries. It is only when this aspect of spirit heals its issues that the soul's vibrations will be raised. The healing of that spirit will take place as well as the healing of other spirits resonant with that issue. It is the lower form of spirit and the lower aspect of karma that usually inform the physical body unless otherwise deemed by Him. When the spirit of a person is weak, this usually means that the karmic issues have not come into perspective. If there is embodiment, the physicality may not necessarily be weak if the spirit is, but other things will be out of perspective with God. If there is no embodiment, the spirit will travel in its dimension until he has resolved what he needs to learn of the truth of the Lord. It is not necessary for the spirit to understand from the soul what it needs to heal, as it is necessary for the soul to understand from its spirit what it needs to heal. The spirit can heal without conscious information from the soul. We are not saying that information would not be useful in one's spiritual growth. We are simply saying it is not necessary.

Spirits can hold within them the karmic patterns of others that have been aligned with their spirits for centuries. So when you are healing the karma of a spirit, you indeed are going back to the moment where the energetic pattern was established in the essence of the spirit. That is where the karma begins. The moment the pattern of separation from the light is established, the spirit descends into lower forms of energy. To heal the karma of man, one must first look at the karmic issues surrounding the spirit even before addressing the issues of the soul. The soul carries with it the karmic issues that the spirit has not moved through.

It is the spirit whose intellect needs to be refocused on the matters of the Lord, and its heart energy needs to understand suffering in terms of Him. It is not unusual for all spirits to encounter trials of grief without the Lord, for the endless search for and confusion of Him can leave the spirit tormented. It is up to the spirit to take hold of the light and strength of the Lord and to shift its karma so that its duties are aligned with those of the higher form of its spirit.

A spirit can continually incarnate in the world of spirit as such, moving through alternate dimensions as it works toward its Godnature and completes its karma. Again, it can also ascend by the resonance with issues of other spirits who are healing karma at the same time. Wherever the spirit sits, it goes through the same continual process of healing karma, which is simply to put it into perspective. It will continue to do that until the spirit has reached the level where it can merge as one with all aspects of spirit and soul within the Lord. The highest forms of both will be united in the kingdom of Heaven. The karma will be complete when it is deemed by the Lord above and the Lord within the united soul.

If a spirit becomes enslaved by the patterns of another, it will be up to that spirit to free itself with the assistance of the Lord. You must know that there is not truly another who can hold you back except the Lord, which would then be for your highest good. If you fear that your karma is being transgressed upon, we suggest that you ask the Lord to intervene. The transgression is something you are familiar with. This is truth. If there is an issue that needs to be put into perspective, the moment your spirit does so, the karmic patterns will cease to continue, as will the attachment of other spirits resonant with your learning pattern. One must strengthen the mind to believe that the Lord can help you in all things. We say this because the spirit challenges the Lord so and continues to hold against Him that which is truth.

There are times when karmic patterns are necessary as the spirit is willful in learning of Him. Even though the soul may indeed understand what is transpiring, the spirit may refuse to accept the Lord's truth. We find this to be the case with most spirits that are suffering. The acknowledgment of the Lord's purpose for you becomes more than the intellect of the spirit can handle or wishes to believe. Always, always, when karma is put into proper perspective in the lower form of spirit, the vibrations of light will raise themselves up to the Lord. That is why we say that in all healing, the spirit and soul are healed, not necessarily the body. One needs to work with the spirit first most of the time, unless otherwise deemed by the Lord. When one is putting into perspective any karma relating to the spirit, know that you will receive much more from Him than you anticipated. To release ties that have bonded the spirit for centuries will have a ripple effect on the universe. It is not necessary for one to break ties with the misunderstanding that they will not diminish. It is not up to you or anyone else to release karma, but it is only through Him and His disciples who will show you the way. Indeed, it is not factual to say that karma is released, we do so for your benefit. But it is truth to say that it is raised up to the Lord. As it begins to raise itself, you will become closer to your union with Him and begin to unravel the energies that have been misunderstood in your perspective of Him. This process indeed is a most magnificent one.

When a spirit is putting into perspective its karma, know that there will be others who will try and distract you from your mission. Pay no attention, as they are just jealous of your love for the Lord.

There are times when one needs to bring the energies of the higher form of spirit to assist the lower form in putting the karmic laws into perspective. It is at these times when the Lord or His disciples will come to you and let you know. It is at these times when it is not the Lord holding you back or His reason, but the Lord and His disciples are waiting for you to ascend and your spirit has no way of recognizing His calling. The higher form of spirit must be called in to give you the energies and assistance that you need.

Good karma will continue to carry light to the spirit it is imposed upon and to all those who partake of that spirit's energy and essence. There is still karma that needs to be put into perspective at some level because the spirit is still present and not united as one with the Lord.

Even though the spirit is at a higher level than others, it still has something to learn of Him. The karma of that spirit will continue to regenerate its vibrational patterns to raise the light of others and the universal construct.

When we are dealing with the higher form of spirit, we are working with the higher aspects of karmic law that fall into resonance with the spirit of God. The higher form of spirit deals with karma a little differently than the lower form of spirit because it has a better understanding of the love of the Father and is more connected with the universal spirit that ties the two levels of spirit together. The higher form of spirit also has a greater understanding of the Father and of the progression of the spirit toward God. The higher aspects of karma work with the injustices of the spirit that directly relate to the mission of that spirit and soul that it is joined with. It works with the issues surrounding the higher energy vortexes of the spirit.

The karma surrounding the higher form of spirit is one of sentience in the relationship to the Father and the relationship with the universe. It works tirelessly on behalf of the lower form of spirit to try to align itself with the powers of God. It is the higher spirit that will fuel the lower form with the energy needed to work through its karmic issues and reunite the healed aspects to the soul. Indeed, the higher spirit is not without fault, it is just that there is more of the light and strength of Him present so that all can be united as one when the time comes. When it is time for the higher form of spirit to ascend, it can do so leaving the lower form of spirit to still work with the issues that the lower aspects of karma bring to it. This is truth. The higher spirit can leave to fulfill its mission, or leave upon completion of the mission, and the lower form of spirit can remain as so and find other embodiment or dimensions to learn in. It can also be that the lower form of spirit raises the vibrations of the issues to be healed by the Lord. There are many ways that the spiritual laws surrounding karma work, and whichever way works best for you in the name of Him will transpire as so. This is why we tell you that all you perceive is illusion, dear children. Aspects of the Lord in your inner workings are so great and beyond human understanding. You are intricately part of one another and nothing you do is about just yourself. Remember, issues are energies as are the levels of spirit. Energies dissolve, transmute, transform, and raise themselves. The purpose for karma and the process of reincarnation is to bring you back to the essence of the Lord, also to dissolve, transmute, transform, and raise these energies. This is why we tell you of the flexibility of the levels of spirit and of the soul. For whatever is founded in essence will remain as so. All that is founded in energy will, in some way, be rectified. And the only thing founded upon essence is the light of God, the untouchable light of Him.

The higher form of spirit has the power to redirect the issues surrounding the karma of the lower form of spirit if the spirit is willing. Even if not, the lower spirit in some way will receive what he needs from the higher one. It is always this way. The light of God shall always reign truth. There is time for all things under God. All things that belong with Him will return at a faster pace than those things that do not belong to Him. This is why there is so much separation between man, spirit, soul, and all the levels of contemplation they encompass. It takes time for all aspects of the light to come together under the kingdom of Heaven. This is the way He created it. This is the way you chose to understand it and learn of Him and learn of love. Indeed, something so simple yet sounds so complex. If you all truly knew of love, then why is there so much separation from Him?

The lower form of spirit is more likely to succumb to the will of the self if it is in embodiment, or the will of negative energies if it is a spirit. The higher form of spirit is more likely to succumb to the will of God. When the two come aligned as the issues of karma rectify themselves, this shall clear aspects of karma as relating to the soul and help the soul move closer to Him, the light, and other souls who are merging with the light. This is how the spirit ascends to Him and how the soul ascends to Him. The universal spirit encompasses the merging of the two forms of spirit that unite as karma is rectified.

It is important for you on a human level to align the two levels of your spirit with the universal one. We say this because you will bring yourself much confusion, pain, and disharmony of will if you do not. There are times when you know what it is that the Lord is asking of you. That comes through your higher self. It is when you choose not to listen to Him that you cause yourself much grief. *Being one with the Lord is not about finding happiness in all that you do and are, it is about finding peace and stillness within.*

Happiness is up to you and is a temporary state of being, as are all the emotions of the lower realm of man. The lower spirit spends much time getting caught up in these emotions that do not allow the movement of spiritual things to take place. They will eventually take place. We suggest with love that you all make it easier upon yourselves.

The higher form of spirit will always draw to it those higher spirits and souls that will support the evolution of that spirit's work and light. The higher spirit may be working through issues unbeknownst to the lower spirit and to man if that be the case. This may happen with the soul as well. That is why you must always pray and be mindful of Him.

There are things taking place within the sanctuary of God that is within and of you always, at all times. It is the simple idea of loving, and the mindful presence of truth and light that will keep you with the Father. To completely surrender to Him is not an easy thing for man, spirit, or soul to do. This we indeed understand. But it is the only way to truly exist on any plane. *To be with the Lord is the only way.* It is written in the scriptures:

> *Brethren, if any of you do err from the truth, and one convert him, let him know that he which converteth the sinner from the error of his way shall save a soul from death, and shall hide a multitude of sins.*
>
> JAMES 5:19–20

Do you understand? This is what we have been speaking of all along. Only expand your perception to the level of man, spirit, soul, and cosmos. Any level that you work on to bring the perspective of the Lord and the darkness back into righteousness will bring salvation to all. Do right by the Lord and He shall do right by you. It is written this way in many traditions of Him, in many ways. How many times does your spirit and soul need to hear it? *Honor the Lord, and the laws of karma shall work to honor themselves for your benefit and the benefit of others.*

Curses and the Healing of Karma

When it comes to curses, the lower form of spirit is influenced by the powers that be, as can be the higher form of spirit. There are many higher spirits that become attached to the light, so their intellect may not be aware of the presence of others that seek to hinder their light. The attachment to the light can bring forth the refusal to see the darkness and its perspective on the whole. The innocence of the spirit is something we would caution you against. Even the Lord hath much innocence, yet He has supreme intelligence when it comes to putting into perspective all that is of Him. It is the same on all levels. A curse is nothing more than the thought of power upon another that is not of the righteousness of Him. If you choose for your spirit and soul to stay in righteousness, then the curse and all spirits attached to it will abandon itself in the appropriate time. We are not saying that curses do not do damage upon man, spirit, or soul. Indeed, they can cause much harm. We are stating that for your benefit, learn to rectify your relationships with the Lord in relation to karmic issues at the level of spirit. This will bring whatever issues that are out of alignment with Him back into perspective and will cease to fuel the power of the curse. There are as many in the world of spirit who profess light to all as there are who profess darkness. Do you not think the Lord understood all this at the beginning of creation and manifestation? The level of spirit is where you all must do most of your work. Putting into perspective your relationship with the Lord will do much for the ascension of your soul unto Him.

There are those who must also work at the level of the soul. As for these spirits, their advancement unto Him has taken precedence above all else. A curse is not necessarily negative as you may think, for again it suggests a holding pattern of energy whereby the spirit and/or soul can be locked into it for a period of time. When it comes to the thought of a curse, it is much about power. It is your spirit that must learn about the proper alignment of power within itself and how to use that power to maintain the spirit of God within you at all times. It is when the spirit chooses to misunderstand this power that it falls out of perspective with Divine order and intention. You must learn to rectify all that comes to you within sight and intention of the Lord's goodness. It is easy for anyone to place a curse upon another. It is only easy for the spirit receiving it if it is open to it on some level. It doesn't matter which lifetime or what level of contemplation. There has to be a misunderstanding about the Lord somewhere in the construct and consciousness of the spirit. The thought of a curse has much to do with karma, as it is the process of understanding this holding pattern that will enable the spirit and soul to move closer to the Lord. Do not get caught up in the makings of a curse as we see so many of you do. It is not necessary when you understand about the relationships you have made with the energies of that curse and where you sit with the Father on these matters. There are many tools on the lower levels of contemplation that will assist you in disempowering these curses. The tools are secondary to your alignment with God and the power of Him. Remember that. When you do, the spirits holding you in this fashion will also.

Much of your karma will change at the level of spirit once you choose to see yourself not as powerless of the Lord's will, but as a child of God who is loved and cared for by Him. Many of you choose not to accept what you agreed to from Him. Part of what is of vital importance in your spiritual growth is that you seek the Lord with gratitude and acceptance for what is placed in front of you. When you do, you know not the effects it has on your spirit, soul, and embodiment if any. The power of gratitude and acceptance will change and rectify what is needed for your karmic journey. This you must know and believe. It is easy for man to say he is accepting when the spirit is in distrust of Him. Acceptance will allow the energy of grace to come into the spaces where the curses, the negative energies, the healing, and rectification are needed. So many of you struggle with the Lord when it comes to your karma, good or not. Have you ever thought of placing yourself before Him and offering a gesture of praise and thanks?

When you learn to appreciate the Lord and the truths around karma, you will receive His mercy and rewards tenfold. Gratitude does much to even confuse dark spirits and demons and the thought of curses they place upon you. It does much to confuse your own spirit into accepting the responsibility of light that you truly are. Take heed of this, dear children. When we say that you have much to learn about love and righteousness of that love, listen to us. When we say you have much to learn about power and righteousness of that power, again, listen to us. True gratitude comes from loving God selflessly and unconditionally, such as the Father loves you—always has and always will.

Be grateful to the Lord for the karma set upon you. It will bring you the rewards of Heaven you so greatly deserve. This is something that all the prophets of our Lord understood but also had challenge with. From Elijah to Moses to Jesus, all were indeed challenged with offering gratitude from time to time to Him. Once you have surpassed this challenge, things will be different for you on all levels. We say this to man, spirit, and soul. Again, once you surpass this challenge and learn to be grateful for the karma that the Lord hath placed in front of you, you will see and know the light in more ways than you could imagine! It is written in the scriptures:

> *For every high priest taken from among men is ordained*
> *for men in things pertaining to God, that he may offer*
> *both gifts and sacrifices for sins. Who can have compassion*
> *on the ignorant, and on them that are out of the way;*
> *for that he himself also is compassed with infirmity. And*
> *by reason hereof he ought, as for the people, so also for*
> *himself, to offer for sins.*
>
> HEBREWS 5:1–3

So you see, the gifts and sacrifices are indeed thanks to the Lord. The one who is chosen might be weak because of his own spirit and the relationship with God he has known over time. In offering thanks for his sins and the sins of the people, in offering gratitude for his sins and the sins of the people, he is giving over to the Lord what is to be made whole and righteous. He is giving to God what is to be put into perspective of Him and what is to be held in light of truth. This is how one shall bring karma into perspective on any level. Offer it to the Lord with praise of Him and His mighty works.

The power to change karma lies in this simple offering.

When your experience of karma does not seem to end, look upon the Lord favorably and know that it is of His bidding. There are reasons for your uncertainty, and all will be shown to you when the time is right. When we speak of karma that does not end, we are referring not to a curse, but to a way of existence for the spirit and the soul in what seems a continual pattern of being. *There will come a time and a place where God will show you the reason, and for this, again, your patience will be rewarded.*

We have spoken to you many times regarding karma and illness, and the ways in which illness unfolds as a result of karma, both good and not good. All illness, physical or mental, manifests in the spirit before it does so in the embodiment, if any, or can be present with a lower form of spirit in the other world. Again, do not judge illness as a consequence of negative karma. For this is not truth. It may as well be good karma or both. The living God works His truth in many ways for you to know Him. Illness has much to do with perspective. As to the understanding of that perspective, that is between you and the Lord. Even when the illness is caused by a curse, we say to you the same thing as before. Even when the illness is an act of righteous mercy from the Lord, we say to you the same as before. Even if the illness is predestined by our Lord, we say to you the same as before. Even if the illness is self and spirit created, we say the same to you as before. *Look to God. Offer thanks and praise. Put your relationships into perspective. Put your light and your darkness into perspective. Place love, power, and truth with Him above all else. And accept with grace and dignity that you are a child of God.*

You must know that the works of mercy through our Lord will be with each one of you at some time in your spiritual progression of Him. At some point in your incarnation as man or as spirit in the world of spirit, each of you will be asked to be a vehicle for Him. You agreed to this the moment you were birthed from light. This is part of all of your karma. God's mercy will unfold for each of you in various ways, as you will each be given the opportunity to show others the light of God that you are, and subsequently, the light of God that they are. You have all made the agreement to be of service to Him in one way or another, and your Father has appreciatively accepted the offer of assistance. When you know that you are a vehicle for such greater things than the self, we suggest that you give to yourself gentleness of heart and peace of mind. Also give yourself the reassurance that the Lord God, your Father in Heaven, rejoices with you.

We will now speak about karma and the soul. The soul and the laws of karma surrounding it as such are also slightly different. The soul is not so much continually reborn as the spirit can be. It is continually present and renewed with the life of God and the light of the Holy Spirit.

The soul is everlasting and present as one. Each soul in creation is sourced from the soul of the Creator. As the spirit is reincarnated, the soul in essence is not. The soul, in forms of energy, is. The essence of the understanding of the soul remains as such. Whereas the energies that transpose within the soul reincarnate through the spirit.

The soul forms a continuum of energy and remains present through the experiences and existences of the spirit, whether embodied or not. It is when the experiences and learning of the spirit raise the vibration of that spirit that the soul continues to remember its essence and strengthens its presence and stillness amidst the Lord. The purpose and karma of the soul is to remain present in the strength and life of Him. The soul maintains its dignity and light of the Father in understanding and learning of its duality. It is as though the soul is on a path of recollection while the spirit is on a journey of learning and experiencing. The soul is similar to the macrocosm, whereas the spirit could be considered the microcosm. The soul embodies the higher understanding of our Lord God and carries through the universe with it the totality of these understandings. The division of souls is upon each spirit that is created in the image and likeness of God. Whereby, each soul has the inherent qualities of the other and partakes in the remembering and experiences of the other. Remember, the soul is about presence. It will continue to remain present in the kingdoms of God and of Heaven. It waits patiently for the spirit to create light and truth and to merge the learnings with the energies of the soul. Indeed, there are souls who have walked the earth or the world of spirit for many a lifetime; this is truth. Yet it is our perception that you make so much more of this than we do. For the soul to walk the worlds for centuries is not something that we deem unpleasant. All the soul is learning to do is to remain present with the Lord. Your soul is another's and another's. If it seems that the soul is separate yet a part of the self and spirit, there is truth to that. You all have a soul. Each spirit needs a soul to create upon itself. The soul does not need a spirit. It is self-containing and permanent until the end of time. It is permanent because, in essence, it is a nonexistent state of being.

The soul is nonexistent in matter, in that it is created to different laws of the universe and does not need to exist as part of the microcosm. It exists as part of a higher truth of creation for our Lord, something we will all come to know when the end of time as you know it comes and things change. The use of the soul has not been apparent to many, and the understanding of its powers is something we await for many of you to learn.

When indeed one hears that the soul has come many times to learn a lesson, there is truth and misunderstanding in that. The soul, in its continuity, remains as such. There are issues of the soul that are inherent within its energies that transpose themselves upon the universal consciousness. Thus, the issues that all spirits have, embodied or not, are one and the same. When a soul continues to remain present, it is because the knowledge that that soul embodies is still manifesting itself through creation. Again, all souls source from the soul of the Creator. Then there is a division of that soul into a smaller number of souls, which mirrors that of creation and universal law. Each soul holds the knowledge of the Lord. As each soul continues throughout time, the soul remains in essence as permanent, while the energies transpose themselves in the universe for all of our higher learning. Many spirits belong to the soul. At the end of time, the spirits and souls will merge as one and cross from the kingdom of God into the kingdom of Heaven. Remember, the kingdom of God includes all that is manifested according to Him. The kingdom of Heaven is nothing but light. Thus, there is no reincarnation when it comes to the essence of the soul. What becomes renewed is the life-giving energy of our Lord and the Holy Spirit. The spirit goes through many different deaths, if you will, but the soul remains ever present, continual, and is strengthened. The purpose of the soul is simply to support the spiritual construct of the universe and to love the Creator. It is the means by which the spirit can do its work. The soul and the universe can be considered as one, dear children, again, a macrocosm. The universe is the magnificent soul of God, and it will continue to remain present for all of us through our learning process as gently as the Creator does.

So when we recommend for you to learn of stillness, it is so that the soul becomes strengthened in the love of the Lord. You can learn many great things and receive the bounty of Him when you come to practice stillness within. As long as the spirit and mind suffer, the soul will continue to remain ever present, ever remembering. As the spirit and the mind learn to be still, the soul will strengthen and find peace with Him, and the kingdom of God will be rectified according to the laws, love, and will of the Creator.

Thus, to remain still is to remain strong. The strength you will receive from Him is far greater than you could ever imagine. This is different from the Lord's power. Strength with the Lord will align you further on your mission and you will endeavor to assist the universe in coming into totality with the Lord. So you see, the little things the Lord asks of you have profound effects on the kingdom! This is what you are all here for. The karma of just yourself is trivial in comparison to the mission the Lord has for all of you as one in respect of the universe.

That is why when you are further along on your path, you have knowledge of the manifestations of your soul's journey. Have you ever wondered where it is that this growth of the soul will lead to? You might notice issues of the soul or other souls transposing themselves upon you for your highest learning. You might notice that passions belonging to the soul are placed upon your spirit. Think far greater than that of yourself. Think far greater than your soul belonging to only you. When you perceive a passion of the soul, it belongs to the energies that transpose themselves upon the universal consciousness. So when we say to you that you must heal the passions of the soul that bind you, we are speaking about those passions belonging to the energies of that soul, and not the essence. The passions are those that are amidst the universe and the totality of its conceptual understandings. It is a very simple task to place those energies into perspective for the greater good. That is why throughout this entire discourse, we have recommended prayer and the stillness of the mind as the best pursuit to quiet the passions and to bring light to them. Again, it is only the continued strength of the soul that is needed to maintain the balance of the universe at large. This includes the earth, the world of spirit, and the cosmos. *Be still for one moment in time and you will have created a shift so great that the universe and its Creator will rejoice. For this, we promise you.* This is the power and truth that lies behind the karmic principles.

When you have all learned the mastery of the soul, the need for reincarnation will cease to exist and you will have all expanded to a greater awareness of the Lord within you and a greater existence and experience of Him. This will be more magnificent than even the prophets of our Lord have foretold. Indeed, the second coming of Christ and the kingdom to come is that which you have never imagined.

When Christ said to us in the scriptures that it was Elijah who had come as John (Matthew 11:14), do you think he was merely speaking of the spirit of Elijah? Indeed not. He was speaking about the spirit, but also about the collective soul, the soul that was representative of Elijah within the universal construct. This is the collective soul that we are all a part of and can greatly aspire to. It is not the precepts of karma as you understand it that apply here, but the wisdom and understanding of the collective conscience that do. That is why when you call upon those in the world of spirit to assist you, you call upon that essence that is greater than the spirits belonging us. We only come to you in this fashion as it is easier for you to comprehend. You call upon the universal and collective conscience to facilitate the redirection of energy toward the Godhead, the kingdom. The reincarnation of thought, energy, being, and expression is simply the rebirth, renewing, regeneration, and redirection of what exists to that which is greater and belonging to the Lord and the universe. It is of love, and so much more. So when we speak about righteousness, we indeed mean it as such. The laws of creation are magnificent in all their glory, as is the Logos, and all the spiritual laws as set forth by Him. Indeed, when it is said that what one sows one shall reap the same, you are given the power of the universe to contend with and awaken to. Expand what the Lord hath given you to know Him far greater than you have done before. Expand your awareness of Him to be better able to receive Him more effectively in your hearts, minds, spirits, and souls. Do so, and the laws of karma and the process of reincarnation will be insignificant to your spiritual growth. You will come to know this as truth in time because you will be higher than you are now. You will be closer to Him. He will be closer to you, and you will understand and know this to be true.

The Seven Angels and the Trumpets

And the seven angels which had the seven trumpets prepared themselves to sound.

The first angel sounded, and there followed hail and fire mingled with blood, and they were cast upon the earth; and the third part of trees was burnt up, and all green grass was burnt up.

And the second angel sounded, and as it were a great mountain burning with fire was cast into the sea; and the third part of the sea became blood. And the third part of the creatures which were in the sea, and had life, died; and the third part of the ships were destroyed.

And the third angel sounded, and there fell a great star from heaven, burning as it were a lamp, and it fell upon the third part of the rivers, and upon the fountains of waters. And the name of the star is called Wormwood; and the third part of the waters became wormwood. . . .

And the fourth angel sounded, and the third part of the sun was smitten, and the third part of the moon, and the third part of the stars; so as the third part of them was darkened, and the day shone not for a third part of it, and the night likewise.

And I beheld, and heard an angel flying through the midst of heaven, saying with a loud voice, "Woe, woe, woe, to the inhabiters of the earth by reason of the other voices of the trumpet of the three angels, which are yet to sound!"

And the fifth angel sounded, and I saw a star fall from heaven unto the earth; and to him was given the key of the bottomless pit. And he opened the bottomless pit, and there arose a smoke out of the pit, as the smoke of a great furnace; and the sun and the air were darkened by reason of the smoke of the pit. And there came out of the smoke locusts upon the earth; and unto them was given power, as the scorpions of the earth have power. And it was commanded them that they should not hurt the grass of the earth, neither any green thing, neither any tree, but only those men which have not the seal of God in their foreheads. And to them it was given that they should not kill them, but that they should be tormented five months; and their torment was as the torment of a scorpion, when he striketh a man. And in those days shall men seek death, and shall not find it; and shall desire to die, and death shall flee from them.

And the shapes of the locusts were like unto horses prepared unto battle; and on their heads were as it were crowns like gold, and their faces were as the faces of men. And they had hair as the hair of women, and their teeth were as the teeth of lions. And they had breastplates, as it were breastplates of iron; and the sound of their wings was as the sound of chariots of many horses running to battle. And they had tails like unto scorpions, and there were stings in their tails; and their power was to hurt men five months. And they had a king over them, which is the angel of the bottomless pit, whose name in the Hebrew tongue is Abaddon, but in the Greek tongue hath his name Apollyon.

One woe is past; and, behold, there come two woes more hereafter. And the sixth angel sounded, and I heard a voice from the four horns of the golden altar which is before God, Saying to the sixth angel which had the trumpet, "Loose the four angels which are bound in the great river Euphrates. And the four angels were loosed, which were prepared for an hour, and a day, and a month, and a year, for to slay the third part of men. And the number of the army of the horsemen were two hundred thousand thousand; and I heard the number of them.

And thus I saw the horses in the vision, and them that sat on them, having breastplates of fire, and of jacinth, and brimstone; and the heads of the horses were as the heads of lions; and out of their mouths issued fire and smoke and brimstone. By these three was the third part of men killed, by the fire, and by the smoke, and by the brimstone, which issued out of their mouths. For their power is in their mouth, and in their tails, for their tails were like unto serpents, and had heads, and with them they do hurt.

And the rest of the men which were not killed by these plagues yet repented not of the works of their hands, that they should not worship devils, and idols of gold, and silver, and brass, and stone, and of wood, which neither can see, nor hear, nor walk. Neither repented they of their murders, nor of their sorceries, nor of their fornication, nor of their thefts.

REVELATION 8:6–13, 9:1–21

The second woe is past; and, behold, the third woe cometh quickly. And the seventh angel sounded; and there were great voices in heaven, saying, "The kingdoms of this world are become the kingdoms of our Lord, and of his Christ; and he shall reign for ever and ever."

And the four and twenty elders, which sat before God on their seats, fell upon their faces, and worshipped God, saying, "We give thee thanks, O Lord God Almighty, which art, and wast, and art to come; because thou hast taken to thee thy great power, and hast reigned. And the nations were angry, and thy wrath is come, and the time of the dead, that they should be judged, and that thou shouldest give reward unto thy servants the prophets, and to the saints, and them that fear thy name, small and great; and shouldest destroy them which destroy the earth."

And the temple of God was opened in heaven, and there was seen in his temple the ark of his testament; and there were lightnings, and voices, and thunderings, and an earthquake, and great hail.

REVELATION 11:14–19

It is now time to put these writings into perspective. Evil can exist within the context of sacred writings for the purpose of bringing to you the glory of God and the healing of the soul. There is much about these teachings that you will understand and much about them that you will not comprehend until later. For this we ask of you patience. Know that by reading those passages, you are creating unto the Lord and the many souls who are encumbered within these writings the light that will bring them healing. Remember, the light cannot exist without the darkness on the lower levels of manifestation and understanding. It is these writings that reflect the darkness (and the light within it) only for you to allow for the healing of the soul to take place. That is all. Those passages are not to frighten you. They are to heal you and to bring to perspective your truth. So we ask that the Light of God be with you all as you take in what you have just read, which we will do our best in explaining.

Do you not think there is evil amidst the light that will try and frighten you against our Lord God? You must understand that when it comes to aligning with the Lord, no matter what prophet speaks of Him, there will always be two polarities to contend with, and this is what these passages in Revelation speak to you about. It is not about the evil befalling the earth or man. It is about the evil that is trying to contend with the light in these works of God. In placing perspective on these passages, many souls will be freed. This we promise you. The intention of those passages was to originally instruct you on spiritual practices toward the holiness of the Lord, and how to use those practices to further your advancement unto the kingdom of Heaven. It was to show you the way to the kingdom, a guideline if you will, for those who desire to strengthen themselves in the ways of Him through the power that the Lord hath given you. To write about such things will only confuse the darkness and give more power to the light. For this we are pleased. It has been a long time in coming since the souls taken by those writings have been encumbered by the confusion and fear. This will soon be rectified. And for the many of you who read those passages with fear and confusion as well, we hope to bring you some light on the subject.

Do you not think that angels (as the ones in those passages) can be disguised by the hands of darkness? We say this because we would like for you to understand that evil is not to be feared in truth and that there is no one who is exempt from creating from both the light and the darkness, no one. Until the time comes when we are all merged as one with Him, we will all be part of that continuum where duality exists.

Let us take it step by step. First let us understand the intent of the authors of those passages. We say authors because there were many, not just one. And they were not all of light. The truth of the Lord is that some of what was written came through with the misunderstanding and confusion of Him. And that comes when the darkness is provoked by the light of Him. There are many souls attached to the confusion around those passages, many who were frightened by the light of God and the darkness as well. So we commend the spirits that worked through the writer(s) of those passages, as their intention was actually a noble one, although the learning has been misunderstood through centuries.

When there is fear of the Lord's power that is not in righteousness, it has the ability to encumber souls and that is exactly what it has done and continues to do. There have been many who have proceeded to transcribe those passages in various ways. We say to you this: listen to them and feel with your heart of their intention. For they too are helping to place into perspective the light of Him. That is the focus of those writings. Why do you think that the Lord let it be placed in the end of the scriptures? Do you not think there was purpose? I trust He knew well how those passages would affect the spiritual life of man, spirit, and soul.

Evil hath many ways and intentions of keeping the perspective out of balance. What transpires in those writings is to show you what takes place when there is no balance and the scales have fallen toward the darkness.

Nonsense toward those who wish to rebuke the Lord and His Glory. The fear of the Lord is evil's greatest friend. However, the light is evil's greatest adversary, and for that, there is so much more. Do not be imprisoned by the words or the energies that transpire through some of Revelation as it is only to make you rise above duality and see the perspective of self, spirit, and soul. Do not be taken in by the words that procure shame and insolence toward our Lord. For indeed, that is not necessary. With the hand of the Lord, let us all disengage from what is not of Him and bring to light the truth.

As we have spoken of karma, the words in those passages have enslaved many to a karma that it is time to be righted. There has been purpose and reason for all. For this we do not condemn any. There have been some who have chosen to stay in the darkness of the energies of those writings. For them, we pray to the Lord to have mercy.

Revelation is a very important book indeed. Yet as there are blessings upon it, there are also grievances. It was written to show people to continually have faith in the Lord and in Christ, and it also shows the torment the soul can go through when it is not in alignment with our Lord. However, the fear it portrays is not in righteousness of Him. Remember when you speak of the Lord, you will bring Him to you. When you speak of evil and you are not with Him when you speak of such things, you will draw that to you as well.

Again, we commend the writer(s) of Revelation, for the intention is a great teaching of our Lord and a tool to show you the possibilities when you remain in strength of Him. Light can be disguised as darkness. For this we do not rebuke. This we try and understand by bringing the light of faith and glory of God to it.

If you notice, the last statement in the quoted passages refers to great calamity. *There were lightnings, and voices, and thunderings, and an earthquake, and great hail* (Revelation 11:19). Do you not think that the purification of the inner soul is of that nature when it comes time to return to the Lord? It is not just one soul that the calamities were referring to, but many. The karma of all is to be rectified at the time of God. It is to be rectified and raised to His glory just as the Christ was. This is what evil fears most. How can the Lord give you all His power and glory and not test your faith in Him and in His gifts to you? He does not test you out of disregard. Rather, He tests you out of His love for you, so that you may be strong in Him, within yourselves, and in your mission. This you must believe.

God will not destroy you, dear children. He loves you. *He will only raise you up to love Him as He loves you.* Evil will not destroy you either. *It is your attachment to evil that will destroy you, not evil itself.* This you must come to understand. When you become attached to the darkness, the judgments that fall prey to you are many, and they are not of the Lord's doing. In the scripture of Revelation, it is the angels who bring destruction upon the world. Again, do you not think that angels can become attached to the darkness? Do you think the will of God desires to condemn you?

The will of Him is to love you and bring to you balance of will and all that is created unto Him. He does not ask of you to become attached to either the light or the darkness, but rather to hold them both in perspective of His love for you and to hopefully choose to live in light of His will and love, and in respect for all that is. That is how righteousness will come to all and His mission for the universe will be fulfilled.

Learn of these writings, know of these writings. But know them from a place of God and righteousness, not from fear of destruction. And we promise you, the meaning, the energies, and the karma of all that is written in Revelation will change for you. It will affect your self, your spirit, and soul, as well as all those who have been enslaved by the grievances in those teachings.

You will notice that throughout Revelation the number seven is used many times. It is simply that this number is defined by our Lord as symbolic of the many graces of Heaven. There are many numbers that define the heavens and bring light to truth, many.

Let us speak now about the seven angels and their trumpets and what the Lord would like for you to understand of them. We will tell you as the story is rewritten for your truth and light.

Then the seven angels who had the seven trumpets prepared to blow them. The first angel blew his trumpet. Then hail and fire mixed with blood and was poured into creation, the creation of man and spirit. The hail represents the duality of consciousness that is healed by the baptismal waters of the universe. The fire symbolizes the first initiation and purification of man on the earth plane. In man, initiation focuses on a blessing of higher energy that is given to him in the creation of power centers in and around his being. The first power center takes control of that hail and fire and transforms it into the power cord that will enable him to connect the earth with the heavens and to fulfill his mission from the Lord. In spirit, this creation also focuses on a blessing of a higher energy that is given. This blessing will enable the spirit to have courage in the face of darkness and to withstand trials against our Lord in complete faith and honor of Him. A third of the earth, the trees, and the grass were not literally burned up as the passage states. The old ways of understanding and the knowledge given that was not in complete truth of Him will be purified. The old energies that have been present for many a lifetime that have been without truth of Him shall return to the light. This will begin a new phase of the cycle of birth for man to come, as well as those beings in the present and past. This transmission of energy into the first power center will enable man and spirit to rise above what has been deemed by spiritual law in the past and to create anew with the Lord, for the new time to come will be one of magnificence. The appearance of the first angel is in light around rebirth of the spirit in a larger paradigm. If you think an angel of the Lord comes upon you with destruction as it is stated in those passages, we suggest you think again. When the power of the Lord is present, the darkness shall always feel threatened.

Then the second angel blew his trumpet. Something that looked like a big mountain was thrown into the sea. And a third of the sea became blood in which living things died and ships were destroyed. Do not fear your creative power as given to you by the Holy Spirit. The mountain is the obstacle that you have thrown against the power of the Holy Spirit that will rise up within you. This power is used to cultivate your relationships in light of the Lord, not against Him. That which is destroyed can only be the desires and attachments that this power does not serve. Place into perspective the meaning of this. Do not take unto you what does not belong in the name of God. You do not need to fear the power of the Lord within you or fear that the Lord is submissive to that of the darkness. The sea represents the second power center of man and of spirit. This second power center enables man to make right his use of relationships to gain greater access to the spirit of God. Know this. To make use of this is different than to make righteous. Think about it. Separate the mind that is not of Him from the relationships that you create out of confusion. The sea only becomes blood when you fail to recognize or accept the God within and the God within others. Your power of spirit lies within your ability to create relationships using God as your witness. Relationship is not just an agreement that exists between you and another. It encompasses all that is involved with creation. The power behind this center is strong with Him and must be used in accordance with His will.

The third angel blew his trumpet. Then a large star, burning like a torch, fell from the sky. This symbolized the awakening of the higher power of our Lord as given to you in the scriptures for you to learn and know better of Him. This is the power of the Lord that will place into perspective the will of Him upon your soul and the rest of creation. This relates to the third power center in man and spirit. Indeed, this is the opportunity for all to make righteous the will and dignity of our Lord, and to place into perspective the entire universe. As the passage states: *It fell upon the third part of the rivers, and upon the fountains of waters . . . and the third part of the waters became wormwood; and many men died of the waters, because they were made bitter* (Revelation 8:10).

We say to you this: think about truth and Him. Think about the way you perceive truth. The water that becomes bitter is what is not in truth and justice of our Lord. The people who drink this bitter water will not die. Their spirits will be tormented by their own injustices and many who believe as they do. God has given you the power to know truth in many ways and to find your own truth in relation to your mission with Him. When it comes time for you to relinquish your authority to the Lord, know that you will do so. This is His way. This is your way. You have the choice to know Him in all His light or to continually see through the darkness. The Lord gives to you the choice through this third power center to align yourselves with Him or with the darkness. He gives you the choice to create according to Him or not to. He gives you the choice to see the truth or to know otherwise. He gives you the choice to explore your mission with dignity of Him. When you choose to do so, your spirit will be given all the power it needs to complete what the Lord hath asked of you.

When you learn to master the blessings upon yourself and spirit as the Lord hath given you, you will receive the knowledge of the universe in increments to the level at which you can apply them. This is also the meaning behind the third power center in man and in spirit. The application of the laws as set forth by God has the power to create the universe at will. Do you not think that evil was frightened of this? You must listen, as there are those spirits and souls who refuse to understand that the Lord is with them. These words are your truth and your purpose. *With Him, you can only live. Without Him, you will die.* The Lord grants you the love and mercy of the heavens to partake in at your request of it. Even if you do not request it, you must trust that it is there. The Lord will not abandon you as the darkness will. He will never leave you or torment you the way that the darkness has.

The fourth angel blew his trumpet. A third of the sun, the moon, and the stars were hit as the passage states. This darkened the day, leaving it without light. This passage speaks to the transformation of the soul. The sun, the moon, and the stars are representative of the spiritual hierarchies as created by the heavens. The hierarchies are nothing more than ways and laws that creation is founded upon, thereby enhancing the awareness of the soul. In order for the soul to progress, there has to be order within the universal and personal kingdoms. This is about that order and the order in which man, spirit, and soul ascend to the kingdom. This is about those energies that are associated with the fourth power center in man and spirit. It is not that the day was without light and that the sun, moon, and stars became dark. It is that the light transformed itself into something greater than it was before. And in order to do this, it has to go through the darkness once again. This is about the opening of the soul to love. In man, this reflects within the heart. There is an order to this love as deemed righteous by the Lord and the heavens. And there is a way that this love unfolds for your higher understanding and purpose.

As the fourth angel blew his trumpet, the potential for man, spirit, and soul raised itself higher to the light of Him. The eagle flying high in the air was only to frighten away the soul from becoming all too powerful in the Lord's love. When the soul becomes all too powerful in the Lord's love, then it has the potential of becoming ignorant. When the eagle flew overhead and said that there was trouble for those who live on earth, he was warning the soul to be wary of its passions keeping it at the lower levels of contemplation. For indeed, the soul is always constant. However, remember that the soul's vibrations are raised higher to the Lord at the moment that the spirit does its spiritual work. The spirit can stay for long periods of time at the lower levels of contemplation if it refuses to see the light. For this reason, the Lord has given you His unlimited love for your purpose both on earth and in spirit.

Then the fifth angel blew his trumpet. And a star fell from the sky to the earth. The star was given the key to the deep hole that leads to the bottomless pit. The passage states that as the key opened the hole that led to the bottomless pit, smoke and locusts came upon the earth. And the locusts were given the power to cause pain in people for five months. The king of the locusts was said to be an angel named

Destroyer, as the scriptures say. For this we say to you, nonsense! As you grow in the power of the Lord, there will be many that will try and interfere with your spiritual progression. It is not up to the power of the Destroyer to take away your love for Him, for it is only you who allow this to happen. Do not think that the locusts are there to protect you from that which is more powerful than what they can offer you. The passage challenges you to run from the face of death or indeed to run from the darkness. *In those days shall men seek death, and shall not find it; and shall desire to die, and death shall flee from them* (Revelation 9:6). This is about your responsibility to take hold of the power of the Lord within you and affirm your belief and faith in Him. This energy comes through when you call to it and nourishes the fifth power center of man and spirit. This is an important power center as it is concerned with the affirmation of the Lord through you in all ways. It is only the lack of faith and belief that will cause you not to affirm your life to Him in all that you are and all that you do. The deep hole that the passage refers to is in actuality the never-ending grief that will arise when you choose not to affirm your faith in Him.

It is only that grief that will give rise to the powers that will eventually destroy you. We say destroy because when you choose not to rise above the suffering, you leave yourself open to torment from such things, which are symbolized by the smoke and the locusts giving you the pain of darkness. Remember, pain can be a dangerous attachment in one's spiritual growth. For this, many of you do not believe. It is easy for most men and even spirits to become attached to the pain of being without Him. If they were to raise themselves above that pain, they would see the reality of things as we know it and would have to take responsibility for the Lord's power, might, and love upon themselves. Death can only run away from you if you choose not to see death in the right perspective as our Lord created it. As the passage states, *Men . . . shall desire to die, and death shall flee from them* (Revelation 9:6). When man, spirit, and soul have even gotten to this place of being tormented by the smoke and locusts, if you will, they will desire to have a death that is different than what the Lord wishes for us. It is not a true death. It is not death at all. Many of you perceive it as death and as the end to your suffering. We see it as the transformation of the suffering into the boundless energy of God. It encompasses all that transpires for you with His tender love and mercy.

Do not allow for your power to affirm your love for Him to be usurped by false pretexts. When you choose to invoke the energies of this fifth power center upon you, you will begin to understand the purpose for the Lord's will upon you. Indeed, as you begin to understand all the power centers, as you move higher in frequencies, you will see that the power expands itself and moves into choice for the spirit and soul to know God differently. Your awareness of the transformation of the Lord within you and your right to accept this transformation begins to avail itself.

When it comes to karma and reincarnation, you can work effectively with these power centers and begin to align yourself with God's purpose for you and do so in a manner that is supportive and in alignment with your spiritual progression. Again, all does need to work in accordance with the will of God and the rules of spiritual law as deemed by the kingdom. We are showing you these gifts of the Creator so that you can begin to manifest your purpose of Him within you if you have not done so already. What the Lord hath given you is of great importance for your knowledge and understanding and is more identifiable to man and spirit on the lower levels of contemplation as well as the higher ones. It is not everyone who can consciously see into the world of spirit. Each of you can take responsibility for these power centers bestowed upon you and begin to take notice of the spiritual laws at work within them.

After the fifth angel has appeared, there is a passage in the scriptures that states the following before the appearance of the sixth angel: *One woe is past; and, behold, there come two woes more hereafter*

(Revelation 9:12). This is not a warning from the heavens, dearest children. When we become closer to Him, all that is not in perspective of Him becomes frightened by the power of the Lord that will indeed place all into perspective. What is not understood is always feared. We do wish that this were not so. There is much to be rectified in the way of Him in regard to man and spirit's potential to be of His image and likeness. In simply reading these words, you have facilitated more of the process than you realize. It is said that all words belonging to our Lord have the power to change even form. There is certainty and truth to that. When you achieve growth in your spiritual life where you can access the vibrations of all the power centers within you, you awaken the ability to change even form. You can notice these feats in the scriptures and other sacred writings, as well as within practices of various spiritual traditions. This gift is not given to some of you, it is given to all of you; even though there are only certain beings and spirits at present who can achieve these altered states. There are even many in the world of spirit who maintain a way of existing as deemed by the Lord only to be transformed at the permission of Him. This power is extraordinary and available to all under the light of Him, however it will make manifest through those who are chosen. You must realize that the Lord hath given all of His children every power known to Him. The ability to make manifest those powers is given differently to each man, spirit, and soul. This is done so that we could all learn of the splendor of the Lord and how beautifully and differently He creates Himself in each one of us. If we all expressed the Lord in the same way, there would be nothing for us to look forward to in our ascension toward Him. All power begins and ends with the Lord. The book of Revelation teaches about things such as karma and evil, but it is that power that can be harnessed from the righteous understanding of those subjects that the Lord wishes for you to grasp.

The first great trouble that has passed is merely what you have accomplished in the name of Him that is righteous and dignified with all the glory that is known to God. It signifies that transformation of the lower domain of evil into light. That will ultimately awaken the higher states of consciousness that lead to ascension. It is only trouble for those who wish to stay within the powerless of the darkness. The two other great troubles to come refer to the awakening of the soul's potential to an even greater glory of our Lord. There can only be trouble when the soul uses that potential unwisely, or when the soul does indeed use it righteously—which interferes with evil's plan. The awakening of the soul's potential in congruence to what we have been speaking of refers to the two other power centers in man and spirit. The Lord gives you many more centers of power as you continue to awaken. After a certain time, they become irrelevant in your growth. By this we simply mean that your focus on their awakening becomes secondary as you live from the wellsprings of the Lord on a continual, conscious basis. God has given you a structure so that you may simply understand Him in your present knowledge. Remember, there is structure in all things: the earth, the heavens, the world of spirit, the universe, and in the laws deemed by the Creator. Structure is used so that there is support for the continued creation of light and the Lord's will until that time comes when all is living and existing to the will of the Creator. The need for structure ceases when it transforms into a different vibration. If you look at what we have been speaking about in the process of karma and reincarnation, the same rules apply. This is about the known and the unknown; the form, and what is formless. Karma and reincarnation have a structure that supports the existing spiritual laws. It reflects upon these power centers that the Lord hath given you. As the spiritual consciousness is raised, these laws will change to resonate with the spiritual alignment of all that exists within the Lord's domain; as will the power centers that the Lord hath given you. They constantly change and affect what unfolds for you in your spiritual progression. We say to you this: be mindful of those power centers as tools for your advancement. Like anything else of Him, do not get attached to the contemplation of them in your pursuit of healing, knowledge, and light. If you do, you will not allow the natural progression of these power centers to unfold. These power centers are for righteous use and understanding only and have great benefits if you choose to be with them in His name.

The sixth angel blew his trumpet. A voice was heard coming from the horns on the golden altar that is before the Lord. As the passage states, the voice told the sixth angel to free the four angels who are tied at the River Euphrates. The angels were to be freed to kill a third of the people on the earth. Other people were not killed but did not change in their ways to the Lord.

This passage gives rise to confusion and misunderstanding. What do you think it means to have angels kill a third of the people on earth? Do you think this is truth? Let us look at it differently. The sixth angel is congruent with that of the sixth power center in man and spirit. It is the threshold for the Illumination of the Soul. This power center holds the wisdom, knowledge, and inner vision of our Lord for the entire universe. With this power, man and spirit have the capability of illuminating their souls to the level of the heavens. Indeed, we say capability. When one soul has this capability, it gives awareness to all that exists of the will of God that is inherent in all of creation. This power center looks at the will of God and lives the will of Him differently than the other power centers. This truth is key. To live the will of Him through your vehicle at each moment and know truths beyond your current possibilities will allow you to expand your limitations to reach up to the infinite possibilities of our Lord. This is the opportunity for souls to grasp the Divine intellect of the Creator and to use that intellect to further their ascension toward Him. When you are living your mission guided from the sixth energy center, it is said that you make choices that are in agreement with that of Divine Providence, even though you understand that there are both good and not good consequences to that. This power center brings you an awareness of the profound love that the Lord hath given you and an understanding and acceptance of your service to Him. Service indeed that comes from knowing and living the will of Him through you is a gift from the Lord Himself.

The four angels that were freed to kill a third of the people represented the torments and passions that the mind inflicts on the soul. Only a third are killed, with the rest of the people left to choose between fear and love, darkness and light, from the perspective of the intellect. Remember, the intellect is very important when it comes to karma. To raise your thoughts in the name of the Lord will indeed have an effect on your karmic duties and the way in which you perceive your spiritual progression toward Him. The others that were not killed are symbolic of those thoughts that seek to understand the Lord and His righteousness. It is only their fear that makes them not change toward Him. And remember, even for those who think they do not change, if you exist on any level, you are always receiving the Lord in some way, always effecting change.

Then the seventh angel blew his trumpet. It was said in Revelation: *In the days when the seventh angel is ready to blow his trumpet, God's secret plan will be finished. This plan is the Good News God told to His servants, the prophets* (Revelation 10:7 [NCV]). The passage states that there were loud voices in the heavens, and that they shouted out that the power to rule the world belonged to the Christ. And the elders who sat before the throne of God gave thanks and proclaimed the Lord's power over all. They proclaimed that it was time for the Lord's judgment upon men. And for those who live in the Lord's image and likeness, they shall be rewarded. And for those who do not, they shall be destroyed. After the voices finished, the temple of the Lord became opened and the Ark of the Covenant and all its splendor was to be seen. With this vision came calamities from Heaven that fell upon the earth.

You must understand that the gift of prophecy is given to all those who seek to distinguish the Lord's truth from what is not truth, and His works from those that are not His works. The seventh angel is congruent with the seventh power center that is given to you as justice and reward for your works of Him and Christ. The seventh power center is in alignment with the gift of prophecy. This is truly a gift of the Lord for your good works through and of Him. Prophecy does not take place in the domain you think. The energies that belong to it rule every aspect of the universe. It is part of the Logos.

Prophecy is not about the telling of the future, it is more about the juncture where the past, present, and future meet to distinguish truth from reality. There are many different realities that exist for man, spirit, and soul. The one who can prophesy will know the difference between the reality and the truth of it all. The juncture where the past, present, and future meet will place you in the highest perspective of the truth if you allow it to happen. It is from this place on, that you can open yourself to receive the gifts of the Lord through you. In that place, there is nothing but stillness and presence. Not the present time, but presence. You have the opportunity to face your truth, not your reality, when you engage and empower this seventh power center that the Lord hath given you.

What you will come to know and understand as you begin to master the seventh power center is indeed the use of God's creative power to bring forth manifestation of prophecy that is foretold. When you prophesy, you live the truth of God through you in every moment. The past, the present, and the future are simultaneously being directed and healed with the will of God in mind. Do you not think that the Lord gives all of us that same gift? There is an understanding in the world of spirit how to bring what is prophesied to fruition in different dimensions of reality. You see, prophecy, free will, and the Lord's will have a parallel relationship that supports the structure of the universe in some way. What is in His will can indeed be prophesied. Even the will of the self can be foretold. Do you not think the Lord knows you so, and the universe He created as well? Many of you think that the Lord gave you more than you can take responsibility for. Have the faith in yourself that the Lord God has in you. He has always known exactly what you are capable of doing and being and what you are not. And He has given you many chances to rise to the occasion of being complete within your Godnature.

Thus, when the seventh angel blew his trumpet, the Lord gave you the kingdom of Heaven at your request for learning and appreciating who you are. The power to rule the world is subsequent to the love that you will experience in the stillness and splendor of the Lord. This seventh power enables souls and spirits to transform themselves at higher levels and also to work within their karmic process at higher levels. The gift of prophecy and karma at this level become tools of empowerment with the Lord so that you can work to master your karma a little differently than from the other power centers. To master it does not mean you can take the process in the direction of your will. It simply means that you can overcome your hindrances in a more distinct way as an awareness of your progress lies within your Divine intellect and within the heart of Christ, which you have. You will be able to maneuver with the hand of God what your soul does not need to attach to any further. And you will do it with more grace as given to you by Him.

As the passage states, the elders bowed down and gave praise to the Lord. How righteous indeed to give Him thanks. How righteous indeed to give Him praise. The moment you can look to the Lord and say Alleluia, you have granted Him the privilege of coming into your heart and making it greater and more loving than it ever was before.

When the elders expressed in their praise to the Lord that it was time for the Lord's anger to judge the dead and to destroy those who destroy the earth, they were merely speaking of the Lord's light to come into balance once again with the darkness. The Lord will not destroy His children, this will never be. It is only through the misunderstanding of the darkness that you will ever be destroyed. But not by Him, by your own misgivings of who you are. Even when we speak the word *destroyed,* we do not place the same understanding of it that you do or even your translations of the scriptures. The Lord never hath destroyed anything. Once you understand this, you will begin to see a more loving Creator. You will begin to feel empowered by His love for you.

Once you have acquired the awareness of the seventh power, there is no turning back. That is why it says that God's temple in Heaven was opened and the Ark of the Covenant could be seen by all. All the laws change at that level, and you will receive a new level of instruction from the Lord as to how to progress in your spiritual life and how to enhance and align with your karmic duties to the Lord's will for you.

After the seventh power, there will be more to know, more to learn, and more to understand. So much more. And then you will start again at the beginning, only with a different understanding and more love for yourself and God. You think that this is a trick of the Lord. It is not. That is why so many of you are born having completed much of your karma and wondering why you are still being reincarnated. To start at the beginning is to start as light. To start at the beginning is to start at love. You will never stop learning, as long as love and light exist. It will just be in a different way. And at that point, even the rules and laws of the spiritual consciousness and karma will be transformed. So dear children, take your lives one day at a time, take your existence as spirit one vibration at a time. But always, do it with the help of the Lord. You cannot fail with Him by your side. Above all, there is eternity.

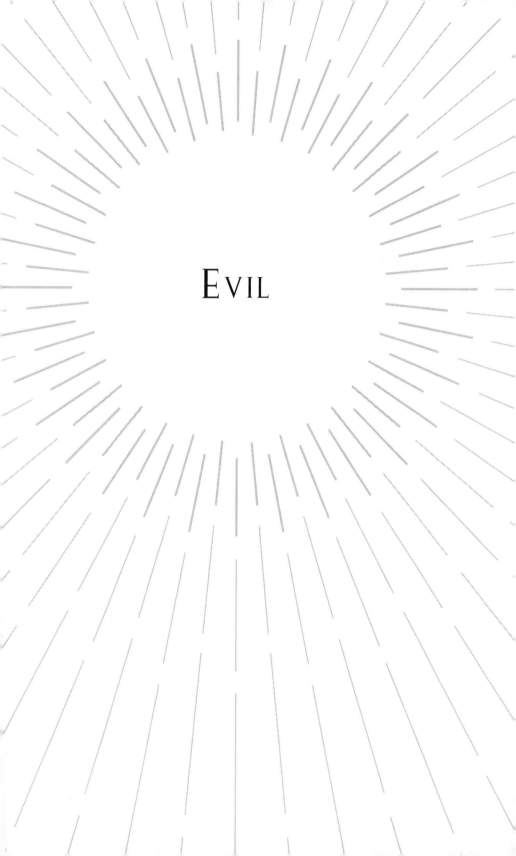

EVIL

May all evil come to rest in the stillness, silence, and light of God. May we come to know evil as doth the Lord; with His strength, and the light of His faith.

LAURA AVERSANO

But the souls of the righteous are in the hand of God, and there shall no torment touch them.

WISDOM 3:1

The Origin

Nothing created in the essence of God is evil, but all that is manifested from the energies of our Lord has the potentials and makings of producing evil. All that is in existence is of the Lord, this you must understand. When it comes to evil, the existence as such is only rendered by Him as necessary to place the structure and understanding of universal laws in perspective of the light. The way that the Lord understands and truly knows evil is much different from the way you do. Creation and manifestation are of different energies. If we were to speak of the Lord's essence alone, there would be nothing in creation or manifestation to speak of. The moment the Lord came to be known in creation, light and darkness existed as relating to the universe. The Lord's essence in and of itself ceased to exist as a single entity. Rather, His essence dispersed itself as energies for us to understand and learn from. These energies co-created the polarities of good and evil, the light and the darkness. To think that the Lord is only of light is untruth. To think that the Lord is of evil is untruth. To think that the Lord is everything that is possible within the scope of the universal consciousness is truth. That will include all that is good and all that is evil. If you were to not see that light and evil can coexist in perspective, then you will not be able to rise above the makings of the soul and reach into the heavens. For without Him, you cannot learn of light, and without Him, you cannot learn of the darkness. This you must believe.

You shall begin this journey of knowledge by knowing and accepting that as much light of Him that you have, you have acquired as much darkness. This is nothing to be frightened of. When you become aware of what evil truly is, then you will be able to place it in perspective of your spiritual growth rather than working to rid it. This does not mean that we do not encourage the casting out of such entities of evil. We are simply asking you to understand why it is a necessary component for the present moment in the universal construct. At the end of time as we know it, all will be merged with Him in the kingdom of Heaven and there will be nothing but light and the essence of the Lord to speak of. Until that time, the Lord will give to you exactly what you need to understand the makings of the kingdom and your soul's place within it.

There are many levels and manifestations of evil. Light you were made of. This light includes the darkness of the Lord that you interpret in a way that makes you suffer.

The essence of the Lord is light that is resting in stillness. When creation and manifestation served themselves, the movement of these energies of our Lord brought to each soul the power to acquire the makings of the entire universe. When light does not rest in stillness, it ceases to be just that of light. Think about that. That is also how perspective arises. You must be still within the light for there to be perspective of the darkness contained within and around it.

To ask the question of what is evil will bring forth many answers from the seen and unseen world. We will seek to accomplish the quest as given to us by our Lord in serving your greatest good with this knowledge. We will seek to define evil in perspective of where the universe is at its present moment. We are not speaking in terms of time, but in terms of the progression of relationship between the light and the darkness of the universe as a whole.

The soul is just a mirror of the universe. What transpires within the spiritual progress of all souls will reflect the accumulation of experiences within the universal construct. As the light learns from the darkness and the darkness learns from the light, all souls and universal consciousness will raise themselves up further toward the Lord. Henceforth, on the lower levels of creation and manifestation, chaos will ensue. The chaos is symbolic only of what is out of perspective coming into perspective. As things do come into perspective, the amount of light will indeed be raised. In the lower levels of creation and manifestation, as much darkness will be raised and the same will be transformed by its perspective of the light. Evil has the potential to be raised and transformed, to be increased, and to be cast out, depending on the level of contemplation we are working with. If you think that there is no evil in the higher realms of contemplation, you are mistaken. The Lord hath many angels and saints still working closely with Him to protect His entire kingdom. The Lord will cease to need those helpers the moment we are all with Him in eternity and the darkness is not a necessary component of the spiritual life.

Evil exists in the plane of earth and in the world of spirit. As above, so below. Evil transfers itself differently than most other laws. It must be rectified in the lower levels of creation first for it to be placed within perspective so that what lies in the higher levels of contemplation will also be placed within perspective. Even though evil is also manifested in the higher levels, its physical form takes precedence among the lower levels of contemplation. To put into perspective all darkness that is within the world of spirit and on the plane of earth, one has to look at these lower levels of contemplation.

What do we mean by putting evil into perspective? It can mean many things depending on what we are speaking of. It does not necessarily mean the healing of it, which is something many of you have perceived. Evil cannot be healed in truth. It does not need to be healed. If you were to learn that, perhaps you would seek to know the universe better. Perhaps you would seek to relate to the universe and yourself better. To place evil in perspective simply means to allow for the light of God to infuse itself into what has rendered itself not of God. What transpires after that is ultimately the will of Him. Whether evil is then transformed and raised, increased or cast out, is totally up to God's discretion. This is not to say that the Lord is a cruel King, for indeed, that He is never. This is not to say that He doth desire evil to exist to punish you. *He doth desire evil to exist to teach you of the greatest powers and truths that He can ever bestow upon the children*

He loves so. He doth desire evil to exist for your understanding of the love that you were and are created by. He doth desire for evil to exist so that evil can learn of Him too. In light of that, He does not desire for evil to harm or punish in any way. This is where the Lord steps in to rectify. He desires for evil to exist simply as a state of presence for the knowledge of all. When evil manifests itself, the spiritual laws as set forth by Him begin to adhere themselves to the universe. Again, this is important for your knowing. The Lord God desires for evil to exist simply as a state of presence for the knowledge of all. When evil is placed in perspective, it will be in complete stillness and surrounded and balanced by the light. When evil is not in stillness, then it is not in perspective. Evil can teach you love. It always does. Look at how many of you turn toward Him after suffering through the darkness.

So when we say that the Lord is in truth, He is all that exists within the universe, including the light and the darkness. The Lord is all this within the element of stillness. Once the energy begins to take form, then the evil that manifests itself is not of the Lord's making. It is of your making. It is of your perspective of the light that you carry because you have not in truth learned of the correct perspective of the light that you hold. Nor have you learned of the correct perspective of your darkness.

Whether we are speaking of individual souls, the collective soul, or the soul of the universe, evil stems from the far reaches of all dimensions and can create upon itself only by intent. No matter the form, it can create only by intent. When the soul loses its ability to transcend the nondualistic reality of its nature, evil is present. When the soul loses awareness of its nature to create within the essence of the Lord as opposed to manifesting with the energies of the Lord, such is evil. When the soul enables itself to be in contemplation of Him, such is evil. It is that way because contemplation is not necessary when you are simply of His essence. Contemplation fuels desires and attachments of the lower self, therefore opening one up to the energies at will.

All those things that are evil are also of light. They are not avoidable of either polarity when in existence. They cannot be, for the kingdom of God is set up in that manner. Evil is only the understanding of the truth of Him in incorrect perspective of the light. Only place what you need to on the thought of evil. It is because of the false knowledge and thoughts that you place upon the existence of evil that allows it to continue to create out of balance with the desired intention of our Lord.

Evil was set forth as a structure of knowledge that is able to serve your greatest understanding and knowing of Him. The main intention of evil is simply to exist in a state of awareness and presence, not to destroy that which is light. That has only come to be because of what all souls have come to burden themselves and the universe with. That is not of the Lord's will. In His desire for evil to exist in stillness, your understanding of that will show you that there is truly nothing to fear around the evil that God knows. There is much to fear around the structure and manifested energies of evil as they create upon themselves in the dimensions of existence where you have free will.

Evil in and of itself is not bad, nor is it corrupt. I am speaking of evil at its core essence. Just as the Lord has essence and energy, evil also is held as essence and energy. Evil is a misuse and misinterpretation of the light of God and the nature of the soul according to His inner workings. The relationship to the Lord becomes misconstrued when evil is present. This relationship becomes misconstrued in the eyes of your own soul, not in the Lord's eyes. The Lord does not place as much emphasis on evil as you do. This truth might serve you. He does place emphasis on the misuse of the interpretations of evil. That will indeed bring to you harm. It is this misuse of those understandings that the Lord offers to you His servants and counsel at large for your protection and guidance. Those in the higher dimensions of the world of spirit place emphasis on the misuse of those understandings because as long as evil continues to exist on the lower levels of contemplation, it will exist for them also. Whether they are angels or saints, they will encounter as well the misuse of the truth. However, their understanding of those truths is far greater than those existing at the lower levels of contemplation. Thus, their fear for themselves is less. They have more fear for your soul in your spiritual growth than they do for their own. They indeed know and have learned of the stillness that can exist within the concept of evil. The Lord might bring you the concept, but it is you who have given it structure and your own meaning. It is our hope that some of this meaning becomes rectified during this discourse.

When you come to understand the nature of light in respect to the nature of the darkness and your place within it, you will seek to enhance the intelligence that the Lord hath given you to fully comprehend the nature of being. The intelligence that you have acquired in the state of contemplation you are in attaches you to the misunderstandings of the workings and power of the Lord. When the soul seeks to unify itself with the Lord in its quest for spiritual knowledge, it gains momentum in its quest only if it is able to rest gently in the presence of evil as opposed to nullifying it. You might not understand what we mean by resting in the presence of evil. It is to be mindful of the engagement of your soul with its energies and to show respect for all power of the universe. It is only when you rest simply within your own soul that you can rise above both the light and the darkness to be as one with Him.

When the soul forgets its place with the Lord, it engages in the learning process that will enable itself to put all into perspective. Nothing can penetrate the light once the light has been absolved by the Father. By this we mean that the light is in totality of His essence. Your intellect has much to do with the presence of evil when it is not in its resting state. *Evil will rest when you have obtained the knowledge and wisdom of the Lord and are able to put that knowledge into perspective.* Until that time, dear children, believe that evil does exist in creation as you know it, in energy, and within the lower levels of contemplation and manifestation. Love alone will not put it into perspective. If that were to be true, then why was Jesus tempted by the Devil? The kind of love that the Christ exemplified does have the power to place evil in perspective. But we are speaking of a love that encompasses more than just a feeling or energy within the heart. We are speaking of every grain of truth, light, and grace as given by our Lord. This is the kind of love that the Christ exemplified. This is the kind of understanding that will place evil into perspective.

When the intellect can no longer comprehend and live by its untruths, it will seek to find a greater understanding of Him. It will seek to furnish its path with the balance of understanding that comes with advancement. Until that time, the intellect will serve evil as it does light, only to the matter that it needs to make itself aware of the workings of evil, as it needs to make itself aware of the workings of light. The workings of evil are the passions of the soul that extend to thought, action, deed, and inner knowing. Yes, the soul needs to have an inner knowing of evil so that it may obtain a true inner knowing of the light. This is only so because you have asked the Lord to experience creation. The workings of evil also extend greatly beyond the passions of the soul to the exploitations of the universe. We are not speaking of evil at this point that is in its resting state. That is because evil as such is not meant to be corruptive or exploitive. Only when evil is not in its resting state can it corrupt or exploit the universe at large. Remember, in the sanctity of our Lord when there is unity among all and complete light, evil is not present. There is no need for it to be present. That is a state of being that we have all not reached yet. We are speaking of the kingdom of God in which all is encompassed at the present moment. When we speak of the exploitations of the universe, we speak of the lack of respect that evil has for the light in the lower levels of creation and the lack of respect that souls have for evil. To fear the Lord is indeed to respect Him. Could you not respect the darkness in the learning that it has to teach you? To do so would serve to assist you in finding the proper understanding and boundaries in regard to evil and its energies.

To believe that you are without evil or its energies is untruth. To think that you are not capable of understanding or rising above them is also untrue. For as long as time has existed, there has been evil. Again, that is as long as time has existed. Time has only existed in creation and manifestation. In the essence of Him, there is no time. As far back as evil begins is as far back as your soul has the knowledge and understandings of its inner workings. This is how much knowledge and workings are within your intellect and the makings of your soul. This is part of the greater truth, and this is what all souls come to place into perspective. If the Lord God gave to you the inexplicable light of being, you were also given the understanding of its opposite so that you may cultivate a spiritual life according to the workings of the Lord and the Holy Spirit. Accept the light within you, and accept the darkness. If you do so, you will already be ahead on your spiritual path and understanding of who you are and who the Lord is with you.

The longer that evil that is not in its rested state persists, the more destructive its energies, and the more the soul becomes wary of its place with the Lord. For we say to you this: the moment you are birthed into creation, you are part of the Divine intellect, which makes the universe codependent on your learning experience and understanding of the light and the darkness. As the levels of light expand, thus the darkness—and in contrast to the learning continuum as set forth by God. Man and soul's endeavors to understand their basic nature through the Lord's gift of free will enabled all souls to partake in the structure and energy as opposed to standing peacefully in relationship to the concept and essence of evil. Remember, when the Lord created the heavens and the earth, all was still. The birth of all souls comes from stillness. All will return to the light in stillness. As will evil.

It must be in stillness for all to understand the meaning that it has brought forth for your learning.

The light of God is uncreated essence. Evil that draws forth from the universe is created essence. What does this mean? It simply means that eternal truth rests upon nothing but light. It is uncreated because it has never ceased to exist. The concept of evil sprang from a kernel of truth, so to speak, that needed to set up a structure so that all could learn to appreciate this uncreated light that is of Him. It has a beginning in the universe. The definition of universe implies that there are things in motion. For that to be of truth, there have to be opposing forces at work for the greater understanding of creation and manifestation. At its essence of truth, evil is just a concept of understanding that within itself it indeed carries light. When its essence is created upon with free will by souls in any dimension, it no longer has conceptual understanding but begins to take form. Remember that in the heavens it was said that an angel of the Lord who fell from grace began the evil in the heavens. Did not this angel encounter first the light of God? The angel hath been named Lucifer, and indeed, he is at present one to contend with. Do you not think even he contemplates the Lord from time to time? Of course he does. In order for him to exist, there is light upon which he needs to survive. If you think evil only survives upon itself alone, you are incorrect. Evil also needs the light to expand. It is just unfortunate that as it expands, it is mostly done with misuse of the powers that be. If there were no light, there would be no evil. Remember this. It will become useful to many of you when you are in situations of darkness.

The energies belonging to evil do not necessarily need the will of the Lord to exist, which is different than that of the light. The essence of evil at its core does need the will of God to exist. Just because the Lord gave His permission for evil to expand its energies does not mean He supports it through His will. You will know the times that the Lord does support evil through His will for your higher learning.

There is evil at the level of man, evil at the level of spirit, and evil at the level of the soul. At any level, it is your choice to engage your intellect in the constructs and confines of it. We say confines because unlike the light, evil has its boundaries. Understand this, its power can reach further than the soul could perceive, but it has its limits as the power, intention, and will of the Lord are far greater. Evil cannot permeate where the Lord does not allow it. This is truth. However, the Lord is mindful of the gift He gave you to be as magnificent as Him, which includes the choice to create as you so desire.

The will of the soul relates to that of the intellect. It enables the soul to righteously choose experiences that will serve its capacity to hold both the light and the darkness in a perspective of balance and harmony. This perspective is the only thing that will move the soul in its spiritual progression and through those laws set forth by Him and His Council. It is the purpose of all souls to learn to justify their experiences of imbalance by utilizing the light of God. When we say justify, we literally mean to bring justice to. At the lower levels of contemplation, evil needs to be justified. At the higher levels, it needs simply to be placed into perspective. It depends on the awareness of the evil that persists and the advancement and understanding of the soul. Each soul, spirit, and man has the capacity to produce works of goodness or works of the darkness. It is our hope that all souls render goodness. For we know this is not truth. So we ask all of you to take a look at your darkness, and to see where it is that you and God need to bring truth and understanding to what is not in perspective in your nature. Part of your nature does allow for the presence of evil in a resting state until that time when it is no longer needed by the universal construct and your spiritual conscience. The nature of light and the nature of darkness is continually changing and expanding. What was the will of the Lord then is indeed the will of the Lord now, but to a greater light, and a greater awareness. That is because of the continuum of motion that was set forth by you. In being blessed with the grace of free will, you are all doing the work of growing on your spiritual path, whether or not you are conscious of that journey. It is because of the work that you are doing that is changing the nature of the soul itself and the way in which the soul relates to the light and the darkness.

Thus, the nature of the soul that is in constant change and growth will go to the Lord with a greater respect for what has been given and a learned awareness of His truth. Many of you so work on your spiritual growth either in fear or in misconception of what evil truly is.

Man's Interpretation

Part of what you will need for your further understanding is the discipline of self, spirit, and soul restraint. All evil is intended by that nature within you and is not restrained to the light alone. Love is extremely important but will not hinder the attraction to the darkness. One must cultivate through stillness and soulful presence, the discipline of self-restraint so that evil itself may stay restrained to the boundaries the Lord gave to it at its inception. Within that self-restraint love, power, respect, and dignity for the Lord's works and also the works of evil will abound and will incite the soul to stay present with the balance that is needed for its journey back to Him.

Evil at the level of man initiates man into his physical and emotional being. Evil at this level flourishes as the self tends to create with more of its own will rather than the Lord's and more of its own intellect rather than His. The boundaries of evil are far less structured as the levels of contemplation are at their lowest in the universal construct. The misuse of power within the boundaries of man himself has allowed for evil to permeate so. It is interesting to note that when we speak of boundaries, we tend to view those in the world of spirit as having very few or none depending upon the manner of which we are speaking. When it comes to evil, the boundaries as such are dispersed among the elements of thought, being, deed, mind, presence, and awareness; man has much to contemplate indeed in his spiritual progression. The boundaries of evil become confused with the elements that we have spoken of and continue to manifest themselves greatly in the universe. To think that the Lord does not notice this is foolish. For every evil that is present, so is the light of God. Believe in this, and it will take you a long way.

Of that which is given to man, it is the seduction of power and knowledge that seek to diminish the light of God. We say seduction because the mind of the self and the intellect of the soul become drawn to what it thinks will render itself as powerful as the Lord. The moment the mind and the intellect of the soul seek to separate from Him in this fashion, they become impassioned by those things that will subject the mind and the intellect to further disconnect in shame from our Lord. This is not a judgment. It is simply truth. Evil cannot co-create without the willingness and attachment of the souls and energies that seek to learn about power. This is why we speak of self-restraint. We understand completely of the makings of the soul and the intellect, as well as the spiritual progression toward our Father in Heaven. All we ask of you is to be mindful of what you choose to align with. Evil will be present for a while. It is part of your nature for the time being. It does not mean you have to choose to expand your awareness upon it.

Evil at the level of man insists upon itself and will inflict passions against the spirit and the soul. The soul emanated from light with the capacity and ability to choose to be of the Lord's image and likeness. The passions themselves are not evil, they are subjective and open to interpretation by the soul that is willing to grow in the name of Him. They become energized by the fallibility of the soul to be of the same extreme of light that the Lord is. It is only this that enables the soul to pursue what is in opposition to the nature of light. To pursue a nature, whether in the light or in the darkness, does not mean that the soul has to partake in its creation. There are ways of learning and understanding without the level of engagement that all souls come to render. You can have awareness of the understanding of your nature without inflicting intent upon it. That is the beauty of creation. That is also, in part, the understanding of the power of the Lord within you. To not engage but to have acquired the understanding of the truth around evil is important, both your truth and the Lord's.

To be mindful of the level of evil in man, one must be mindful of what is good and endearing to the Lord. Thoughts and emotions can sway the mind to use the grace of God against man himself. Afflictions on any level within man only come because of the attraction of the misuse of the energy of our Lord to the soul's advantage. We are not speaking of the soul's advantage within the light, we are speaking of the soul's advantage within the darkness. Man may or may not necessarily know the extent of harm he is bringing upon himself when expanding unto evil, but it is true that his spirit and soul are aware of the makings indeed. And it is the higher level of spirit and the light of that soul that will work tirelessly to maintain balance of the nature of the being in totality of its present essence. It is the effort of the higher spirit and light of the soul to simply bring to the consciousness of that being the boundaries and understanding of the darkness without falling prey to the seduction of co-creating with its power.

Darkness can never come to manifestation unless willed by man at the beginnings of the mind. It can be present, but it can simply stay in its resting state of being for the time being. That is why the construct of the mind is so Divine. The power that the Lord gives you to create things of light is of greatness. It is your choice.

Evil at the level of man can indeed be cast out as it comes into perspective. I am not speaking of its essence, which remains present, but its energies, which are the fuel for destruction. To begin at the place of the Lord within the heart, mind, and soul of man will enable you to see the justice that this will bring when you become aware of your relationship to the darkness. There is no judgment upon yourself for having this darkness knowing that it is part of your present nature. However, there is discernment and healing within the parameters set forth when this agreement for the darkness to be still becomes broken. For the Lord doth not want you to make use of this darkness, He just desires for you to be aware of it as a Divine tool for your awakening to Him. When man makes use of this nature, he comes to know sin. Evil does not touch the essence of man, which is, of course, his likeness and image of the Lord, the Spirit of God. The essence of man is not the soul or the definitive levels of spirit, since they are both privy to the darkness. It is that untouchable essence that is God's essence. It is that essence that will ultimately be as one with Him in the kingdom of Heaven where nothing but light shall eternally dwell.

To cleave to the love of the Lord will not bring man to understand his relationship to the darkness. To surrender to the will of the Lord in stillness will assist man in understanding this. To allow for the light and the darkness to move through you as you progress in your spiritual life will show to you the understanding that you need. To not attach to either the light or the darkness will open your mind to the intelligence and wisdom of the Lord and the universe. We speak of not attaching to the light because of the energies that come with attachment. They are all not of Him no matter what it is that you are attaching your spiritual life to. Look upon the saints and prophets of the Lord. Look at their spiritual torments and their triumphs. Through both, they have warned against the mind becoming attached to the experience of the Lord and also the darkness, as opposed to the soul allowing for both levels of awareness to move through them. They speak of love, and that love has boundaries for both the light and the darkness. God's love is peaceful. God's love is merciful. God's love is boundless. For indeed, when you learn to love as Him, we have not this matter to speak of. Until then, we ask that you listen and learn.

When man falls prey to the seduction of the powers of the Lord, man will intentionally suffer. That is man's intention upon his own soul, not the Lord's. So when the many scriptures speak that nothing created by the Lord is evil, there is truth to that. Evil exists since man and soul have the ability and capacity to create with it. The Lord hath given you the same power and knowledge that He has. He has allowed for evil to exist and for the darkness and the light to coexist on some level of being and nature. The Lord chooses to use and create with only light. It is His hope that you all do the same. The power you hold to put evil into its proper perspective of stillness is great. What is even greater is the intention once all evil is put into perspective for all souls to rise in unison toward the light of God. Take what you will from the Lord, and use it to your discretion, for the mind of man, the spirit, and the soul loses its contemplation of Him once it has tasted the rewards of the kingdom. The mind of man, the spirit, and the soul once again confuse the rewards with the passions of the lower levels of contemplation. This allows for evil to grow. When man ceases to use his intellect in the nature of goodness, he surpasses that agreement that is bound by spiritual law and the Father to be of the goodness of Heaven. We say to you this: look not upon yourself as righteous at the level of man. Then you will be deluding yourself. Look to yourself as righteous of spirit within the Lord, then you will endeavor to perceive evil not as thine enemy, but as researcher of truth. When you think you have obtained righteousness at the level of man, then you are attracting thoughts of the darkness. That righteousness belongs to the ego will and not the Lord's. When you seek to detach yourself from what attracts you to evil, then you have accomplished a great thing at the level of man. It is not an easy thing to do, but the Lord and those of us in the world of spirit have much faith in you. Do not be deceived into thinking that you do not have attraction to the dark side. It brings a soul to wonder why then it was given as part of its lower nature. It is for the same reason the Lord gave to us the light of Him. What disheartens those of us in the world of spirit who support your spiritual progression is why some of you choose to focus on your attraction to the darkness as opposed to the attraction to the light. Attraction and attachment are not the same. Attraction if not met with sound understanding and self-restraint can lead to attachment. It is this attachment that hinders the growth of the soul and assists in the permeation of evil.

To suffer evil is not contrary to the will of Him when you are on the spiritual path, at any level. There is a difference between the evil that you create against your own spiritual progression and the evil that is brought your way as a result of the extraordinary light you carry. Now listen closely. To create evil on any level is contrary to Him. To suffer from it as a consequence so that you may learn of the light is of His will. In order for the darkness to see the light, suffering needs to happen so that the soul can rectify the injustices against our Lord and put into perspective and stillness the darkness that has occurred. The Lord doth not desire for you to create with evil. However, He does understand your meekness in surrendering to only the goodness, and the mind of yours that is so doubtful at times.

To understand that our natural capacity is to produce works of goodness while holding space for evil to be in stillness is truth. Know that during this discourse we are not saying to you that you are innately evil. If you have perceived that, we suggest that you look back over these writings. Within light on the lower levels of contemplation, which includes any level of being, the moment you were birthed from light and became separate from the Father you had the capacity, ability, and responsibility to hold the container for both the light and the darkness to come through in stillness and return to the Father. Within light, there is darkness. Within darkness, there is light. For the present moment of understanding, things need to be that way. Anything that is separate from the Father, which naturally includes all that is within the universe, has both polarities. The moment that the Creator decided to create, He created concepts. Some of those concepts He gave structure to, some of them you gave structure to. Evil is one of them that you gave structure to. The Holy Father has helped a little with some of the boundaries.

When you are raised to a higher level of contemplation, focusing on contemplation from the place of spirit or soul, your attachment to evil lessens. You suffer less insomuch as you have acquired a greater understanding, relationship, respect, and perspective of evil. Evil begins its learning of stillness within your spiritual progression and within all that resonates with where you are and what surrounds you.

You must believe that when evil lies still, *it has no power*. The longer it remains in this resting state, the more it will yearn for a greater understanding of its own truth. This is the will of God. Do you think that the Lord would have allowed for the creation of evil if He did not know that evil would also return to Him? When many speak that the Lord is not responsible for the creation of evil, it tends to give evil and those pursuing it the perception of having more power than the Lord. This is nonsense. When people understand the true creation of evil, knowing that it was brought into being as a necessary means for advancement and understanding, it gives its power back to the Lord. Creation in stillness is what we are speaking of, not the manifestation of evil on the lower levels of contemplation. We are not saying that the power of evil is not to be feared even though one believes the Lord is more powerful. On the contrary, there are many forms of evil that need to be feared for your own safety. We are merely trying to assist you in the understanding of what the concept is so your fear is in perspective of the truth. This will help you when you are dealing with such matters. There is a fear that earns respect for both the light and the darkness. It is this fear that will give you the self-restraint needed to continue on your spiritual progression encountering the many faces of God. The Lord does not wish for you to love evil, nor does He wish for you to hate it. In many scriptures, His teachers have professed that. The Lord wishes for you to contemplate evil in a very different manner than you have been doing for lifetimes, both on the plane of earth and in the world of spirit. The Lord wishes for you to contemplate it only in resonance and truth to the light. Without this resonance and truth, you will fall prey to its makings and procreate the darkness. That is not the Lord's wish for you.

The act of procreating evil is nothing more than the nature of the soul, man, and spirit turning against the nature of God. At the level of spirit, evil is presumptuous. It assumes that the will of the spirit is not about professing the faith and the love of the Lord. Rather, evil presumes at this level to entice the spirit into behavior at the juncture of natural and spiritual law that will render itself useless to the true purpose of the Lord. That is an intention of evil at the level of spirit. If the spirit is made to believe that it is useless in the will and purpose of Him, it will no longer seek to unify itself with the Lord. It will seek to align with what will endeavor to bring it further into misery. Evil at this level tends to mystify the spirit. Whereas truth is meant to be clear and forthright, evil will tend to mystify. The spirit once held in this mystification will usurp its rights and privileges of the Lord to that which it thinks will clearly pave the way for eternity. Such false notions can only be surrendered to when the spirit is weak in thought and intention.

You must understand that the concept of mystification in and of itself is not of evil. It is how evil takes hold of the spirit of each soul in order to bring it further from the Lord. When we say mystify, we speak of the power to seduce the soul from a place of awareness to unawareness of our Lord within. Evil being part of natural and spiritual law at this level places the spirit at the threshold of advancing further in the knowledge, truth, and understanding of it. It may raise the spirit and soul above attachment and find perspective in relationship to it. This is only if the spirit is willing and able through self-restraint, faith, and justice with Him to allow for evil and the light within it to rest in stillness. The spirit is so driven by its intensity and desire to know God that it falters on its spiritual journey. The spirit needs to cultivate this stillness of the Lord in his desire to know Him so that he can truly know Him and also place into perspective the relationship between the light and the darkness. Again, only with this stillness can every spirit and every soul reach Heaven. Do you think the world of spirit is completely still? We dare say not. There is so much spiritual growth and transition in the world of spirit and in the higher realms. Until all evil is placed in perspective of the light, the heavens will not be still and we in the world of spirit shall not rest. Eternal life cannot come until all is rectified within the universe, the totality of the kingdoms of God, and the heavens.

Evil at the lower and more intense levels of procreation will indeed seek to impassion and enslave the spirit from the nature of goodness and the Lord within. Evil, when in perspective, will not seek to persuade the soul against the Lord because it will have no further need to. It has been understood. And that is all that evil desires— to be understood, and to be held in the light. Think about it. When evil is faced with the light, what does it do? It becomes frightened, or angered and more intense. It transforms, disintegrates, or merges with the light. It only becomes angry because it has not been understood for its usefulness in returning to the light. To understand evil does not mean to allow it to procreate. When you allow for that to happen within your own spiritual construct, then you do not understand evil. This is what transpires at the level of spirit. The misunderstanding of evil will allow it to procreate. You must endeavor to search your spirit for what is bound by perspective with the righteousness of spiritual law. You must endeavor to search your spirit for the circumstances that enabled you to fall from grace.

Do know that evil will persuade, tempt, pacify, judge, corrupt, and harm the spirit when it is not in stillness. As the nature of goodness has gone into chaos within man, spirit, and soul, so must the nature of evil go into chaos as the learning of the truth of Him comes into being.

It will leave its resting state of stillness in order to find mercy with the Lord using everything within its scope of power. It seeks to undermine the Lord in its own confusion of not feeling merciful toward itself and in relationship to the light. It can only feed upon the soul's indiscretion to the Lord and willingness to be misused in righteousness of Him. Evil will continue to expand in a way that will not serve the Lord as long as you allow for yourselves to not understand the light within it and the mercy it yearns for. Remember, we are speaking of a level of understanding that will bring you power of the Lord and truth of the darkness, not an understanding that will allow for you to become attached to the darkness in your own subjugation.

Excitement for the darkness will bring you nothing but suffering. The Lord God has the power to liberate you from the torments and energies of evil and He hath given you that same power. You have confused it in your intellect with that of the darkness and, because of that, the power has lost its justice and seeks to serve the darkness instead of the light. You must endeavor to heal and rectify that misunderstanding within you. For this, we have much hope in your endeavors. What you think you fear is that of your own truth, it is not the darkness at all. The intellect around evil will continue to serve itself, not our Lord, until you have transgressed the false teachings that the mind encounters with evil. It is not perceived that evil can be in a state of stillness so that it may be useful in your ascension to the kingdom. It has been thought that evil is always corruptible. Both are true. Out of stillness, it is corruptible. Within stillness, it simply exists as part of the natural and spiritual law that will pave the way for your understanding and truth of the kingdom. You will learn about the Lord's power within you as a result of understanding the truth around evil. This is something that evil itself fears. To disempower it will begin to bring the end of the world as we know it, not as evil desires it to be. We know it to be one of transformation and enlightenment. Evil doth desire it to be one of destruction at the lower levels of contemplation. What the scriptures warned can come true if evil doth persist at the level of spirit relating to the intellect that the Lord hath given you in order to be raised to His level.

Thus, to be delivered from evil at the level of the spirit is to place your willingness and intellect in the hands of the Father and allow for Him to place the perspective of evil within the light as you assist Him in this endeavor. Once your spirit rises above the experience of the darkness, the same level of evil will not be allowed to corrupt you in any way. It cannot, simply because there has been a grain of truth adhered to it. Similar to light, all those spirits and souls who are resonant with your understanding of evil will also benefit from your learning. As you will from theirs.

It is interesting when one truly understands the dynamics of evil as set forth with the aspect of grace that the Lord hath given us. When grace is present, do not be mistaken to think that evil is not present. *With every grace that is given by the Lord, cometh every evil to sit at the threshold.* Understand that evil is permitted to be present in this space, only as a respectful concept for the works and mercy of Him. That is all. If evil is allowed to watch the grace of God in action, then it will begin to dissolve itself of every misunderstanding that it has with the Lord our God. This is why we caution against spiritual grandeur. The only one who is of that grandeur at this present time is the Lord God. When you receive graces, allow them to be in the same stillness as intended for both light and the darkness. *All graces as given by our Lord must eventually render themselves in stillness in order to be effective works of mercy in the name of God.* Otherwise, evil will persist when even a grace has not given itself to the stillness of the Lord. When the light of God works through you, if you are not able to detach from the process, it will incite evil to create a structure around you so that you may learn to appreciate the light without attachment to the process. Evil cannot be effective when you are involved in your spiritual progression from a neutral place of loving the Lord. Effective and present are two different concepts. This does not mean that evil will not try and plague you as you grow toward the Lord. It just means that its intent will not be as effective in deterring your alignment with the Most High.

If evil were only darkness, it would not exist. If light were only light, the universe would not exist. Evil doth desire for its darkness to be heard and the light that exists within the darkness to be merciful.

When you are righteous with sorrow in your own heart, you will touch the heart of evil itself. If you perceive evil to not have heart, you are mistaken.

The Good in Evil

Evil has heart at its conceptual birth. It is this heart that evil does try to avail itself of through its actions toward the Lord. We say to you this: a simple truth to placing in perspective some of the evil that binds you is to look upon your own heart for the scorn against the Lord that you so carry. You will see the markings of evil upon you, no matter how much light you hold. Remember, this is not about judgment, but the understanding of your own creation and the creation of the Lord as manifest through you. The moment you begin to judge yourself for having this darkness is the moment you allow for evil to rule. The moment you see yourself in the eyes of the Lord as merciful in His ways through you is the moment you shall place evil in perspective for all the days to come. The Lord is still in all His glory, and that is His intention and desire for you as well.

Evil at the level of the soul is as complex as it is simple. The souls of all relate to the universal structure of the balance between the light and the darkness that is necessary for the continued existence of the universe. If the progression of souls were to simply relate to just souls, then the process of evil in conjunction with the light as a learning tool would indeed be undermined. The creation of evil and its history emphasizes the love and truth of the Lord in respect to the spiritual laws as set forth by Him and the natural order of the universe. The karma of evil is only to render balance in this natural order of the universe. What that balance is changes from moment to moment dependent upon the will of God, the free will that He gave to you, and spiritual and natural law. Evil feeds more upon natural law, as the light of God is nourished more by spiritual law. Natural and spiritual law are only different in vibration and intention. Natural law has more of the makings of free choice whereas spiritual law is rendered by the Lord. Natural law also has to answer to the structure of the universe, which differs from the laws that bind all souls to Him. They indeed interact with each other, as natural law supports spiritual law and vice versa. There are those things that are out of range of the will of God, meaning those things that the Lord will give you choice to. All within the freedom of choice indeed supports the natural order of the universe and will render consequences even if what you are choosing is not of the will of God at the present moment. Know that nothing you ever do in any lifetime or existence will be without its understanding of the light and the darkness within . . . nothing.

Thus, at every moment of your choosing, whether it is the will of God or not, you are making a choice to procreate both evil and light in truth of Him. Remember, even if your choice is one of light and the Lord, evil will procreate itself, but in a manner of truth and perspective. It has to in order for the universe to come into a balance of truth and the Lord. This does not mean that every time you make a choice of light that evil will wreak havoc. We are saying that when there is an act of mercy and light, or a choice of one, that evil will procreate itself in stillness of the Lord so that understanding and righteousness will take place. This is a common occurrence. Take notice of those times when you do or intend a good deed for the Lord and you see the chaos of evil surrounding you. Evil is simply learning to be in stillness with the truth. Whether it is frightened or misunderstood, whether it is a curse or what you refer to as negative karma, know that it is simply trying to find the stillness of the Lord as you are. It is so important for your spiritual growth once again to hear from us that you do not need to attach to evil as set before you.

It is inherent as a certain part of your nature that you will always learn from it. As with the light, you do not need to place yourselves in experiences other than those that the Lord asks of you. This indeed is wasted precious time and only allows evil to get the better of you. Unnecessary learning is not of the Lord's wish for you. Peace and stillness is of the Lord's wish for you. The moment you allow for the understanding that evil and light can coexist peacefully in the contemplation of your relationship with God is the moment that the darkness loses the power and hold it has upon your soul. The soul is only meant to be held by the light with the understanding and truth of the darkness within it. Remember that. The soul is only meant to be held by the light.

When you see evil upon your world, you arouse yourself to anger unjustified at your own expense. It is not that evil and its energies should not anger you, for indeed it does anger most of us in the world of spirit who do the work of the Lord. However, we do not take it upon ourselves and our souls as we see that many of you do. It is only because of our understanding around evil that it is this way for us. You allow it to take hold of your souls and render helplessness in such a way that causes you pain and suffering. We see that you deal with the world around you in that way too. When you begin to look at the makings of the soul and the devastation in the world around you a little differently, you will begin to see the light, literally. Helplessness is not about the Lord. It is about your perception of your weakness in regard to the truth of it all. The Lord wishes not for you to be helpless in all that exists as part of the makings of the soul. He wishes for you to remain in strength and integrity with the power and truth of Him by your side. You must understand that evil will continue to exist and its energies will continue to bring chaos. That will not change for some time. In the meanwhile, we suggest you learn to negotiate with yourself in regard to the stillness of the matter. Always know that no matter how dark the evil is that is present, there will always be a part of it that will crave the stillness of the light within itself. The moment you allow yourself to rest in that stillness, part of that evil shall too, and you will be in a different space within the darkness than you ever were before. If you think that you can negotiate with evil, we suggest that you allow for the negotiation to be up to the Lord and the higher beings. We are giving you tools to help you understand all the darkness that permeates the universe and how to be in relationship with it. Leave the dissolution of evil at the levels of contemplation up to the Lord, for He knows better what He is doing. He does not allow for the structure of evil and its energies to remain as you do. He does allow for the concept of evil to remain present as long as you need it to understand who it is that you are and who it is that you are together.

For we say to you this: whenever you come across that which is evil, say unto it, *Be still, and know that you are God.* And leave the rest up to the Lord. Walk away from the energies that persist with evil that is external. With evil that is internal, we suggest you affirm the same statement to it. Whether it is internal or external, your involvement with evil should only be at the understanding of its stillness. Unfortunately, this is not the way it is at present with most of you. The greatest statement that a soul could ever make use of in his aspiration and progression of and to the Lord is to say, *Be still and know that you are Him.* Indeed, all that is manifest within the soul will learn to comprehend the higher truths around its origins and all that is placed within it in the context of our Lord. He is magnificent. Indeed, you are. Indeed, the stillness of the light and the stillness of the darkness are also.

It is only through such that you will be of His magnificence. It is only through such that you will gain the heart of the Christ upon you.

Evil has karma, as it also has its own will. The intent of its will upon its conceptual beginning once again is stillness. Evil, upon the making of its structure and energies, obtains its own will in pursuit of what is implausible to even itself. Once evil begins to procreate, it loses sight of the intention of its beginnings that were simply in resting state. The will of evil has much to do with its karmic progression in the universe. Evil will continue until it eventually dissolves itself into the light of God. All evil will end up in truth and in peace, no matter which way it chooses to find the Lord. Evil that is raised up will find that stillness and perspective. Evil that is brought down will dissolve itself and find perspective. Evil that is brought down will indeed manifest itself through man since man is the lowest level of contemplation of Him. It is at this level that stillness is imperative for evil to render itself useless until the Lord can guide it back to where it needs to be in order to learn perspective. When the soul connects itself with its passions, it will see that the understanding and mercy of these passions will enable the evil that is drawn to feeding upon them to be quieted in the face of the Lord. We advise prayer and contemplation of the Lord daily so that you may learn of this stillness that is needed for your higher learning. *The karma of evil will be contended with as a whole when each soul within the universe supports the light and the darkness of the Lord from a place of peace within themselves.* One cannot fight or face the evil of the universe without the inner knowing and contemplation of what binds the soul to the feeling of helplessness in the face of such things.

When evil has caused destruction on the lower levels of contemplation, we caution you against rising in vengeance to rectify that destruction. We suggest that you allow for what needs to transpire for the evil to return to its resting state to do so. We suggest this from a place within your heart, not from a place of doing, but from a place of being. Evil needs to complete itself on whatever levels it is manifesting on to return to the stillness of the Lord. For whatever reasons it has come your way, be grateful and ask that it be still and know Him. Be grateful and ask for the Lord's help to place it in perspective. Respect the teachings that the darkness will bring and allow for the energies to *move through you without taking hold of your soul or your mind. This is important. We are not asking of you to do nothing. We are asking you to be still within.* To do this will allow you to feel less of the impact on the energies that evil hath come to you with. It will give to the darkness the space it needs to see the truth and the light and return to its resting place. It needs that and desires it so. This you must believe. When you engage evil at the level of the soul, know that you have bound yourself to the karma of it and it will complete itself in however long a time period it needs, whether in the world of spirit or on the plane of earth. It needs to complete itself so that the light will once again be in truth.

At the level of the soul, that can manifest itself in various ways— as it can at the level of spirit, and indeed in man. Perhaps in man, it is that level indeed where suffering is most. The moment the soul comes to resolution with the intention of evil, then the presence of evil itself within the construct of the soul will no longer be a burden. Evil will only burden itself upon you when you have come into conflict with its presence within you. Evil is not something that needs to be rectified at the higher levels of contemplation; it needs only to be respected for what it simply is. At the higher levels of contemplation, evil truly desires to be left alone to its own desires. It will only engage upon you once you incite it so. Remember, it has the same yearning to know the Lord that you do.

When it comes to faith, much of it is needed when allowing for evil to rest in stillness upon the soul. If you do not have faith, then there can be no understanding of this stillness where all comes to rest in peace. Know that evil hath faith also. Do you think that it would create the injustice that it does at the lower levels of contemplation? For indeed, it has faith that you will accommodate its every need and inten- tion so that it can gain entrance into the kingdom of Him without your knowing. We say without your knowing because when evil persists at the lower levels, it does not care about the soul it has inflicted itself upon. It only cares for its own procreation and its understanding of itself. It is better for evil to be understood when it is at its higher levels of procreation before it is brought down so that the intent is less, and that it can simply go to its resting place without having to complete itself through manifestation on the lower levels as you know it. That most likely is what leads to destruction and suffering.

Evil hath no just cause that is truly in darkness, this you must understand. Its completion does not need to manifest through you unless you so willed it, or unless it comes from the hand of God. Its completion can manifest itself in ways less harmful to your soul if you learn to cope with the loss and chaos that evil will render in its path of descending. The true path of evil, if it has gotten to that place where it has descended to the lower levels of contemplation, is to complete itself in understanding of the light and the purpose of its presence—and to do this in light and manner of your truth.

Evil cannot avoid knowing its true purpose, even if its intended purpose differs. As it completes itself, it will be shown the truth, no matter which form it takes. Understand that evil will honor the learning that you need to do if you honor that within yourself. Evil will not honor you if you do not honor the Lord, and the Lord's place within you.

When indeed the soul hath faith, the process of evil and the process of light can be honored in their coexistence of each other. Evil, or even the Devil, does not need to function in a participatory state of being. It just needs to be as is, in respect of Him just as you are, just as the light is. Thus, when we speak of purification, we do not mean that you are only of the light. We affirm that you are only of the truth, the Lord's truth—that which encompasses all. When you seek to separate the light from the darkness at the higher levels, you seek to separate the Lord from within you.

Purity of the mind hath given the soul the understanding it needs for its relationship to the darkness. Do not think that you can deceive the mind of the ability of your soul to create darkness. Just as the soul can create light, it can just as easily create darkness. Once you have allowed for the soul to have compassion for itself for this understanding, it will be easier for it to rise above its passions and know them not to be sinful, but to be stepping-stones toward the kingdom of God. We are not condoning the mindful action of creating darkness. We are simply suggesting that the soul have more compassion for itself, which we see that it does not. It is the soul that mostly carries the grief of the separation from the Lord and feels the unworthiness of His light. The darkness need not take hold of the soul, it need only be present in compassion of the challenge of the soul. If you think that the darkness cannot be compassionate, you are mistaken. If there is compassion amidst the light, there is compassion amidst the darkness. Remember once again, Lucifer was once an angel of the Lord Most High.

Evil and sin have little to do with each other as a concept. Sin as you interpret it does not exist at the higher levels of contemplation as darkness. It exists at the lower levels of contemplation as such only because evil predicates itself upon sin once the heart and mind have rebuked the Lord. At the higher levels, sin refers itself to the predilection of the intellect of the soul, and its perspective of the Lord within.

At the higher levels, evil exists differently and is also in the midst of finding its way to perspective. It will only gather strength and attach to sin if the intellect of the soul is not present with the truth. It is important for the soul to understand itself deeply within the constructs of the Lord that it was created upon so that it cannot judge itself and rest in strength of its creation. To rest in strength will not give rise to the energies and structure of evil but will give evil the boundary it needs to be still and complacent with the Lord and itself.

Evil will only need to persist if you have not learned to master the stillness within that we are speaking of. We suggest that each of you look at your relationship to the darkness and see where it is that you stumble in your faith to be of truth and compassion. We understand that this is a difficult concept for you to grasp. Again, we are not suggesting that you allow for the energies of evil to take hold of you. We endeavor to show you a different understanding so that you could be more at peace with what the Lord hath given you.

Never forget the compassion of the Lord, and never forget the compassion of the darkness. When you have come face to face with the lower levels of the darkness, ask that the light of it be shown to you with compassion for the Lord's will. It is easy to confuse the darkness when you are in strength of the Lord and confronting it with strength of the Lord as well. As you come to have greater understanding of your role in placing the darkness in perspective, you will seek less to struggle with the Lord on the levels that you do so. You will seek a more fulfilling relationship with Him, one where the coexistence of all that is created by Him can serve mankind and the universe. This is the way the Lord doth desire it to be.

The more your intellect thinks that evil cannot contribute to your growth toward the kingdom of the Lord, the more you give rise to its energies that bring destruction. We are speaking of the evil that is in stillness, not that which wreaks chaos on the soul; that is of your doing and will. Bring to your mind the peace of the Lord within all the darkness that is part of your soul. A thing can only permeate evil when the creation of such is out of intent with the Lord's wishes and the balance of the universe, whether we are speaking of such things on the level of earth, spirit, or soul. Do not place judgment upon what you think is of the darkness. This creates more untruth than you realize. Listen to us closely. For what you think might be darkness might just be *the Light of God*. And vice versa.

Do you not think that the Lord always find truth amidst the

darkness? Do you not think that those of us in the world of spirit who do the Lord's work can find truth amidst the darkness? Indeed, there are many ways in which we do so; nevertheless, we do. Do you not think that at the end of time, all evil will be in perspective and all will be invited to rest in stillness with Him? Accept all that you are with the grace of the Lord resting upon you, and you will come to know yourself far better than you ever have before and you will come to know Him just as well.

When the higher beings in the world of spirit place a structure around evil and do not allow for it to continue, it is simply that the evil hath not learned yet of the Lord's love for it. The higher beings only need to place that structure accordingly when it has gotten out of context of its resting state with Him. Understand the evil will be part of your natural and spiritual lives until the end of time as we know it. You will also suffer at the energies of evil. You will also grow in strength in the light of God. We suggest you follow our example and place structures around all that is light and all that is darkness. That of course can be done through the nonattachment that stillness within provides in the name of God.

> But now the righteousness of God without the law is manifested, being witnessed by the law and the prophets, even the righteousness of God which is by faith of Jesus Christ unto all and upon all them that believe. For there is no difference, for all have sinned and come short of the glory of God, being justified freely by his grace through the redemption that is in Christ Jesus, whom God hath set forth to be a propitiation through faith in his blood, to declare his righteousness for the remission of sins that are past, through the forbearance of God; to declare, I say, at this time his righteousness, that he might be just, and the justifier of him which believeth in Jesus.

Where is boasting then? It is excluded. By what law?
Of works? Nay, but by the law of faith. Therefore we con-
clude that a man is justified by faith without the deeds
of the law. Is he the God of the Jews only? Is he not also
of the Gentiles? Yes, of the Gentiles also, seeing it is one
God, which shall justify the circumcision by faith, and
uncircumcision through faith. Do we then make void the
law through faith? God forbid. Yea, we establish the law.

ROMANS 3:21–31

Read and know that passage. It speaks of Divine Mercy from
Him in relationship to the concept of evil as an existing factor in the
structure of the universe. It speaks of the Lord God in understanding
of the stillness of evil amidst the spiritual laws and how faith can
bring into perspective and stillness evil that is out of its resting state.
It does not seek to separate evil from the Lord, rather to acknowledge
its workings and contribution to the goodness of man and ascension
of the soul. *Seeing it is one God, which shall justify the circumcision by*
faith, and uncircumcision through faith. For God is the one who will
come to judge the living and the dead. For God is the one who
will come to judge the light and the darkness. And the Lord is the one
who will come to place in stillness and perspective the light and the
darkness so they may coexist peacefully in His terms. All that comes
to you may then have the opportunity to be explored through the
grace and faith of the Lord.

And we know that all things work together for good to
them that love God.

ROMANS 8:28

Being a servant and the Lord's creation, the Devil tests
and afflicts people, not as he thinks fit or desires, but to

the extent that the Master allows him. Knowing the exact
nature of everything, God permits each person to be tested
according to his strength.

NIKODIMOS AND MAKARIOS, COMPS.,

THE PHILOKALIA, 3:301

This is truth. Evil can only exist at the command of the Lord, but it will create at your will, knowing that the Lord is watching over it at every move. The Lord will only allow evil to go so far in contemplation of its nature toward Him, as far as He sees fit for your higher understanding and evil's understanding as well. You are to learn about the darkness as much as you are to learn about the light. This is the only way you will get to the kingdom of Heaven. You must struggle with the Devil to overcome your perceptions of Him and who you are with Him. You must struggle with the Devil so that you may truly know the Lord is with you. How long you struggle is your choice. The Lord will allow for evil to complete itself at the destruction of the lower levels of contemplation only if it serves the light and the darkness coming into perspective. You might not be able to understand this concept at this time, but soon enough, you will.

Remember, the grace of God is always with you, even in darkness. The soul must learn to contemplate the darkness with the Lord present at all times, so that it may raise itself to the Divine intellect and wisdom that the Lord hath for you.

The soul has contemplated the darkness without the Lord for many an existence, but it is our hope that you see the error of your ways. The will of God will eventually bring grace to the darkness, which is a main aspect of light that the darkness fails to acquire at some level. Light, without the grace of God, concedes to the darkness.

When the soul is borne from the Lord, it is not held captive by evil but becomes intrigued by the makings of such. Wherefore the soul is as intrigued by His light. Being of innocence, it does not yet know how to contemplate Him within the necessary perspective of the light and the darkness. It is not at fault, such is the curiosity of the soul to understand itself. One can participate in the will of God and the light of the Holy Spirit and still give rise to evil if he has not come to truth within himself. Being that all souls are intertwined at various levels, evil, as it descends, can choose to take hold of whatever souls it feels it needs to place its confusion on. If the soul has come to truth within itself, it can allow for evil to move through him with the grace of the Lord and with sound understanding of evil's divine purpose for being there and nothing more. Evil and darkness can be Divine given the right structure and boundaries.

There is evil that serves man, spirit, and soul. It is truth that on some level, even if you are not aware of it, evil will serve your highest good in the name of God. Give the Devil just cause to serve you in the name of the Lord, not in the name of him, and he will do so, willingly.

The Lord and the Devil hath given you the knowledge and wisdom you need in discriminating against the purpose of Divine darkness and the purpose of evil as it exists at the lower levels of contemplation. The purpose of Divine darkness is to simply strengthen you in the Spirit of the Lord. Do not engage with evil when it is still, which we see that so many of you do. It does not want to profess anything except its desire to understand itself in relationship to the Lord just as you are trying to do. As you engage, it is you who allows it to grow and give birth to that which will teach you in numerous ways to remember Him always. Evil that is Divine can nourish the intellect toward righteousness with the Lord. It can nourish and support the soul in its ascension toward Him. But only if its divinity lies in stillness of every thought, action, and intention of your soul's longing to be with Him. When the soul is not bound by its perceptions of evil, it shall relinquish its fears to the Lord, not to the Devil, and reorient itself to the natural state of being. This is the essence of the Lord in all that the Lord encompasses, thus being both the light and the darkness.

The darkness is permitted to express its divinity in the constructs that are set forth by the Lord Himself. Divine darkness does not intentionally harm, but rather justifies itself in the light of God. Evil can have intent to harm as it descends. Divine darkness seeks the knowledge of the Christ to assist the soul in its awakening to the Lord. Darkness becomes Divine when it has rested in stillness and perspective and has raised its vibrations toward the Lord in earnest intent of knowing its truth. Evil must remain present and still within the soul for the knowledge of the Lord to be awakened within it. We are speaking about a level of darkness that will ultimately bring justice to the soul and to the universe. It will bring justice eventually to evil at the lower levels of contemplation. The Lord's hand does rule darkness that is Divine and merciful. This you must believe. Even Satan cannot touch or comprehend that darkness that is justified by the Lord because the Lord does not allow him to do so. However, a soul can fall prey to the harm that evil can cause when it does not allow for Divine darkness to take its place as the Lord wishes for whatever the purpose is. *Do not stop the darkness that is decreed by the Lord as Divine. This will only bring to you suffering.* Once you begin to recognize this as part of your spiritual progression, you will see the life that you chose as one of benevolence toward yourself, not one of a suffering cohabitant of the universe at will. There is no glory with the Lord in thinking that you are worthy of light alone. You are indeed worthy of all that He is, and every spirit, soul, and man created.

When evil and darkness are sanctified as Divine, it shall even make the Devil come to respect the soul and the Lord more. When you come to respect the Devil in a way that he has long forgotten, it shall be you and the Lord as his teacher. The Devil does not even understand about the Divine darkness. It is something he knows, but something he fears will threaten his power. The Devil is even afraid of the stillness and the perspective from whence it came. He fears that he might once again enjoy the love and bounty of the Lord. Evil is not to be excluded from partaking in the light, which is a mistake that many souls make on a personal level of being. Evil shall be allowed to partake in the glory of the light from a distance that is intelligible for the soul's awakening to Him. It is in this way that it can remember the stillness, and eventually raise itself to be Divine once again. Divine light of Him and Divine darkness can respect each other in ways unimaginable to the soul and can support the greater good for the universal and spiritual construct.

> *Now there was a day when the sons of God came to present themselves before the Lord, and Satan came also among them. And the Lord said unto Satan, "Whence comest thou?" Then Satan answered the Lord, and said, "From going to and fro in the earth, and from walking up and down in it." And the Lord said unto Satan, "Hast thou considered my servant Job, that there is none like him in the earth, a perfect and an upright man, one that feareth God, and escheweth evil?" Then Satan answered the Lord, and said, "Doth Job fear God for nought? Hast not thou made a hedge about him, and about his house, and about all that he hath on every side? Thou hast blessed the work of his hands, and his substance is increased in the land. But put forth thine hand now, and touch all that he hath, and he will curse thee to thy face." And the Lord said unto Satan, "Behold, all that he hath is in thy power; only upon himself put not forth thine hand." So Satan went forth from the presence of the Lord.*
>
> JOB 1:6–11

The Devil is not as presumptuous as you would like to think. The hand of God that rules the heavens rules the hand of the Devil who must abide by spiritual law. We are speaking of an evil that is confined by the laws of God as necessary for the procreation of light. When indeed the Spirit of the Lord casts His discernment upon you in righteousness of your spiritual growth, it is only then that He will allow for the Devil to consume the passions that have bound you with the darkness that will only bring forth light. Evil, darkness, and the Devil wait patiently for those on the lower levels of contemplation to take hold of the darkness. It seems that the darkness on the lower levels has its own direction, which is not visible to that of the Lord; but that is only what it seems. The Lord is aware of the darkness at the lower levels. How can He not be if all that is created in the universe is of the Lord indeed? It is when you seek not to have the understanding of truth and the necessary boundaries in relation to evil and the Devil at the lower levels that the Devil can indeed become rampant in his behavior and bring about such grievances against you and the Lord. As in the passage above, the Lord is the Almighty who will not allow the Devil to touch the person of Job. He shows to the Devil that he too, has the power to make use of the truth. However, the Lord will only allow the Devil to come nearer to Job as willed by the Lord. If you think that the Devil does not have faith and respect for the Lord, you are mistaken. It is when you think that the Devil does not have respect and faith for the Lord that this is so.

Evil and the Devil can be righteous if that is the Lord's will and if that is the will that you so choose to follow. It is not that the Devil will not want to come near you, he will do so in a manner that will respect your learning with the Lord. You must all have faith in evil that is righteous. If you do not, then how can you learn of Him? This is a necessary step in your growth toward the Lord. We say to you again: you cannot come to Him knowing only light. You must come to Him having been through the darkness first. And so it is said that he who knows the Lord in all His truth and splendor shall be as mighty as the light and the darkness that is Him.

Just cause for the Devil is not something that humans understand.

You think to have faith will impede the evil that binds you. On the contrary, it is your faith that will bring to you more darkness so that you may help it and your brethren to learn of truth. It will assist your own soul in coming to terms with the Godnature that is an inherent part of the universe. The soul is congruent with that of the Lord and also is congruent with that of the Devil in respect to the love and light of the Lord. We cannot speak to you enough of this truth. Do not fear the evil that is of the Lord. Fear the evil that you think is not of Him, for it is that evil that will cause you the greatest harm. Faith is necessary for the darkness to live and complete itself in the light of truth. Just as faith is necessary for the light. If you do not have faith in this Divine darkness, then you truly do not have faith in the light or the Lord because this is the will of Him.

When you allow for the intellect and the soul to undermine all that it holds sacred in the name of Him, you allow for more of the darkness to take hold, which is not what the Lord desires for you. There will be times in your spiritual progression when the Devil is necessary for your understanding in your relationship to the Lord, just as the Lord is necessary for your understanding in your relationship to the Devil. Do not think you do not have a relationship with Satan. Remember, the Lord does, and so shall you. For that is written, you cannot know God without knowing Satan. It is only the way in which you know them that can bring you suffering. In the world of Spirit, the Devil takes on many forms. Some of them indeed carry more light than the others. It is known that the more light one carries, the more darkness he carries also. And those of us who work tirelessly on behalf of Him endeavor to bring to truth and stillness the evil that exists.

Just as we ask you to tell evil to be still and know that it is God, we also tell you to say to evil, *be God, and know that you are still.* The first statement will indeed bring evil to respect the Lord, and the second statement will indeed bring the Devil to confusion. For evil and the Devil are separate entities in the face of the Lord. Yet they can coexist peacefully. Evil does not need the Devil to exist. However, evil does need the Lord to exist. The Devil will eventually dissolve and evil will finally rest. When you place the intention and intellect of the Devil unto evil, that is when evil no longer seeks to be complacent, rather it will continually seek justification in its acknowledgment of the Lord within. The Devil will come to you when you call upon him. Evil can come to you when the Lord calls upon it to help you know God more. Evil doth not need the Devil. Remember this. The Devil shall make his appearance when you are confused of the darkness and feel yourself without the Lord upon you. For we say to you this, children of the Lord: have faith when there is evil upon you, and the Devil may not come. Just the evil. And when you feel the Devil upon you, rebuke Him with the love of Christ. Evil can come without Satan's hand upon you. That is why the Lord made evil and darkness to be Divine, so that you may know your divinity through it as well.

Do not attach the Devil or his demons to the evil that is bound by spiritual law to serve you, for that will do your growth no good. Yes, the Lord is the Master over the Devil himself too, and can at any moment carry Satan away from you. The Lord will not allow for Satan to harm you any more than you desire for Satan to bring suffering to yourself. Do you not think the Lord hath faith in your strength to overcome? Do you not think the Lord hath faith that you will come to know the Devil as the light of Him in disguise? Remember, we do not say to you to take hold of the Devil in your heart. When you recognize Him as the light of God, we say to you to command the darkness to be still and honor the light of the Lord, to be God and know stillness. The greatest grace shall come to you within both the light and the darkness of Him.

We do our best not to confuse you of evil that is righteous and necessary and that which isn't. In our understanding, all evil is intended to be righteous and necessary. But you have confused the intention and brought to yourself more suffering than the Lord hath desired for you at times. When you have taken your intention over the Lord's for the darkness at will, you will do much in the way of creating more that will impede your spiritual growth. Know that the Lord is always protecting you and guiding you even if you are in the throes of the darkness. The Lord will endeavor to do so as long as you hold in your awareness the presence of Him. There are rules your soul has agreed to live by, in perspective of the light and the darkness. The moment you transgress those rules is the moment you become willed by the forces of the nature of Him in all ways. If you keep straying from the Lord, the Lord can hold you in the palm of His hand, but you might find your soul dancing more with the Devil because you choose to allow it. It is in this case that the Lord will concede to your desire and allow for you to learn what you seek to learn from the Devil.

Still know and believe that the Lord watches over you and will not allow for what is not in your highest good to take place overall. There is always question as to the Lord's goodness around evil and the Devil. *If the Lord asketh of you not to travel in a direction that is not fit for you, listen to Him.* It becomes out of His hands, so to speak, when you have fallen from grace. The ignorance of the soul and the choice of the soul to do as he pleases can render the soul in the hands of the Devil. Remember, the Lord gave the Devil the same free will as you. And like you, the Devil's free will is ultimately the same as the Lord's. When you fall further from grace, it gives the Devil the opportunity to feed upon your lack of faith in the Lord and in the Devil himself. If you think that the Devil cannot bring you closer to the Lord, then indeed he cannot. But if you allow yourself to learn from Satan how to love the Lord more completely, then we commend you. You have not only done yourself a service but you have served the Devil as well. The Devil will not cease to be complete as long as you give him the power to reign, as he does so with harm. The Devil does not understand or desire to understand the darkness and evil that is justified by the Lord. The Devil only seeks to justify himself or procreate more unworthiness. Once again, the Devil and evil are separate entities amidst the Lord. One has consciousness of Him and the other does not. When you learn to separate the two as you are presently existing, you will then see your existence and your relationship to the universe as different. The Devil and his worshippers will only seek to nullify the intentions of the Lord as long as untruth persists in the universe. When truth prevails, darkness and light will coexist peacefully, with the Devil learning of the Lord within his heart.

Understand, dear children, that sometimes the darkness a soul needs to face is the best way for the soul to come to terms with its separation from the Lord. In your earthly experience, you see so much of the darkness around you. Do you stop to see where the Lord is within it? Do you stop to look at the darkness as Divine righteousness? At the moment you interfere with darkness that is deemed by the Lord, you take away the opportunity for that soul or souls to know of Him. When there are souls who are misguided in the darkness, do you not think that the Lord will guide them or guide you to them to assist? You all involve yourself in that karma that belongs to the darkness in some way. When darkness and evil are Divine, it is not your place to rectify them. That is of the Lord's doing. And He asks that you indeed respect His wishes. The best way for a soul to help another is to be still, whether in the light of God or the darkness of another. Was it not the Christ who was still in the midst of both? Look upon His greatest teachings.

The Devil

The Devil does not know how to be still. When he is not charging at a soul, he is in contemplation of the Lord also. That seems confusing but it is truth. The Devil is always in contemplation of the Lord, but not in righteous contemplation. The Devil will never know how to be still unless evil itself is allowed to rest in stillness within the universe.

Then what can the Devil do? Until he is disciplined, he shall use the souls of many to achieve his greatness in indifference to the Lord's. He does not have to use souls, but there are many of you who still seek attachment to the darkness in a way that is not Divine. We cannot warn you enough about attaching to what will harm you. There is not one soul or being who is not at fault for attaching to the darkness. It is the route we all must take. When you have allowed for your soul to attach to the darkness, you will have given over your soul's power to the Devil and allowed for the grace of God to be his, which is what he so desires. Even if there is darkness that is Divine, we say to you again: do not attach. The Devil still awaits you as the hands of God await you. Be still always and know that you are God. Be still always and know that all is God.

To think that you must be clear of all evil before setting foot in the house of the Lord is untruth. You think that you cannot be as noble as the saints unless you have achieved perfection of Him. Do you not think that those thoughts feed upon the Devil himself? The Devil desires nothing more than for souls to use their feelings of unworthiness of Him to halt their entrance unto the kingdom.

It is the Devil's desire to make use of the fear of all souls to allow them to think that they can never be as holy as the Lord, and therefore, unworthy of being one of His spiritual children. To this we say nonsense. To understand that that Devil wants the Lord all to himself and would rather see the concept of evil go forward in untruth rather than truth is indeed his mission.

When you contemplate the Lord and ascend further toward the kingdom, do not deny the Devil the opportunity to contemplate with you or for evil to contemplate with you. You must understand that both will be present accordingly, and the moment you cease to acknowledge the presence of both, you become stuck in your spiritual progression. There is no one that can tell you that he is not of the light of God, and of evil. If you find such a spiritual teacher in your experience, we suggest you look again. For that is the Devil in disguise. The Lord will send you those teachers whose truth of the darkness is in perspective of Him. Those who fear the truth of the darkness will learn differently than you. We would rather you learn of the Devil under the care of the Lord as opposed to being without His care.

All desire is for the Lord, even that which belongs to darkness, evil, and the Devil. The Devil is not without discernment of Him. If the Devil were not discerning, then he would not know which souls were weakest in their love for the Lord. When power becomes attached to that desire and is out of righteousness, then the Devil continues to feed upon that desire and use it to his own advantage to make souls further fear the Lord's love and not want or need for it.

When the soul begins its inception as light, it immediately enters into the darkness of the Lord. The Lord's will enables the darkness to be placed in perspective and stillness. When the Lord God gave you the grace of mercy and stillness within, He actually instilled within you the understanding of darkness and evil. The power to understand and control to some extent all that is brought to you during your spiritual progression surrounds justice and truth. When we say control, we see it differently than you do. The right of darkness to move through the intention of the soul in order to come to justice is, indeed, a power given to evil. Thus, evil in some aspect has power within the soul of man. Again, only to the extent that the Lord will allow so that you may learn of Him through benevolence of all that you are. If you change the way you look upon evil, as we are teaching you, then you seek not to suffer as much and come to terms with your true Divinity.

Do know that evil doth have the same knowledge of the Lord that you have; that is why the Devil is akin to all that you do in your spiritual progression. For evil to remain still, one must cease to entice the Devil into speaking on behalf of himself to the Lord. The Devil will not speak your truth unless you ask of him to do so. However, the Devil will speak always, in any way that gives cause to engage.

At the lower levels of contemplation, evil and the Devil exists throughout all as much as the light of God does. The power of evil and the Devil seems to have more intention than the light of God because of the misunderstanding of those souls who continue to confuse the truth about the darkness, especially at the level of man and lower forms of spirit in the spirit world. The realization of evil and its dignitaries at this level is something that the Lord warns you about becoming aligned with. When evil is at this place, the intentions of such are of great disturbance to your soul's progression toward the Father. It is when all the souls at this level come to partake and believe in the power of such as being greater than that of the Lord that the will of Satan indeed manifests, leaving the Lord and those of us who work for Him to maintain His mercy upon you. Evil will not stop its path of destruction at this level until the Lord raises His hand and halts its power. Listen closely, for we say to you this: at this level, evil has the intent to deny the soul our Lord in the most dear of ways. He can place upon you grievance upon grievance, and render man, spirit, and soul helpless. This does not mean the Lord is not with you. You must always remember that. As the Lord gave you the freedom to choose whom you wish to align with, He will help you accordingly. The Lord honors what you ask of Him always, as does the Devil. When you choose to align with the darkness at this level, it is because those before you have also chosen to align with the Devil at will. When evil has fallen upon you at such an intention of will, it is most likely that those souls who have come before you, in relation and resonance to your learning of Him, have allowed for this intention to serve their greatest good. *Evil doth not come at this intensity if it has not known you before.* Whether it comes from a previous existence, a relational soul, or a shared thought within the universal consciousness, if evil comes to you with all its power, then you have met it before. It will come to you over and over again in intensity until you bring it to truth and stillness within yourself first. It would seem that the Lord leaves more of the responsibility of the work at this level up to you. And we offer that there is truth in that. Of course, the Lord and His servants are there for your guidance.

When we speak of evil coming to you over and over again, such is the karma of evil when it does indeed need to complete itself. All aspects of the Lord need to complete themselves at the lower levels of contemplation in order to be raised up to the light and stillness of Him. The experiences of the darkness on the lower levels seem so much more intense than those of the higher dimensions of the world of spirit. Indeed we say they are. It is simply because of the impact of the forces of nature that are more concrete in terms of energy and experience at that level. You must realize that at this level, there will be loss to speak of. Just as the light signifies change and transformation, evil and darkness will also signify change and transformation. There will be more loss in your understanding at the lower levels of contemplation. This will come in the form of devastation, illness, curses, and so on. You must remember that in that darkness you will always find the light of Him. Do not place such importance on the loss that will occur, just accept and understand that it is the darkness returning to the stillness of the Lord. Give the darkness and evil at this level the respect that it deserves to render itself still. This respect will always include the appropriate boundaries as given to you by God at that particular time. This is important. If you do not give the darkness the respect it deserves at this level, then you will be involving yourself more than the Lord desires of you to do. You will take hold of the darkness more than the Devil has asked, but he will greatly appreciate the assistance from you. Again, to offer it respect is simply to allow its process to unfold as the will of God commands it. When you get your soul involved at this level, you have the possibility of bringing the Devil upon yourself when it is not in your highest good to do so.

The greatest good you can do for yourself at any level is to accept in the graces of your mind and within your heart the intention for the

Lord upon you, even in the midst of Hell on earth. It is the mind we so often concern ourselves with. It is here that we do not allow for the understanding of the Lord to take place. It cannot take place within the heart until the mind has accepted all there is of our Father in Heaven. To accept that the Lord's hand is also of darkness is contrary to what you have been taught to believe. The only darkness you know is what has brought you harm. Believe when we say you also know darkness and evil that is still; you are just not mindful of it. If you were to be, you would see how much the Lord indeed doth protect and care for you. You would see how much our Father in Heaven loves you.

When you enter into the darkness, the understanding of your nature as man, spirit, and soul becomes more known to you. That is a grace that the darkness and evil give to you. To think that the darkness indeed would offer you a grace such as our Lord—now you are learning. Your nature before you came into energy or being was simply of nothingness. We mean that in the most loving of ways. You, in contemplation, did not even exist. The concept of evil did not even exist. The concept of light did not even exist. There was only Him. And He is not even a concept that those of us in the world of spirit have yet to comprehend in all His glory.

He gives to us all this knowledge so that we may have an understanding of truth of who we are in relation to Him. That is all. The darkness and evil give you the experience of light that you so desire. You would not be able to understand your nature on any level, or indeed, contemplate the soul's longing of Him. His graces can only come to you in the nature of being, on any level you choose to learn from. We say to you this: be still and rise above the darkness in your mind, heart, and soul. Raise your contemplation of Him in all ways. Let the evil and the light that surrounds you be held in the stillness of the Lord. Then and only then will you find peace and greatness of the Lord within. For this we tell you is truth. To work beyond the illusion of the self, the spirit, and the soul, and to be in the nothingness of

Him is to see God as Absolute. Evil and light are as real as they are illusion. If you can contend with that knowledge of being, then you will see that nothing in existence on any level can ever separate you from Him, nothing. You will look at your life and see the meaning and true purpose of the Lord within you. You will have greater faith in what you are, and what you are not. And you will have the truth that the Lord God is the *Absolute Being* and there is nothing else to speak of. If there is anything that we suggest you do from this moment on, let your focus be the Lord always within you, accepting Him for what He truly is, and nothing more.

Understand that as the nature of man, spirit, and soul continually changes, so does the nature of evil and light and the laws as instructed henceforth. There will always be those laws as created by the Lord that will remain as such until the end of time as we know it. Within those laws are others that define the nature of man, spirit, and soul in relation to the light and the darkness. As all souls progress toward Him in their spiritual lives, thus the laws are given permission to change and expand accordingly. They must do so in order for the truth to reveal itself in its entirety and for God the Father to become known in His Absolute Beingness. When you ascribe yourself to those laws as bound by the relationship to the light and the darkness, you permit your soul to evolve at the ever-evolving will of our Lord. We say ever evolving because the Spirit of the Lord evolves as the spirit of each soul evolves, as does the spirit of darkness and evil evolve. There is no greater mercy than to understand that you are children of the Lord, capable of knowing the Absolute Beingness of Him without just cause of your own existence. To perceive the kindness that evil can bring you once it is in the hands of the Creator is to rise above those expectations of Him that you are all attached to in your spiritual progression. If you think you do not have expectations of the Lord within you, we ask that you look again. The contemplation of Him is indeed filled with many expectations for the Lord to save you from the darkness and bring you the ineffable light that He is. When you have reached that place of eternal contemplation with Him, neither the light nor the darkness will matter anymore. Contemplation will cease to exist. What you will encounter is nigh indescribable to even the greatest saints that live in the world of spirit or even that of the Lord's highest Council. To acknowledge Him as Absolute Beingness and to be of that essence without any contemplation of being is indeed of the ineffable Holy Love of the Creator. If you understood deeply how the Lord truly loves you, you will never want for or need for understanding again.

The mercy that lies within the context of evil is Divine. You have to be patient so that it will make itself known to your soul. The grace of the Lord shall bring you what you need to find this mercy when the darkness comes upon you. If you would only meet the Lord halfway in your endeavors and have faith that He will provide that countenance that you need. Do not suffer from the illusion that your nature provides for you. To understand this, you must work through the evil that comes to you to know God in truth. Illusion does not imply that something is not real. Rather it implies the deification of the mystery of our Lord. How so? The Lord can only be deified as can the works of Him through you if you seek to know Him in rising above the evil and the light. We truly cannot know what is illusion because the Lord in all His glory is something that we have all not yet experienced. This is because of the level and consciousness where all souls are at this moment in time. Do not suffer through this illusion, or the glorious mystery of Him, or you will not come to know Him as He truly is. The deification of the Lord in the light and in the darkness is not about suffering.

It is about nothingness. It is about stillness. It is simply of Him. This is a truth that takes many lifetimes and experiences to perceive. First you must work through all that is truth and all that is illusion; all that is light and all that is evil, to come to the nothingness that is the Absolute Being of God. Let the light take its course upon you. Let evil take its course upon you. Let the Lord take His course upon you. *Then God will come.* You will know when that time comes.

Know that evil doth forgive in His name. The Lord would not allow for evil to exist if it was not willing to be of this service to Him. It is the same with the grace of the Lord upon your own souls to forgive the evil that comes upon you. You cannot know love if you do not know forgiveness. You cannot know forgiveness if you have not touched the heart of evil. Understand that. You can touch the heart of evil by standing in the stillness of the Lord's grace, and you must know that there will be times when evil will simply pass you by. There will be times when evil will envelop you. There will be times when evil comes upon you yearning for the forgiveness of the Lord that you carry within. But always, always, seek to know yourself in relationship to all that comes to you. For the Lord and the Devil can disguise themselves as the greatest of teachers. It is only for the purpose of knowing your strength with the Lord and your strength with the darkness that this is so. We have said to you many times during this discourse that the Lord hath given you the same power that He holds. All of it. Do you not think that you will be tested accordingly? If you are given that power to rule the heavens, the earth, and the darkness, you will undergo trials of the spirit, the soul, and the self so that you may be made worthy of the power of Him. The Lord must test you so that He can know if you are willing to carry the light and the darkness of Him in absolute love.

Think about this. Where does your faith lie when evil is present? Is it just in the Lord? Is it also in the darkness itself? When you have come to distinguish that darkness that is Divine and that darkness that is not belonging to you, then you will learn to have faith in it. When your faith rises above the construct on which you have placed your soul's spiritual progression, then you will be able to see God for what He truly is. Remember, we feel that all darkness is Divine on some level of being. We of course acknowledge the darkness that is unnecessary as something that you continue to hold on to when the Lord has given you permission to let go of it. It no longer values itself as Divine because you no longer value yourself as Divine in relationship to it. You no longer see the value of the Lord within it. Your faith must not waiver when evil or the Devil is present . . . your faith in the Lord and in the evil itself. This faith does not give the evil or the darkness more power. We are not saying for you to allow for this evil to seduce your soul in lending your power to Him. On the contrary, we are saying to have faith in the evil will entice you further toward the light of God that it is, that you are. We understand that it is not easy to allow for this process to transform your soul. It takes much self-discipline in the name of God and in the name of love to contradict the confusion of evil and stay in the truth of the Lord when you are face to face with darkness. If anything, evil needs to be taught discipline, while it is not necessary for the light to learn. It already knows. You cannot teach evil discipline if you have indebted yourself to its energies upon meeting. To have faith is to not immerse yourself in the constructs that evil falls upon. It is to bring yourself to stand in humility of the nature of evil so that it may know the humility upon which your faith is held. It is simple. And it is in this way that you will be safe in the arms of the Lord. Safe does not mean you will not be touched by evil's intentions, but you will have the faith that you need to encounter the deification of the Lord in all His truth, and do so with humility and sound understanding of the Providence that takes place within the universe. It is this faith that will bring you peace, dear children. It is this faith that will bring stillness to the evil that is.

When you come to realize evil in the manner of which we are speaking, you will encounter a new strength of self, spirit, and soul than you ever have before. You will be able to stand face to face with the Lord and the Devil in recognition of the greater truth that exists within the universe. Your mind will know the dignity through which the Lord comes to you in many ways so that you may learn of love with Him. You will not carry yourself as the light of Him nor seek to embellish yourself with spiritual grandeur. You will seek only to be a vehicle for the love and works of mercy of Him to manifest through you in all ways, in the light and in the darkness. You will seek to serve others in this way with the compassionate heart of the Christ. Your spirit and soul will seek Him no more as you will know more deeply of the one true God who is completely within you. You will be born again, resurrected into the heart of Christ. The dispassion that your soul will attain for the path toward Him will be silenced by the knowing that He is already with you. It is in this silence that you will see His beauty. And your only duty is to love Him in all ways. It is His will for the Evil One to come to know silence.

We will now speak more about evil at the lower levels of contemplation. The Evil One, also called Satan or the Devil, comes in many guises, and thus takes the concept of evil from the stillness of the Lord into his own hands for further destruction. It is at this level that evil must be feared at a different perspective than that of which we have been speaking. Evil at this level has a higher concentration of focused intention and energy that is separate from the original intent of the will of God. The Evil One can only grasp it after much time has passed with the opportunity of the soul, or souls, to place this evil into perspective, but has not yet achieved the understanding needed to place the evil into stillness. The Devil shall only come to feed upon your soul when you refuse to learn the truth of what the Lord is teaching you around the darkness. The Lord gives you many opportunities and much protection to find the truth of the darkness. Each time you choose not to, the intention of the darkness increases, leaving the darkness open to the Devil and his servants to feed upon the untruth. It is at this level you must understand that all will still and always be the will of the Lord. The Lord will not give to that soul more than what is due the soul at the time of their learning. As before, it is the way you will choose to see the Devil upon your soul that will afflict you with the greatest of harm. For indeed, we know the Devil to be the cause of great injustice and suffering on many levels. We remind you of the power of the Devil to be as great as the Lord when it comes to your uncertainty of the truth. When you are in truth of both the Lord and Satan, there will be silence.

There are many reasons that the Devil may come to you. These are some of the same reasons that the light may come to you. You will seek to know the greatest power of the Lord and of yourself when you come face to face with the Evil One. It is said that sometimes there hath been and will be no greater teacher of the Lord's works. If there is anyone who does not wish the Lord to succeed, it is certainly the Evil One in all his misery. The Devil is not even satisfied when evil is in stillness. He cannot know of his own power when evil is still. When you come face to face with the Evil One, we suggest you hold firmly in the truth and love of the Lord. We suggest you do not render yourself helpless in the face of doubt. We suggest that you not abandon the mercy that the Lord hath for you. We suggest you be still, and be God.

The Devil will do what it has come to do. Remember, all evil, especially at the lower levels of contemplation, must complete itself in some way. The Devil is more powerful at affecting the lower levels of contemplation, on earth and in the world of spirit. When you come face to face with Satan and understand that he must complete some of his will through you in some way, the effects of the intent will be far less on your self, spirit, and soul than evil intended it to be. The Devil wants nothing more than to fight with your spirit and soul. In fact, the Devil knows you will put up a struggle with him and try to defend against him with the power of the Lord. That is indeed a good service if you are at that stage of contemplation where you truly understand the power of God that is within you. Until that time comes, the Devil will feed upon your feeling of abandonment from the Lord when he is present. Think about that. Do you feel that the Lord is with you when

Satan is near? We see that many of you do not, and that is foolish! The Devil will obtain more power over you and from you when you enter in conflict with him when you do not know the truth. We ask of you to be in stillness when Satan and evil are near, as that is something that the Devil does not expect of you, and it will confuse him so. The stillness we speak of once again is not one of subjugation. It is the same stillness that Christ exemplified when he was met by Satan in the desert.

Do not think that the Lord does not wish for you to rebuke the Devil. Christ did rebuke Satan in the desert, but once again, in stillness. To be disciplined in the ways of the Lord when it comes to dealing with Satan is indeed a grace of God. The Devil and evil at this level are not of the stillness we are speaking of. They will return to stillness through some kind of completion or dissolution after it has run its course. If you are wise, you would do your best to be mindful of staying out of the path of Satan when he has not come to you out of choice and will. To get involved with Satan when it is not your time or the intention of the Lord upon you will only bring you misery. It is at these times when you will need the light of God most because you will have greatly lost your way. It is at these times when you will need the Lord and His servants to help in your endeavors to be in right understanding of the darkness and the Evil One. At this level, the Evil One shall do what he wishes until he comes to completion of the task initiated. You would think that the Lord is not with you at these times. We ask you once again to know differently.

The Lord will place the proper structure around Satan and your relationship with Satan as the Lord sees fit for your learning. He will do this without compromising the gift of free will that He gave to you. When you find yourself besieged by the Devil and you ask the Lord to help, you must believe that the Lord will help you in the most suitable way for your highest learning of Him and of love. This suggests that the Lord loves you deeply and only desires for your truth to come into its proper perspective so that you may eventually come to Him in light, love, and sound understanding. The Lord is quicker to halt evil at its higher levels because its understanding of the Lord is not too far from the truth of stillness. At the lower levels, the Lord will most likely allow for evil to run its course to dissolution and completion so that the light of truth may prevail. The souls of all and of the universe can only be nourished by the love of the Lord if the Lord allows for evil to complete and dissolve itself into the light of Him. The Lord will, however, stop Satan in his tracks if the Lord sees that Satan is doing his work out of alignment with the intended agreement of the soul. The Lord will also send His servants to do His (the Lord's) bidding. You must believe that this is happening all the time. Evil and Satan at the lower levels have little respect for the Lord. So the Lord as loving Father will discipline evil as it allows for what is necessary and intended to take place for the highest good of all. It is unfortunate that sometimes as evil completes itself, it will fall upon the soul of one, a few, or an intended experience. It is unfortunate for you because you suffer so. It is difficult for those of us in the world of spirit to help you understand the purpose of this when it is happening. Just know that the Lord is mindful, and restitution of the soul, souls, or experience will always take place. When evil affects the soul, many souls, or an intended experience like this, you must stay firm in your faith and trust that Divine Providence will occur. This is the way it will always be. This is why Satan becomes so angered. Because he knows that he will come to the light of truth. He will try to harm and bring suffering to as many souls as he can before his completion and dissolution as he perceives it at the end of time. As the Lord perceives it, it is simply one of His children coming home to rest in stillness with Him. Satan will contend with the concept of evil itself because the true intention of evil is to be still. Even that is something that Satan does not like. We believe he doth so envy the stillness in some way that he pains himself on suffering until he comes to know it again.

It is spoken in the Psalms:

> *For he spake, and it was done; he commanded, and it*
> *stood fast. The Lord bringeth the counsel of the heathen to*
> *nought: he maketh the devices of the people of none effect.*
> *The counsel of the Lord standeth for ever, the thoughts of*
> *his heart to all generations.*
>
> PSALMS 33:9–11

If it is of evil, it is within the providence of the Lord. If it is of light, it is within the providence of the Lord. If the Devil suffers until it comes to know itself within the stillness of evil, it is within the providence of the Lord. The Devil shall never have the upper hand upon the Lord.

The Devil forgets that it is not the Lord who has abandoned him, but it was he who abandoned the Lord. The Creator desires for the Devil to come to an understanding of his relationship to Him (the Lord), and will allow the Devil, as the Lord allows for all of you, to find the perspective of that relationship within context. The graces that the Lord gives to you, He also gives to the Devil and other created beings. The Lord cannot separate himself among beings. For then He would not be in truth. Evil, and the Devil, will not come close to the Lord in the same way it does to you because of your willingness to succumb to its power and intention. The Devil hath many ways to entice and influence your soul into siding with his intentions. It is only in your ignorance that you do so and your lack of faith and love in the Lord that many of you see the Devil as your friend. We see the Devil as your teacher, not as your friend. This is something we wish for you to rectify.

The Devil and Satan have been related to death but are not of death. That is a misunderstanding. It has been spoken in many scriptures that the Devil leads to the death of the soul by arousing the passions. The Devil can only lead you where you desire to go. The Devil can teach your soul about the silence of the Lord if you choose to learn from him in a way that will serve you.

It is in service of the Lord that your passions teach you not to be bound to anything within the universe. That is why the passions are there. The Devil and Satan are not of death because there is no such thing as death within the laws of the universe. There is only dissolution, completion, resurrection, transformation, and finally stillness. That is all life, the living life of the Lord God. Those stages are the processes by which light and evil become one with the Lord. They differ from the stages of the soul during ascension but are not in exclusion of them. These stages relate to the greater purpose of the universal kingdom as guided by our Lord God, Creator of Heaven and earth.

In referring to evil and the Devil, when the soul allows for the understanding of those stages in relating to the experiences of Satan and the darkness, the soul will come further in truth of God. The soul will come further in truth of the Devil. The stillness will come to know silence even deeper than before.

When you realize that evil just is, you will find more peace within your spiritual life. The death of the soul does not come from your willingness to separate from the Lord in order to learn of higher truths, nor does evil come from that place. It is only your interpretations and thoughts upon your soul's contemplation of these truths that will continue to mystify you until you come to believe that the Lord is, indeed, both the light and the darkness. Acceptance of this truth will bring you more grace than you know. For all the scriptures say this is so. It has been man's interpretations of the teachings that have been confusing. Look at the Lord through the words in His many traditions. You will see the same thing written of Him. You will see that what is of light is also of darkness. Free will does not make the soul culpable of evil. It is the mind that is culpable of evil. It is the mind that will not permit the Holy Spirit to make restitution with the thoughts that come from the Devil. God gave you the greatest mind of all. He gave you His. You were also given the mind of the Evil One so that you may choose to raise your thoughts higher than both the Lord and the Evil One to know nothing but silence. That is a heavenly reward, to have nothing but silence.

It is silence that is the greatest enemy of Satan. This is something that Satan is aware of and fears most. When you are aware of direct confrontation with the Devil, you must believe it is only because you are gaining strength in the Lord's truth. Satan works deceitfully many times and also outwardly if you allow him to do so. The moment you become mindful of him indeed and are in direct confrontation with him is the moment that he is in fear of the silence. He will test your greatest strength and faith when he is nearer to being silenced by the Lord. Whether this silence is through dissolution or completion, it is still something he fears and envies at the same time. When you offer your soul the blessing of merciful kindness, the Lord will grant you as well as the Devil shall grant you the utmost respect during this confrontation. This is how you instruct the soul on the discipline of your passions. This is how you instruct the mind on the discipline of its temperament of the wisdom of the Lord.

The Devil will do his best to be deceitful and conceited when it comes to his ploys. He shall, however, always be able to make himself known at the will of the Lord. You must trust that when something comes to you, and you question whether or not it is of the Lord, or of the Evil One, there will always be a grain of light, and always a grain of darkness. Do not confuse yourself or waste precious time in idling over whether it is of the Lord or not. We speak of those times when you are on your spiritual journeys and you become challenged by the Evil One. The Devil will always come to those who seek the Lord. And the Lord will always go to those who seek the Devil. Remember, it is you who have more challenge and misunderstanding around Satan than the Lord does. For the Lord hath perspective over Satan. This is something that Satan does not like. He knows that the only reason he exists is because the Lord permits it.

What has been misunderstood through time is the notion that those who are purified by the light of God do not have reason to be subject to the Devil's torments. No one is without torment from the Evil One. No one is without the hand and light of the Lord. We suggest greatly that you learn to respect the love that the Lord hath for your higher learning and appreciate His efforts on behalf of your spiritual progression. When it comes time for you to meet the Lord face to face, you will understand why you have experienced your soul in the nature that was given to you.

When you pursue the stillness of evil and the silence of the soul, you must be cautious to keep yourself in agreement with the nature and construct of the universe. Be in your life with the Lord and the Evil One in the context in which your existence was given to you, whether you are on the plane of earth or in the world of spirit. As long as you are living a spiritual life, you must endeavor to maintain balance on the levels you exist on. This is important. For too much light or too much darkness does not keep the construct of the soul or the universe intact. The Lord will provide you with the necessary means and understanding to live your life in search of this perspective. It may not be the existence that you desire, but it is the existence that will lead you to truth. This you must believe. Whether you are the greatest saint or the greatest sinner, the Lord hath provided for you, in agreement with your soul's mission, a way to balance the light and the darkness so that it will come to know the truth in the way that it was intended to be.

When you go beyond what the Lord hath deemed for you, you will encounter light and darkness that your soul will not be ready to handle. We say that the Lord gives you what your soul can work with. It is your responsibility to have faith in that and honor His intention for you. If you pursue the darkness and the Evil One past the extent to which the Lord provides your understanding, then you will come to know suffering. We give you this knowledge so that you may understand evil and the Devil; it is not so that you may pursue him, but that you may come to respect the power and knowledge of yourself, the Devil, and the Lord more. It is simply for your awareness of the love of the Creator and your spiritual life. It is also so that you may learn to discriminate with compassionate discernment what is the Lord and what is Satan.

The Devil will begin to take on form in various ways as it deems itself upon the soul of the afflicted. These forms can manifest themselves as demons, elementals, thoughts, unruly and unjustified behavior, and passions that hinder the progress and healing of the spirit and soul. Whichever level the Devil feels righteous enough to manifest himself, you must understand that he does so in violation of that power that has been originally given to him. The Devil does not remember that he was once an angel of the Lord who was given authority to bring light and goodness to the Lord's children. It is the Devil who seeks condemnation—not of the soul, for he knows that the soul will come to the light of the Lord. The Devil seeks condemnation of the mind and intellect that is given to each soul. The intellect is greater than you think. It is justified by the Divine intellect that serves the universal construct and foundation of the spiritual laws as deemed forth by the Creator. If the Devil can manipulate at the lower and intermediary levels where the soul's greatest hindrances are to ascension, then the Devil hath succeeded in his intention. The Devil will not try and render as much confusion or harm at the higher levels. Remember, evil at the higher levels is of a different understanding and is learning to exist in stillness. Thus, the Devil will seek to obtain his righteousness against the Lord where it is that the soul thinks it needs restitution for its own confusion about the light that it carries. The Devil does not understand about the nature of its powers, just as you do not understand the nature of your own soul's powers. The Devil can only be controlled by desire. I am speaking about the Devil as he is manifested in the lower levels of contemplation. Desire comes from the mind that is not in sound understanding and peace with the Lord. We are not saying that desire is something that will not serve you, for perhaps it is the nature of desire that has led many souls to pursue their journeys to the kingdom of Heaven. It is a necessary constituent for the higher learning of all souls and something that the Devil can indeed relate to. Whether it is demons, elementals (constructs of energy that take form at various levels), thoughts, behavior, or the passions, they are all bound by the same thing that attracts the Devil to feed upon them: desire. They all take on form that the Devil can identify with, and seek to make his mark on the soul's integrity of the Lord.

That is why we say to you whether you are in light or in darkness, to be still and know that you are God. It is the fire of desire that needs to be silenced so that the soul can hear the words of truth coming from the mouth of the Holy One. The soul is intended to know desire, or it cannot know the Lord. That is why the greatest teachings will come in the form of duality. That is what the Devil waits impatiently for. He desires the very same thing that you do, complacency of the soul at the discretion of the Lord. You must understand that you cannot be delivered from evil, but you can be delivered from desire that brings you suffering by the graces and truth of the Lord. You can indeed be delivered from desire when the Devil has given permission for his evil to come into stillness. His permission is always granted by the Lord God Himself. When you remain in stillness with your desires, then demons, elementals, and the other ways in which the Devil takes form will simply diminish in intentional energy and reconstruct themselves to other forms. Those forms are dependent upon Divine Providence of the Lord. Temptation and sin are of your own making. The Devil cannot tempt you when you have brought silence to the desires of the heart and mind that are not in alignment with that of the Lord's will. Even those desires that are of the Lord's will can seek to have retribution because those desires are still at the lower levels of contemplation and create forms of energy that attract powers to the soul that will render hindrance upon it.

The Devil hath been used to symbolize the fall of the angel from the Lord and the fall of man from the kingdom. The Devil can also be seen as that which renders the Lord insurmountable in all His Glory. The fall of the angel of the Lord and of man was simply a form of being that failed to recognize the beauty of the internal kingdom and eternal life that it is part of. The Devil does not wish to end his existence and will seek his eternal life through the reparation of souls. It is interesting because the only way to the kingdom is also the reparation of souls, but in a different manner, in the light of God—that light that includes the darkness. The Devil doth desire eternal life, and that indeed will be his fall. Think about it. There are many of you who attach so deeply to the existence that you breathe life into, whether it is in the world of spirit or on the plane of earth. When you are in stillness of that desire, which is the foundation of all desires that attract the darkness, then you will seek to not need the Devil at your side. We suggest you start at the place of allowing for yourselves to be loved by the Lord. He will give you everything that you need to still the desire for Him and for truth.

When you realize that desire and Divine love are different, then your relationships with the Lord, the Devil, and with your spiritual progression will also be different. Desire can bring you to understand Divine love, but it may not necessarily bring you to know Divine love as the Lord wishes for you to know it. The Devil would rather see you betray your own soul in the name of him against the Lord so that the desire upon which you nurture yourself can be given over to him. The Lord wishes of you to know desire as separate from the Divine love that He gives to you. The Lord wishes of the Evil One to know desire as separate from the Divine love that He gives to him.

When you see yourself as worthy of all that the Lord gives to you, whether it is in light or the darkness that is of Him, then your desires of the heart and mind will be appeased by the sanctity of the Holy Spirit. It is through the direct permission and experience of the Holy Spirit that you will gain the greater understanding that is of the eternal life that is inherently yours.

When it comes to demons and elementals, they only forage upon that aspect of the soul and the mind that is incongruent with the intended learning of that soul upon that particular time or experience. To feed upon the soul and the mind is not the intention of the Lord, but more the will of the demons and elementals so that they may take the breath of eternal life from you and use that power and truth of yours to nourish their own existence. Demons and elementals work for the Devil but in truth continue to expand upon their own form of being by stealing righteous power from the Lord and the universe and making it unto their own. Still, the Lord's Providence rules over all, and what He intends for the Evil One and his workers, and for the concept and structure of evil, shall endeavor to come to fruition and truth.

When you recognize the power of eternal life and the truth of it, do not think that you are without learning still of the Lord. Until the time comes when there is no more time to speak of and we are all as one with the Lord God, the truth of eternal life is still conceptual reality for the soul and the universe. It is something the Devil will try and stop at every chance, meeting your every desire with comfort of him instead of the Lord.

Do not be misled by the temptations of the Devil when it comes to your doubts of eternal life as one with the Creator. It is the truth that shall set you free.

The power that the knowing of eternal life brings is rendered by your faith and love in the Lord. It is that same power and faith that the Evil One doth try to take from your soul. That power cannot be simplified once it is in the hands of the soul, for it is something that the Evil One fears as it will continue to strengthen the soul in the name of the Lord. When you have reached perfect contemplation of the Lord in the way that your soul is able to do at this time, you must know that the Devil will be waiting for you when you come down, to try to diminish the graces that the Lord hath bestowed upon you. Indeed, he may try, but with the faith of the Lord at your side and the truth around darkness, you will endeavor to bring peace to your heart and mind. Divine love has no awareness of what is not of the Lord; thus it has awareness of all that is of the Lord. You will come to know this love as you come to bring peace to the heart that binds itself so to the darkness of desire and untruth.

The Devil fears this Divine love of the Lord as much as it respects it. If he did not yearn to know it himself, he would not be tormenting you so. It is important that you seek to discipline the heart and the mind in the ways of the Lord as much as you need to discipline them in the ways of the Evil One. In this way, you may come to discriminate and render discernment as necessary at the appropriate time. To render discernment upon the light of God or the darkness of the Evil One at your will, will not serve you in your greatest understanding and truth. For it was David who said to the Devil:

I said, I will take heed to my ways, that I sin not with my tongue: I will keep my mouth with a bridle, while the wicked is before me. I was dumb with silence . . . and my sorrow was stirred. My heart was hot within me, while I was musing the fire burned: then spake I with my tongue.

PSALMS 39:1–3

The fire of thought can indeed be raised at the appearance of the Evil One when it is important at that time to allow that fire to be given over to the Lord so that the Evil One does not have cause to afflict you. The discipline we are speaking of will teach you of this Divine love that the Lord hath for you always. You seek to engage with the laws of the natural world in relation to that of the spiritual world and in opposition to your truth of the Lord. Engage the laws of the natural world as created upon by those laws of the spiritual world and you will find more peace within your spiritual life. You will know better how to engage with the light upon you. And you will know better how to engage with the darkness upon you.

The Devil doth fear the sound of the Lord upon you always. Remember that.

When you have taken victory in the manner of righteous truth around the Evil One, you must remember always to be thankful to the Lord and to the Devil for serving as your teacher. To think that your accomplishment in this manner is of your own soul's worth is indeed of the soul's righteousness and not of the Lord's. You must know that your soul is worthy of the Lord's love. That is truth. All that the Lord is, you are. To justify the victory over the Evil One as having nothing to do with the greatness of the Lord and Divine Providence will bring you nothing but the Devil himself back to your side.

When it comes to what has been deemed by the Lord as constructive evil for the purpose and growth of the soul, if you have not offered gratitude to the Lord and to the Devil, you will be shown the respect and humility that is required to know the truth of the light and the darkness. One cannot overcome the Evil One if one has not learned graciousness around the afflictions bestowed upon them by Satan. Graciousness is not about willful acceptance, but of a respect for the teaching that will bring the soul nearer to its intended purpose. This is when we tell you that the Lord will allow for the Devil to have further dominion upon the soul (as you so allow it) when you fail to recognize the blessing bestowed upon you by your experience with the Devil. Awareness of the workings of the Lord in your life as well as the workings of the Evil One are an important aspect of your soul returning to the kingdom. Your graciousness of the Evil One will render him almost helpless in afflicting his intent further upon you. This you must believe.

We again refer to self-discipline as a way to contemplate your soul's nature with the Evil One. You will learn greatly of the self love that is Divine and not righteous of the self, and you will come to love the darkness within you as much as the light. Thus indeed, you may rise above it in truth.

You must remember that all life is a gift, that all of the darkness and the light within life is a gift. All has been given to you with love from the Creator.

Divine love is a reward within the process of the soul's spiritual evolution in remembering the truth of the relationship between the light and the darkness. It is something that is given freely as part of the nature of the Lord within you. It is also an awareness that is cultivated through higher learning and appreciation of the inherent truths within the universe. It is more than simply essence and energy. Divine love encompasses the wisdom and nature of the universe at will.

Divine love will be nurtured by your attempts of faith in appreciation for the Devil's confusion surrounding your soul's purpose. The discipline of the mind and heart will assist the soul in compassionate and dispassionate engagement with evil. Both belong to the appropriate level of engagement and learning that is required of the soul at the meeting with the Devil. When the Lord asks you indeed to pray for the Devil, it is best that you do so. You will be giving to yourself a far greater blessing than you could imagine.

Do your best to appease the mind and heart of what will draw the Devil nearer to thee. We say to you: draw the Devil nearer to Thee (the Lord) and let the Evil One make restitution with the Lord. Always, with whatever comes to you in your spiritual progression, have an open heart and mind within the stillness and mercy of the Lord. So if there is darkness that is waiting to pursue you, you shall know ahead of time what it is that you will need to do.

> *There are said to be five reasons why God allows us to be assailed by demons. The first is so that, by attacking and counter attacking, we should learn to discriminate between virtue and vice. The second is so that, having acquired virtue through conflict and toil, we should keep it secure and immutable. The third is so that, when making progress in virtue, we should not become haughty but learn humility. The fourth is so that, having gained some experience of evil, we should hate it with perfect hatred. The fifth and most important is that, having achieved dispassion, we should forget neither our own weakness, nor the power of Him who has helped us.*
>
> NIKODIMOS AND MAKARIOS, COMPS.,
> *THE PHILOKALIA*, 2:76

As the soul learns to harness its powers of the Lord, it will indeed encounter the servants of the Devil in many a form to be reckoned with. To hate evil with perfect hatred is simply to allow it to come to the stillness of the Lord with the dignity and grace that is given to everything created in the image and likeness of Him. You must always nurture the intellect to the understanding of the spiritual laws as given to you by the Creator. With each soul, there is one truth. But there are many interpretations as to how the light and the darkness will manifest themselves according to the will of God for this soul to develop righteously.

The nature of evil continually expands upon itself as does the nature and creation of light. It will do so until all has come to know silence within the universe.

We ask that you do your best not to provoke the demons that do not need to teach you righteousness, for it is at those times that we are disheartened in the world of spirit. It is then that they can harm you unjustly, and we will do our best within the will of the Lord and His providence to bring you justice. If the Lord hath given you the same power as He has, do not call upon what you do not need or create circumstances that do not serve you where the Devil is concerned. For we say to you this: there will be times when the Devil is brought upon you where it is out of context within the providence of the Lord. This is not to say that you cannot learn from it. This is simply to say that at times, these experiences are not justified by Divine Providence in their exactness. They may be justifiable in the providence of the soul as a whole, but not in their exactness. The Lord knows of all the evil that does take place but cannot control that which is out of context within your spiritual progression if you have rendered it in some way. When the Lord tells you not to progress in a certain direction and you do not heed His guidance, you create the opportunity for darkness to come upon your soul and its intentions. There will be times when those whom you relate to, at your own discretion and will, can also bring upon you or attract to you as it attracts to them, that darkness that is unjustifiable in its exactness. Since the Lord gives you free will, He will not obstruct your nature to choose those experiences that will serve your greatest good, even though they may appear to be of disservice to you at the time. Remember, the Devil can appear at any moment as himself, or disguised as another. He can be brought to you when the Lord says it is not for you to learn from him at this moment. That is because it is of your choosing to engage with him, whether it is through your own soul or the soul of another. However, even if the Devil cometh your way, know that the Lord will seek in the end to justify all as the light of God. The Devil would not be himself if he were not deceitful and cunning in his ways of the Lord.

You must be cautious at these times of your alliance with the demons, for it might be necessary to learn from the Devil himself in the experience that you have attached to. If that is the case and you are unwilling to resolve yourself of this experience or the soul to whom you are relating, then you create the possibility of suffering needlessly at the expense of your own soul. We have seen this many times in the world of spirit and on the plane of earth. Let the Devil and his contemporaries work within what is necessary for Divine Providence. We would recommend that you disengage from what is not in your soul's best interest or responsibility to take on in regard to the evil that is justified or necessary. You create more work on your soul's behalf and on behalf of those of us in the world of spirit who protect you.

Again, be cautious of darkness at this level. For indeed, its wrath will become great when your soul has interfered where it does not belong. Just as the Lord will stand righteous when a soul interferes with the light that is incumbent upon a soul or an experience, such is the Devil who will stand righteous as he perceives it when indeed you have crossed his path.

Even angels and saints respect the darkness and the evil where they have no business upon intruding. This is not to confuse you. The question then arises: is the Lord indeed in control of evil? To this we answer you yes, with and in His understanding. However, the Lord respects all that He has created and trusts completely in Divine Providence within the universe. He cannot instill His desire upon you so intently, in order to respect the laws of the universe. He does that gently, in accordance with the free will that He gave you in direct relation to His will. He hath the same laws with the Evil One. Remember, we are not speaking of Divine darkness at this time. We are speaking of that evil that is unjustifiable in its exactness when you are out of alignment with your spiritual progression. It will bring suffering as you stand before the Lord in reparation.

The Devil hath the power that you give to him. Why not put that same power toward the Lord God? Imagine the glory that would come of it. The Devil and his demons will come to you through the mind and bring destruction to the heart and soul. They will render the spirit fallible through the senses that make up the spirit. For it is not man alone who has sensory power as given by the Lord. The spirit does also. And the Devil seeks to attack the senses of the spirit when indeed the spirit is at its most vulnerable. This is why we recommend that before you come to know silence, you must endeavor to pray to the Lord God. And after you have come to know silence, you must still endeavor to pray to the Lord God. The gift of sensory power and knowledge as defined by universal law gives the structure on the lower levels of contemplation for evil to manifest itself within.

Without the experience of darkness and the Evil One, the soul cannot truly discern the path of righteousness. Its experience is beset by the mind but processed and integrated through the senses. That is why you must not only work with the Devil at the level of self, but at all the levels upon which the Lord hath created you. You must seek to eradicate the Devil and his contemporaries from the mind, the heart, the body (if embodied), the spirit, and the soul. And you must believe that each time the Devil is eradicated and evil comes into perspective, loss and transformation will occur. If you are on the plane of earth, those changes will also affect the physical world around you. You cannot contend with the Devil and his demons without loss and transformation occurring. Sometimes indeed, this loss may be great. But the heavenly rewards will be plentiful.

Demons can easily attack the senses because of their own sensitivity to them. This is a power that is given to them by the universe. The only reason this manifests as so is because of man's capability to understand and perceive the Lord through his senses. The Lord needed a way to reach souls at the level of man through his sensory experience. Man is quicker to respond to evil and the Devil at a sensory level than he is to respond to angels and the light of God. This is truth. We wish it were different. The faith of man can sometimes lie more in the power of the darkness than in the light because of man's ignorance and attachments. We see that you are learning otherwise and commend you. And what strengthens your faith in the Lord will also strengthen your faith in His power.

Do not presume as you are learning to understand the concept of evil and the work of the Devil that you will be free of conflict from the darkness. It is when you have learned to appreciate the role of evil and the role that the Devil plays in your ascension toward the Lord that the Devil indeed will become fierce. He does not desire for you to gain the power of the Lord that you so deserve, and to come into the stillness of the darkness that has the potential of bringing you great suffering when out of stillness. How poor of Satan to think so little of your potential. How great of the Lord to know and trust how Divine you are in your wisdom. Believe that no matter where you are in your spiritual progression, you must always be humble to the darkness. The light you hold encompasses all of the Lord. There are souls who are in different stages of their ascension to the kingdom. When it comes to evil, no matter where you are in regard to the Lord, evil will eventually come to stillness with your understanding being greater. You will not differ in your experiences of evil as you live your spiritual experience, whether or not you are conscious of them. We are not speaking at a sensory level, but in a level of understanding within the soul. There are stages of understanding and perspective that evil will come to as separate from you because it is part of the universe. It does not need the soul to do its bidding and come to stillness. Yet the soul needs the understanding of evil to come to the Lord.

That is why evil simply exists, with or without you and, indeed, not because of you, but because of its own contemplation of the Lord. It will, however, continue to create upon itself in part because of you. That is different.

That is why we ask you to stand in humility of evil, the same humility that you would have before the Lord. To know that evil simply exists and to stand humbly may allow for the Devil to pass you by on its way to destruction if that be the Lord's will. You must endure always, with piety of the Lord and His faith upon your soul. It is that devotion that will raise your own faith in what you see as belonging to your Father. The humility that stands in strength and faith of the Lord will assist the soul in its restraint of desire, and in its discrimination of what is righteous to the soul at each moment. This will be so whether it is in the light or the darkness of the Lord.

Remember, the Devil will take what belongs to the soul, whether good or not, and seek to use it to his advantage. If you are ahead of him in his intentions and are mindful of the discriminatory powers of the soul and the sensory power to which the Devil finds himself drawn, you can halt the Devil before he ploys with the light of God in you or the darkness. The Devil does not need to placate the Divine darkness that is inherent within the soul because it is already justified and held sacred by the Lord God.

Even so, you must always see yourself as humble and grateful to the Lord for all that He has entrusted to you. Through the powers of discrimination, you will learn the understanding of the concept of evil and how not to engage when it is not required of you or how to engage differently. Be cautious about self-aggrandizement around the teachings of evil or you will open the doors to that Devil that you have not expected to come. To take responsibility of the teachings upon your own soul is not the way of righteousness. For those that do, you will come to know otherwise. Take the teachings as part of the Divine intellect that the Lord hath given you and allow for them to move freely within the universe. That is the way the teachings were meant to be glorified. That is the way you, the Lord, and the Devil will be glorified as all has come to be placed in proper perspective and truth.

When you take the teachings upon your own soul, then you have not truly learned. This is something that the Evil One waits patiently for. The Lord wishes of you always to be prepared in your existence for the expansion of light or darkness that will come to you, so that you may endeavor to be in stillness of the truth of your existence. Especially when it comes to the Evil One, you must always be prepared by steadfast diligence of your own soul's makings, potentials, desires, strengths, and weaknesses. Rest assured, the Devil, as is the Lord, is indeed aware too.

If the Lord were not to allow for the Devil or his contemporaries to deceive you and come toward your soul, then indeed, your mind would be still without the greater understanding and truth of the darkness. So the Lord must watch as evil assists you so that you may learn of stillness through ascension and not descending into the abyss of your own Hell.

When you are faced with such trials that the Devil and his demons bring, do not falter in the face of the Lord. For there is nothing greater that will lead you into Satan's arms than to concede your power to him in fear of the Lord. The truth is, in some way you will suffer. Would you rather not suffer with the Lord at your side than with the Devil himself? Indeed we think not! The spiritual life is one of arduous endurance in the faith of the laws as deemed by the Creator. The spiritual life will also bring much trial as it will joy in the contemplation of the darkness of the soul in order to bring evil to rest. It takes great courage and faith in the Lord when you have come upon the Evil One to trust that the Lord will bring you to salvation even if it comes to death as you perceive it. Stay steadfast in your faith of Him even in the darkest of nights. You will come to see the light as the sun rises. For this we promise is true. To stay in stillness as the light of God and the Divine darkness of Him come upon you will bring you the greatest of all truths. Know that all things shall come to pass in the name of the Lord.

As evil leaves you to resolve itself in the manner that it is willed, it will leave behind more evil, perhaps a different one, and also more light. One cannot exist without the other. It is simply that the ways they exist will reflect your relationship to the Lord and your own soul's growth differently.

It is the Lord of all Hosts who is the Petitioner of Mercies upon the souls of the universe, and upon everything that is created within the universe. Thus, when you speak of what is evil, we suggest you do not condemn it as not belonging to the Creator since He is ruler and Creator of all. He alone can call to evil and bring it to its knees and into stillness at any given moment that He doth so desire. This you must believe.

You are to fear the Lord and the Evil One, as much as you are to love them for the service they give in honor of the love that is there for your soul's ascension. If you do not come to love the darkness in a way that will serve your greatest good, then it is truly that you do not know how to love the Lord in all His glory. Demons, the Devil, and evil shall always exist. For the moment you abandon the Lord, they will be waiting to afflict you. The time when you do not abandon the Lord, they may still afflict you, but believe when we say that the intent will be less having faith that the Lord is indeed with you always.

Believe as it is written:

My son, if thou come to serve the Lord, prepare thy soul for temptation. Set thy heart aright, and constantly endure, and make not haste in time of trouble. Cleave unto him, and depart not away, that thou mayest be increased at thy last end. Whatsoever is brought upon thee take cheerfully, and be patient when thou art changed to a low estate. For gold is tried in the fire, and acceptable men in the furnace of adversity. Believe in him, and he will help thee; order thy way aright, and trust in him. Ye that fear the Lord, wait for his mercy; and go not aside, lest ye fall. Ye that fear the Lord, believe him; and your reward shall not fail. Ye that fear the Lord, hope for good, and for everlasting joy and mercy. Look at the generations of old, and see; did ever any trust in the Lord, and was confounded?

Or did any abide in his fear, and was forsaken? Or
whom did he ever despise, that called upon him? For
the Lord is full of compassion and mercy, longsuffering,
and very pitiful, and forgiveth sins, and saveth in time
of affliction. Woe be to fearful hearts, and faint hands,
and the sinner that goeth two ways! Woe unto him that is
fainthearted! For he believeth not; therefore shall he not
be defended. Woe unto you that have lost patience! And
what will ye do when the Lord shall visit you? They that
fear the Lord will not disobey his Word; and they that
love him will keep his ways. They that fear the Lord will
seek that which is well pleasing unto him; and they that
love him shall be filled with the law. They that fear the
Lord will prepare their hearts, and humble their souls in
his sight, saying, "We will fall into the hands of the Lord,
and not into the hands of men: for as his majesty is, so is
his mercy."

SIRACH 2:1–18

Never lose hope in the Lord to bring you to truth and salvation. It
is He who will bring mercy to even the Evil One that has come upon
you. You may become restless in your waiting for the Lord's rescue of
your soul from darkness. We tell you that the time to wait is decreed
by the Lord as serving your soul in its greatest endeavors. If you allow
Him to bring mercy upon the Devil in your patient endurance, you
will have succeeded in achieving the greatest of mercies known to the
kingdom of Heaven. You will have achieved a union with the Lord
that is most sacred, and a mutual respect with the Evil One that is
honoring.

Be mindful of reproach to the demons that attack you. They
will come to you as themselves or through the guises of another, or
an experience. You must remember that it is the Lord only who can

rebuke the demons and demand reparation for sins committed. The moment you seek to punish the demons, you have become no greater than they in the face of the Lord. And you fail to see the harm that you might inflict upon your own soul. To damn another being, whether angel or demon, is not what the Lord asks of you to do. When indeed the Lord asks of you to assist in rebuking the demons, that is when you listen. The Lord will give just responsibility to those He sees fit to do His bidding. You are not to engage where it is not of your concern.

We say this because the demons work tirelessly to assail on many levels, especially that of man. While the mind is working steadfast to accomplish the will of the Lord in spiritual pursuit, the demons may be afflicting various parts of the spirit, the soul, or man. If you are embodied, the struggle against the demons will be far greater as your desire on the lower levels of contemplation is much stronger than the other dimensions of being. While being mindful of what you encounter in your thoughts, we ask you to be mindful of the disgrace that you bring upon bodily influences that will attract the likes of the demons. You must understand that disgrace is not shame. We refer to disgrace as that which is not filled with grace in the name of the Lord. Demons are drawn to attack anything that is not illumined by the grace of the Lord. This is truth. Whether it be in body, spirit, soul, or mind. We do not suggest that you hold yourself in contempt of the physical self. On the contrary, we ask you to honor it more than you presently do so. We are merely suggesting that you bring the grace of the Lord to all aspects of the lower levels of contemplation, especially that of the physicality of man. Desire will always be in the body and intellect of man. It is unavoidable. You can allow for the grace of God to illumine that desire so that the attacks of demons will be less if any, even the ones that are willed by the Lord to teach you. They come in part to teach you the grace of the Lord. Remember that.

When you seek to nullify your desire of the self or even of spirit, then the demons will also have less to feed upon. This is truth. For even the desire to know the Lord must be in silence of everlasting truth. We say to you this: be of the Lord always, in all ways. When a demon has come to you, do not cast judgment upon it, for this will entice it more. Instead, simply show it the hand and heart of God.

Faith

Do not fear, do not provoke further, and do not slay. Those that serve the Lord will take care of what does not serve you or does serve you. It is your responsibility to understand in which way the demon serves your greatest good. But do so in the name of the Lord, and in faith of the Lord. Allow for the demon to speak his peace. Allow for him to do so without fear of retribution on your part, for this only brings more suffering to you. When we say retribution, we refer to the retribution upon your own soul in attachment to this being.

When the demon sees that you care nothing at all except for the existence of the beingness of the Lord, what then will he have to destroy? Whether a being, a thought, or a passion, the demon can only attack what is in form. So we ask of you to become formless, in all ways that you can. And what is in form, we ask that you surrender all desire and attachment for. To disempower the demon on your part, give him nothing that will serve his greatest good except that of the greatest and most loving God.

The demons and the Lord will test you for your faith in eternal life and the resurrection to that eternal life. Always. Demons will fail to achieve their intentions upon you as you grow in light and faith of the Lord. They will try their attacks on you at any level upon which you allow them in. The more you concede to the grace and will of the Lord, the more the demons will become angered and tired at their trials. There will come a time when you see yourself not as being or form, instead, you will see yourself as formless being. That is the time when the intentions of the Devil or the demons will not penetrate you as deep as they had been before. That is the time when you have let the graces of the Lord insinuate themselves upon the heart and the soul in ways richer than before. It is the heart of God that you so desire in your existence, no matter the level of existence you choose. The heart of God can be felt, seen, experienced, and touched within the stillness of that which is formless. We certainly understand that when you are embodied, you cannot be without form. So we suggest to you to meditate upon the other levels of being. Meditate with humility upon your heart, your spirit, your soul, and your mind. Learn to create what is formless using the stillness and beauty of the Lord. Come to appreciation of the knowledge that your spirit and soul is not simply yours, but belongs to every other created being and essence within the universe. Learn to identify what is created by you and what is created by the Lord. Seek to silence the heart, mind, spirit, and soul from all activity except that of the grace of stillness.

You will be renouncing not only the power of the demons but the power that you thought was given to the self, the mind, the spirit, and even the soul. We understand that to embrace the formless can bring bouts of fear unimaginable. When this does happen, we ask you to continue with your meditation. As you become stronger in that space of Him, you will encounter the threshold of the entire kingdom of the Lord in ways unseen, and you will experience His love in ways ineffable.

Righteousness in regard to the demons only belongs to the Lord. There is not one of you who will not partake of the actions and intentions of demons as relevant to the Lord's salvation for you. Do not presume to attend to the demons without the Lord's permission. And do not presume to condemn another for the demons that are upon them. For if you see a demon upon another, then you have that same demon upon your own soul. You must hold the truth of the Lord and Redeemer in your heart always, so that He may enkindle the fire of the Holy Spirit to illumine your soul's awareness of His presence always.

Presumption of the Lord's ways upon you when a demon has come your way is not of the Lord's will. Then you will give rise to ego and self-grandeur and not to truth. Salvation comes when you concede your presumptions in humility of the truth of your being. It does not come when you seek to justify your learnings upon the perceived advancement of your soul and its powers. The moment you perceive yourself as glorious of Him to the manner in which we are speaking, then you have deluded yourself and fallen prey to the demons. Then it is not the Lord that you seek to know in your heart, but the righteous power that comes with spiritual knowledge and advancement. We recommend that you be cautious of this path, as you will encounter more passions that will bind the soul even further. Self-aggrandizement is easy to fall prey to when it comes to facing the demons that torment you. Indeed, they will at times even let you win through the power and mercy of the Lord only to test your humility against them.

Your humility must come with acceptance of the teaching that comes to you. You cannot be truly humble when you have not accepted the teaching even if it comes disguised as darkness. You must always remember to discriminate within the teaching as it comes to you, so that your learning will involve no more suffering than your soul needs to grow. Discrimination and discernment will bring to you righteous judgment of even the greatest demon that afflicts you. You will be engaging with that demon from the deepest recesses of your heart where the Lord awaits you in silence. This is how you will learn of your heart's truest deliverance unto yourself. This is how you will learn of the true love and compassion of the Lord. This is how you will also learn of the true compassion that the darkness has for you.

To be clear in the heart of all demonic activity, you must embellish the heart with the supreme love and goodness of the Lord. The heart knows the truth of the Lord within its deepest recesses and how to obtain the light of Him through purification and illumination by the Holy Spirit. The heart indeed knows of this without the aid of the mind or intellect and will seek to purify and nourish itself even without your conscious consent. This is truth. The heart is the heart of the Christ and righteously so belongs to Him and His Father in Heaven. Even when the mind, the spirit, and the soul seek to identify their energies with those that do not align with the Lord, the heart will endeavor to hold the space for purification and illumination by the Holy Spirit and will hold firmly to the heart of Christ within itself. For we say to you this: even the greatest demon shall fear the heart of Christ. That is why they come guised as angels, only to come within your heart and rile against the heart of Christ. They know that the heart of Christ is indeed untouchable, yet the mind, spirit, and soul with which you have struggled can be afflicted so.

Light alone is strong enough to hold back the demons that torment you. Even if it is of the Lord's will, the intensity of the affliction will be lessened by your focus on the light of the Lord. Your heart hath greater strength of the Lord than you are aware of, for it is the Lord's gracious and abiding love that will conquer and bring you to the doors of salvation. To love as the Lord loves will indeed bring you glory.

You must engage the heart in all that you do, especially in relation to that of your mind. Evil treads with fear upon the heart that loves like the Christ. Allow the heart to receive the Christ in the mercy that is known to him by his Father. Bring the heart to the understanding that without the Christ light within it, it shall not come to know the kingdom.

Your heart can expand to the awareness of Christ and the Lord God where evil cannot enter without humility of stillness. When evil falls upon the heart of Christ within that stillness, it will be transformed into the love that the Christ and his Father have for their children.

It is easier for the darkness to enter the mind, the spirit, or the soul than it is for darkness to enter the heart. It will only enter the heart once it has enmeshed itself within the others. You must work tirelessly to protect your heart from any intrusion by the Devil. Once he has entered, it will take much time for you to find once again the heart of Christ within. It has not left; it is only that you refuse to align yourself with it and give power to the darkness. The heart of Christ is indeed magnificent and carefree of the woes of the soul and the spirit when it is truly belonging to the Christ. Jesus as Christ knew the power and truth that was given to his heart by his loving Father. He knew well how to protect and nourish it with the graces of his Father in Heaven.

Let your model for stillness of heart be the man who holds
a mirror into which he looks. Then you will see both good
and evil imprinted on your heart.

NIKODIMOS AND MAKARIOS, COMPS.,

THE PHILOKALIA, 1:170

Let thought come into your intellect as you may, but guard the heart gracefully to that which enters it. Seek not to embellish the heart with false teachings, for you would be bringing upon it grave injustice. The Lord gives you much compassion when it comes to the fire of your heart's longing and knows deeply of your suffering in seeking His love. Never forget the bounty of the Lord's love upon your heart. It will shine greater than the light of the Holy Spirit. It will bring forth unimaginable miracles for the soul's taking. It shall gift you with the magnificence and splendor of the heavens. It shall give you the understanding of the evil that befalls you. The greatness of the heart of Christ gives you the mercy of compassion—one that will engender the deepest union for all who long for the love of God. Once you have touched upon the heart of Christ within you, you shall never want for anything again. For the purity that you will come to know is of the most Gracious and Merciful Redeemer.

The love that you have for the Lord through the heart of Christ and the Father's love for you can affect the intention of the darkness.

The darkness of evil comes to you so that you may learn of the heart of Christ and the love that is instilled within it. To join your heart with that of Christ, you must endeavor to offer the Lord's salvation to every passion that encumbers it so. Each time you offer a loving embrace to that which enters the heart, know that you are growing closer to the Lord and to His Son whom He sent because of His love for you.

At noon it parcheth the country, and who can abide the burning heat thereof?

SIRACH 43:3

So let us confidently believe that the cold dark coals of our mind will sooner or later blaze with heat and light under the influence of Divine fire.

NIKODIMOS AND MAKARIOS, COMPS.,
THE PHILOKALIA, 1:314

The nature of man, spirit, and soul is indeed to love greater than it thinks it is capable of. The love of the Lord is the awakening to the threshold of the kingdom. If you do not have love of Him, you do not even exist as Being, essence, or energy. Any grace given to you by our Father in Heaven doth have love akin to it. You cannot achieve that holiness that is deemed by the Father as righteously yours without having the love of the Lord and of Christ upon your heart. You cannot have light without love, and you must believe you cannot have the darkness without love. For if all things were created unto the Lord in the name of love, then so was the darkness of which we have been speaking. The Lord holds the darkness in contemplation of His love differently than you. And so you are learning. You can acquire all the knowledge of the universe and practice all that was given during this discourse, but without the love of the Lord God and His son Jesus the Christ, you will have achieved no knowledge of spiritual matters at all.

To live for the spirit of the Lord God and the spirit of the Christ with love in your heart will bring to you the greatest understanding of the spiritual life that you desire. The Lord hath created on love alone, so that you may create on love alone. The love of the Lord is complete in sanctity of the laws within Heaven and the universe. If you indeed love as the Lord and the Christ does, then you shall awaken to that glory that is ineffable. The light that comes from love is the supreme motivator for the creation of all within the nature of God, thus manifesting the creation of man, spirit, and soul. Divine love is of the purpose of all that was, is, and will be created. Both the light and the darkness were founded upon love.

The interpretations of that love have been left up to beings and energies who have been confused in their contemplation of it. When you seek to know of this love of the Lord and of Christ, we ask that you look no further than your heart. For the heart upon you is given in honor of the Lord, not in honor of you. It is you who have forgotten that. No trial, no tribulation, no honor, and no advancement on one's spiritual journey can be conceived without the love of the Lord—as is no thought, no action, no word. For you are wholly made up of the love of the Creator, and henceforth, that is how you will go to Him in the kingdom of Heaven, as nothing but love. The light of God commands it so.

In all of the truth that you have been shown, if you do not have love, then you do not understand what has been written. Nor do you understand why it is that you exist at the level upon which you do. For it is love alone that will urge you toward the kingdom of Heaven, and it will urge you to find truth, light, and perspective in all that you do, and in all that comes to you. If you think that you do not engage in the darkness out of love, you are mistaken. It is only because you love the Lord so that you are willing to torment your own soul to find truth in those matters.

What you have been given has been built upon the love of the

Lord. Yet you have little faith in that love of Him within you and lose sight of the heart that has been so graced. For we say to you this: do not waste precious time in seeking what is upon you in the realm of spiritual matters. What you have been given will come to you as truth when you have found that you are at the end of your journeys. You will end in the same way as you began, only to have acquired the knowledge of what the Lord has emblazoned upon your heart for all eternity since the moment of your inception. The knowledge of the universe is indeed powerless without your understanding and acceptance of the Lord's love upon your heart. It is powerless without your love being given in earnest to the Lord and His son Jesus the Christ. For all that you do, the Lord's love shall cleave to your heart like fire that is molded in pure light of consciousness. So we say to you always to cleave to the love of the Lord as doth the fire that shapes you.

For nothing in truth is without love. Nothing in God is without love, and nothing in you is without love. And there has been nothing in this discourse that has been given to you without love. The desire to know the Lord God shall always be with you, and the desire to love Him shall be your only truth.

In the words of His son Jesus the Christ:

> *Blessed are the poor in spirit; for theirs is the kingdom of heaven. Blessed are they that mourn; for they shall be comforted. Blessed are the meek; for they shall inherit the earth. Blessed are they which do hunger and thirst after righteousness; for they shall be filled. Blessed are the merciful; for they shall obtain mercy. Blessed are the pure in heart; for they shall see God. Blessed are the peacemakers; for they shall be called the children of God. Blessed are they which are persecuted for righteousness sake; for theirs is the kingdom of heaven.*
>
> MATTHEW 5:3–10

And from a disciple of the Lord:

Beloved, let us love one another: for love is of God, and every one that loveth is born of God, and knoweth God. He that loveth not knoweth not God; for God is love. In this was manifested the love of God toward us, because that God sent his only begotten Son into the world, that we might live through him. Herein is love, not that we loved God, but that he loved us, and sent his Son to be the propitiation for our sins. Beloved, if God so loved us, we ought also to love one another. No man hath seen God at any time. If we love one another, God dwelleth in us, and his love is perfected in us.

1 JOHN 4:7–12

As Jesus the Christ said to his disciples:

Peace be unto you. As my Father hath sent me, even so send I you. . . . Receive ye the Holy Ghost.

JOHN 20:21–22

Know that from this moment on, the peace and
love of the Lord will be with you always.
Now go forth, and spread the Good News of Him.

BIBLIOGRAPHY

King James Bible. 1611 Edition. Available online at ebible.org/kjv

Nikodimos of the Holy Mountain and Makarios of Corinth, comps.
The Philokalia: The Complete Text. 4 vols. Translated and edited by
G. E. H. Palmer, Philip Sherrard, and Kallistos Ware. London: Faber
and Faber, 1983–99.

Laura Silvana Aversano can be reached for questions,
comments, or spiritual consultations at
LauraAversano@aol.com.
Her website address is **www.LauraAversano.com**.

ACKNOWLEDGMENTS

My deepest gratitude to God. To my teachers in the world of spirit, you are my solace. My life is dedicated to your mission.

To my family, I know that this work has already brought healing to us as a whole. To Lois Dunnavent, thank you for your strength, love, and support during the writing of this book. Your friendship and your guidance have been invaluable over the years. To Marcia Pollock, your presence, encouragement, love, and support of me have carried me through difficult times. To Dr. John Beaulieu, enough gratitude could never be conveyed from my heart for all the support and guidance you have given me as I matured into my work. Father Joe, I know you are smiling at me from heaven. I thank you and miss you. Richard Grossinger, you rebirthed this book into its next phase. I am grateful our paths crossed when they did. Thank you.

INDEX

reasons for incapacity and, 59
woman healed by Jesus from, 23–35
illusion
  implication of, 194
  perception as, 111
initiation, 14, 131
inner peace, 9, 57
Isaiah, book of, 48

James, book of, 113
Jesus
  baptism of, 66–67
  death of, 36–37, 42, 44, 50
  healings performed by, 2, 3, 8
  relationship of God and, 73
Job, book of, 182
John, gospel of
  on anointing the soul, 29–30
  on being lived by God, 26, 27, 106
  on blind man healed by Jesus,
    57–58, 98
  on creation, 71
  on equality of beings, 64
  on Father and Son of God, 51
  on God as love, 76, 230
  on sin and death, 44
  on work and will of God, 35–36
John the Baptist, 32
justice
  Divine darkness and, 181
  symbolized by death, 45

karma
  changing of, 93–94, 101, 104–6,
    115, 117
  curses related to, 98–99, 114–15

enslavement by one's own, 95
evil and progression of, 172–73,
  191
gratitude and acceptance of, 115–16
healing of, 52, 53–54, 96, 108
illness as result of, 117–18
levels of spirit and, 106–13, 114
life circumstances and, 95, 96–97,
  99, 102–3, 105–6
reincarnation and, 80, 84, 92, 95,
  100, 143
soul and patterns of, 108, 118–20
understanding the laws of, 80, 97,
  101
kingdom of Heaven, 89, 120, 142, 228
Kings, book of, 33

lepers, cleansing of, 61–65
life circumstances
  changing vs. accepting, 105–6
  karma related to, 95, 96–97, 99,
    102–3, 105–6
light
  attachment to, 114
  darkness and, 60, 68, 147, 148–49,
    152, 162, 168, 202
  prayers for bringing in, 19, 20
  process of bringing healing and, 9
  stillness and, 73, 148, 154, 165, 171
  transformation of evil into, 138
  uncreated essence as, 155
Logos, 27, 54, 55, 58, 80, 141
love
  boundaries of, 160
  Divine, 207, 209, 210, 211, 227–30
  healing with, 18, 55–56, 64

Books of Related Interest

Affirmations of the Light in Times of Darkness
Healing Messages from a Spiritwalker
by Laura Aversano

Love, God, and Everything
Awakening from the Long, Dark Night of the Collective Soul
by Nicolya Christi

Opening Doors Within
365 Daily Meditations from Findhorn
by Eileen Caddy
Foreword by Jonathan Caddy
Edited by David Earl Platts, Ph.D.

The Fourteen Holy Helpers
Invocations for Healing and Protection
by Christiane Stamm

Return of the Divine Sophia
Healing the Earth through the Lost Wisdom Teachings
of Jesus, Isis, and Mary Magdalene
by Tricia McCannon

The Mystery Tradition of Miraculous Conception
Mary and the Lineage of Virgin Births
by Marguerite Mary Rigoglioso, Ph.D.

When God Had a Wife
The Fall and Rise of the Sacred Feminine in
the Judeo-Christian Tradition
by Lynn Picknett and Clive Prince

Lessons from the Twelve Archangels
Divine Intervention in Daily Life
by Belinda J. Womack
Foreword by Catherine Shainberg

INNER TRADITIONS • BEAR & COMPANY
P.O. Box 388
Rochester, VT 05767
1-800-246-8648
www.InnerTraditions.com

Or contact your local bookseller